Creating European Citizens

Europe Today

Series Editor: Ronald Tiersky

Scandinavia in World Politics
  Christine Ingebritsen

The Politics of Economic and Monetary Union: Integration and Idiosyncrasy
  Erik Jones

NATO and the Future of European Security
  Sean Kay

Contemporary France: A Democratic Education
  Anne Sa'adah

Creating European Citizens
  Willem Maas

Euro-skepticism: A Reader
  Edited by Ronald Tiersky

Europe Today: National Politics, European Integration, and European Security, 2nd Edition
  Edited by Ronald Tiersky

Uniting Europe: European Integration and the Post–Cold War World, 2nd Edition
  John Van Oudenaren

Creating European Citizens

Willem Maas

ROWMAN & LITTLEFIELD PUBLISHERS, INC.
Lanham • Boulder • New York • Toronto • Plymouth, UK

ROWMAN & LITTLEFIELD PUBLISHERS, INC.

Published in the United States of America
by Rowman & Littlefield Publishers, Inc.
A wholly owned subsidiary of The Rowman & Littlefield Publishing Group, Inc.
4501 Forbes Boulevard, Suite 200, Lanham, Maryland 20706
www.rowmanlittlefield.com

Estover Road, Plymouth PL6 7PY, United Kingdom

Copyright © 2007 by Willem Maas

All rights reserved. No part of this publication may be reproduced, stored in a retrieval system, or transmitted in any form or by any means, electronic, mechanical, photocopying, recording, or otherwise, without the prior permission of the publisher.

British Library Cataloguing in Publication Information Available

Library of Congress Cataloging-in-Publication Data

Maas, Willem, 1972–
   Creating European citizens / Willem Maas.
   p.   cm. — (Europe today)
   Includes bibliographical references and index.
   ISBN-13: 978-0-7425-5485-6 (cloth : alk. paper)
   ISBN-10: 0-7425-5485-6 (cloth : alk. paper)
   ISBN-13: 978-0-7425-5486-3 (pbk. : alk. paper)
   ISBN-10: 0-7425-5486-4 (pbk. : alk. paper)
   1. European Union. 2. Citizenship. 3. Citizenship—Europe. 4. Citizenship—European Union countries. 5. Freedom of movement. 6. Supranationalism. 7. Supranationalism—European Union countries. 8. Political rights—Europe. 9. Political rights—European Union countries. I. Title.
JN30.M22 2007
323.6094—dc22

2006031617

Printed in the United States of America

∞™ The paper used in this publication meets the minimum requirements of American National Standard for Information Sciences—Permanence of Paper for Printed Library Materials, ANSI/NISO Z39.48-1992.

Contents

	Preface	vii
	Introduction	1
Chapter 1	Introducing European Rights	11
Chapter 2	From Rights to Citizenship	29
Chapter 3	Maastricht's Constitutional Moment	45
Chapter 4	Europe's Homogeneous Space	61
Chapter 5	Toward a Constitution	77
Chapter 6	The Limits of European Citizenship	95
	Conclusion	115
	Notes	121
	Selected Bibliography	143
	Index	171
	About the Author	179

Preface

Since the end of the Second World War, an extensive set of supranational rights has been created in Europe. These rights extend entitlements, impose obligations, and have increasingly been designated with a term traditionally reserved for the relationship between individuals and states: citizenship. States have historically been defined in terms of insiders (citizens) and outsiders (foreigners). European Union (EU) citizenship supersedes this traditional distinction by removing the ability of European states to discriminate between their own citizens and those of other EU member states. Thus European citizenship represents a distinct rupture with the historical tradition of state sovereignty. This fundamental transformation is particularly evident in the realm of free movement. Nothing in international law requires a state to automatically allow citizens of another state to reside on its territory, nor to grant them wide-ranging civic, political, and social rights. Yet European citizenship not only provides Europeans with choices about where to live and work but also forces EU member states to respect those choices.

Freedom of movement for individuals is only the key first step and most visible manifestation of the emerging European rights regime. Seeking to explain this emergence—why states cede their sovereignty and eradicate or redefine the boundaries of the political community by including "foreigners"—this book analyzes the development of EU citizenship and advances more general hypotheses about the evolution of rights. Most explanations of European integration focus on how it meets the economic interests of states. By contrast, I argue that postwar European political development also reflects the drive to create not simply a free trade market but also a community of people. Examining the rise of European citizenship elucidates the political nature of the European project: the goal of building, in the words of the European Coal and Steel Community (ECSC) treaty, a "broader and deeper community among peoples" with a "destiny henceforward shared"—the project of creating European citizens—has informed European integration since its origins. Its prospects will determine the future of Europe and provide lessons for political integration elsewhere.

Research for this book was generously funded by the Yale University Graduate School of Arts and Sciences, a doctoral fellowship and Federalism and the Federations supplement from the Social Science and Humanities Research Council of Canada, and a Mackenzie King Travelling Scholarship. The manuscript was written at New York University's Center for European Studies, chaired by Martin Schain and then Katherine Fleming. Leah Ramirez, Jennifer Denbo, and Zoe Ragouzeos provided excellent support, while my students at NYU and the resources of New York City proved inspirational. Final revisions were completed at Glendon College, York University, and I thank my new colleagues for their warm welcome. Many more people have aided this project than can be thanked here, but my advisors at Yale—Seyla Benhabib, David R. Cameron, Geoffrey Garrett, and Rogers M. Smith—as well as Bruce Ackerman, Elise Auvachez, Sheri Berman, Christopher Chivvis, Hugo Cyr, Bob Dahl, Katherine Foshko, Walter Goldstein, Gilles Grin, Leah Haus, James Hollifield, Pauline Jones-Luong, Hussein Kassim, Janet Laible, Elise Langan, Jonathan Laurence, Matthew Light, Juan Linz, Heather MacRae, John McCormick, Margaret McCown, Behrooz Moazami, Thomas Ort, Berthold Rittberger, Glenda Rosenthal, Ian Shapiro, Jo Shaw, Debra Shulman, Beate Sissenich, Dagmar Soennecken, Alec Stone Sweet, Phil Triadafilopoulos, Amy Verdun, Maarten Vink, Antje Wiener, Steven Wolinetz, and Aristide Zolberg provided special insight and encouragement at various stages. I also thank Kimberly Twist, Sylvia Zareva, and especially David Harper for research assistance at NYU.

The idea for this research originated at Leiden University, where I am indebted to Herman van Gunsteren, Peter Mair, Andreas Kinneging, Galen Irwin, and others, and where I benefited from the inaugural year of the Leiden-Oxford honors seminar on European governance. At Yale, Ivan Szelenyi, Hannah Brueckner, and other members of the comparative research workshop and the Center for Comparative Research provided constructive criticism, and I also benefited greatly from workshops in political theory, political economy, sociology, legal theory, history, and international relations. A year at Nuffield College, Oxford, provided a congenial environment in which to write, and I am grateful for Oxford's amenities. The European Commission is a fascinating place to work and conduct research, and for granting interviews to a sometimes perplexed researcher, I thank Giuseppe Callovi, Fernando Pereira, and Angela Martini from Directorate General (DG) Justice and Home Affairs, Jean-Claude Séché from the Secretariat General, Robertus Cornelissen from DG Employment and Social Affairs, and a number of anonymous sources. I particularly thank Auke Haagsma from the Internal Market DG for arranging a *stage atypique*. I also thank the librarians of the European University Institute in Florence, Italy, as well as those of its Historical Archives.

Much of this book started as conference or workshop papers or presentations, and I thank the discussants and commentators, as well as several anonymous referees. Unless otherwise noted, all translations are mine. Furthermore, in an effort to simplify the bibliography, I have grouped institutional works under their current overarching institution. Thus, works by the *Commission administrative pour la sécurité sociale des travailleurs migrants*, for example, are found under European Commission, works by any ECSC organs are found under European Coal and Steel Community, and works by the former Parliamentary Assembly are found under European Parliament. As for language, I have generally opted for the terms "prointegration" (rather than pro-European, Europhile, or Euroenthusiast) and "Euroskeptic" (rather than anti-European or nationalist) to refer to the two sides of the spectrum of opinion relating to integration, though there is much nuance within these positions. This book reflects research current through December 2006, but an earlier version of parts of §1.1 and §1.2 appeared as Maas (2005b), an earlier version of part of §5.1 appeared as Maas (2006a), and a related overview will appear as Maas (forthcoming). The book benefited from Ron Tiersky's encouragement and, at Rowman & Littlefield, Susan McEachern's expert advice. My family provided much-appreciated love and support, especially my wife, Deborah, who was not present for this project's start but read every word at the end, improving this work in countless ways.

Introduction

The first thing that must be sought is the citizen; for the city is a certain multitude of citizens. Thus who ought to be called a citizen and what the citizen is must be investigated.¹

—Aristotle

Union citizenship is destined to be the fundamental status of nationals of the Member States, enabling those who find themselves in the same situation to enjoy the same treatment in law irrespective of their nationality.²

—European Court of Justice

Citizenship, exclusive territoriality, and sovereignty define modern states: citizenship would be meaningless without states, and states would not be states without citizens.³ Since the Maastricht Treaty (1993), however, citizens of European Union (EU) member states have had at least two citizenships: that of their member state and that of the Union. The political communities of notionally independent states thus blend into one, though EU citizenship is superimposed onto populations that already possess national citizenships. Historical comparisons are suggestive: the unification of Germany or Italy; the development of the United States, Canada, or Australia; or even the formation and rise of nation-states themselves. But these cases differ because sovereignty, territoriality, and citizenship had in each instance not yet developed into their late twentieth-century forms. Furthermore, the second half of the twentieth century witnessed many *disaggregations* of citizenship—for example, from Czechoslovak citizenship into Czech and Slovak citizenships, and from Yugoslav or USSR citizenship into the citizenships of the successor states, to say nothing of the postcolonial independence movements that created scores of new states around the world—but no other amalgamations.[4] Other regional integration efforts such as the North American Free Trade Agreement (NAFTA), Mercosur, and the African Union have provided individuals with some rights, but such rights remain very limited when compared with European rights—and none have developed into citizenship.[5]

Given its apparent uniqueness, an overarching question central to any examination of EU citizenship concerns the conditions necessary for citizenship itself to emerge, crystallize, and develop. As doubts about the future of the nation-state have grown, particularly since the end of the Cold War, citizenship has received renewed attention because it promises to capture contemporary transformations in political relations while also retaining the essential link between individuals and states that was evident already in Aristotle's definition of the state as a composite comprised of citizens.[6] Citizenship can range from "thick" to "thin," depending on the degree to which states affect individuals: for the citizen, thick citizenship entails many rights in and obligations to the state, while thin citizenship denotes a relative lack of such rights and duties.[7] This continuum has been the subject of vigorous debate, with some authors (often termed liberal) advocating thin citizenship and others (often termed communitarian or republican) countering that citizenship must rest on thicker notions of shared duties and common identity.[8] Citizenship remains a contested concept, but one understanding of citizenship emerged from western Europe to dominate others and spread around the globe: a homogeneous political status within the context of the state. In contrast to complex historical patterns of variegated and multitiered citizenship, this understanding of citizenship denotes a single pattern of membership: to be a citizen is to be a member of a legally uniform (usually national) group of people, with attendant rights and duties. Consequently, the idea of dual, plural, or multilevel citizenship is problematic: if only states can confer citizenship, then the notion of an overarching EU citizenship is jarring as long as EU member states continue to exist as states and the EU itself is not a state.[9]

But perhaps the EU *is* becoming a state, depending on what one means by the term. Contemporary states result from a long evolution dating back at least to the Peace of Westphalia (1648), but there has been much variation in their development. Any definition of the state is itself subject to change over time: ideas change about what states look like, and how they should or do behave.[10] Citizenship is a similarly contingent concept. Indeed sovereignty, citizenship, nationalism, and state development are interrelated: modern states are expected to incorporate their people as individual citizens, educate and mobilize them around shared goals, and promote welfare through public programs and the expansion of citizenship rights.[11] Achieving these goals requires establishing boundaries. Political communities are systems of exclusion as well as inclusion: while the control of movement was not a sufficient precondition of statehood, control of movement was a necessary precursor of the sovereign state.[12]

Rights and Citizenship

Citizenship, in its definition as a legally homogeneous status within the context of the state, is comprised of rights and duties. These evolve through a process of contestation among individuals, groups, and institutions, shaped by and in turn transforming the political order. Rights that evolve through political pressure are legal rights, not the natural or divine rights that characterized Europe until the seventeenth century: law was seen as founded on God's authority, and monarchs, subservient only to the Pope as God's representatives on earth, could interpret the law. Starting in the seventeenth century, however, the individual came to be regarded as the primary unit upon which the rest of society is constructed, and political thinkers based their theories of law on the rights of individuals: Grotius, Hobbes, Pufendorf, Locke, Rousseau, and others all shared the belief that consent constitutes the sole source of legitimate authority and the basis of political obligation.[13] The notion that the rights of a people derive from their institutions of government fits the redefinition of the state as a body of free individuals united together in order to enjoy common rights and advantages, the redefinition that informed the Peace of Westphalia and the European political order that evolved since. Since Westphalia, there was a strong relationship between rights and state formation, though the development of rights differed greatly from state to state. In the meantime, the vacuum left by the rejection of divine law as the foundation of rights was filled by positivist theories claiming that the state is the only foundation for rights and law.[14]

If rights indeed depend on laws, which in turn depend on states, then it might be argued that European rights cannot exist if Europe is not itself a state. States do remain central in guaranteeing the basic rights of citizenship because rights are respected only in a system governed by the rule of law. Yet dismissals of European rights ignore the reality that European legal instruments now constitute an autonomous system of law. The European Court of

Justice adjudicates real laws that give rise to real rights. In this sense, it is indeed true that "the status of 'Community citizen' [was] officially recognized from the moment when the Treaties granted rights to individuals and the opportunity of enforcing them by recourse to a national or Community court."[15]

The emergence of European rights since the Second World War echoes another historical development: that of individuals demanding rights as citizens rather than subjects.[16] Rather than simply accepting authority bestowed from on high, individuals increasingly demanded a voice in the shaping of that authority, a voice that finds expression in the modern idea of rights. People who cross jurisdictional boundaries—such as the Italian workers who in the 1950s and 1960s sought work elsewhere in Europe, the millions moving about the Union more recently, or indeed migrants elsewhere around the world—tend to demand rights in their new place of residence. In this way, establishing rights to free movement and residence alters the political environment and generates demands for extending and expanding the content of the original right. In a story that parallels the development of democratic states, one right follows another—civil rights foster demands for political rights, which in turn foster demands for social rights—in a process that can eventually lead to the extension of citizenship, a status bestowed upon those considered full members of the community.[17] The rise of EU citizenship reflects the fact that Europe is no longer simply a community of states but has become a community of individuals with a common status.

Rights are fundamental and unalienable; policies are freely altered. The precise distinction between rights and policies is sometimes murky, but extending rights to individuals is different than changing, say, agricultural or industrial policy. Policies can be relatively easily modified by governments, whereas rights are more basic and fundamental. Consider the right to education, which is enshrined in the European Charter of Fundamental Rights as well as the Universal Declaration of Human Rights. It is unclear what precisely this right entails: imagine that a (short-sighted) government decided to reduce its education budget by providing only a few years of schooling, so that students past a young age would receive schooling only by paying tuition. It is unclear whether this would constitute merely a change in government policy or an infringement of the right to education.[18] Many governments around the world have been naming "rights" procedures and principles that are better understood as policies. For example, threatened political elites may attempt to "constitutionalize" policies as rights. Labeling a policy a right matters because doing so makes it harder to negotiate and compromise—as is becoming evident in democratic states around the world.[19] But the content of rights *does* change, as countless historical and contemporary examples remind us.

Free Movement, Markets, and State Building

Political commitment can create supranational rights in any context, but such commitment is more likely to occur and to result in supranational rights where there are economic reasons for introducing them. Community free movement rights were first introduced at least in part in order to facilitate a freer labor market. Strong links between the state and the market may be necessary to the elaboration of rights in any modern context. Indeed, many rights evolved via processes of adaptation to the evolution of markets.[20] To the extent that rights developed in tandem with markets, it should not be surprising that the emergence of a European market has led to European rights. But one of the arguments of this book is that the introduction of economic rights was coupled with a political project.

Free movement is the bedrock upon which the entire construction of European rights has been built. Citizens of one member state who move to another one to take up residence or employment are caught up in the creation of European rights because they are the beneficiaries of free movement, practice it, and push for its expansion. Free movement rights for workers launched the process of European political integration, and the further development of European rights is central to the entire project of integration. Robert Schuman's aim of reducing the rigidity of borders while not eliminating them or inventing a rationalized geography captures this objective.[21] Driven by the goal of opening up Europe's borders, the development of European rights significantly alters the traditional role of states in controlling immigration.[22]

Some commentators claim that free movement rights had to be introduced in order to ensure a common market, just as the movement of goods, services, and capital had to be liberalized: thus a former Commission vice president argued that the "establishment of a common market implies free movement of persons, if not as such then at least as labour."[23] He characterized free movement as "the final abandonment of the traditional concept of emigration based on the system of bilateral and multilateral agreements" and presaged that "full and absolute equality of treatment [would] lead to the rapid replacement of the notion of the 'emigrant' by that of the 'European worker.'"[24] But even if worker mobility is desirable in a free trade zone, it does not automatically follow that free movement provisions should be enshrined as individual rights. Certainly free trade arrangements in North America and elsewhere have not resulted in extensive supranational rights for individuals.

Because extending European rights constrains states to respect them, states should prefer bilateral or multilateral agreements (which can be altered relatively easily) to individual rights (which cannot): arguing that domestic policy concerns could result in supranational policies with the same impact as European rights cannot explain why national governments should be willing to enshrine *rights* rather than simply working out ad hoc intergovernmental bargains.[25] A free European market does not require European citizenship: in fact, citizenship makes markets less free because it forces governments to regulate the markets in order to satisfy rights.[26]

Since there was no market requirement for individual rights, an important reason why European leaders chose to introduce free movement and then other rights was commitment to the "European idea," discussed below. In making this choice, they followed the historical examples of most states—particularly France (where one of the first effects of the French Revolution was to ease restrictions on movements within France) and Germany (which in the nineteenth century had gradually reduced barriers to free movement as part of its unification process).[27] Indeed, democratic states around the world typically guarantee as one of the first articles of their constitutions their citizens' rights to free movement within state territory.

Removing barriers to trade often generates demands for freer movement of workers, and political leaders can *choose* to translate those demands into individual mobility rights for workers. Doing so alters the political environment and may create further political pressure to broaden the original free movement rights. Leaders who share a common political commitment can continue this process of extending rights to its logical conclusion: a common supranational citizenship. This process, the subject of this book, is what occurred in Europe. As long as the resulting supranational citizenship continues to be based on a political bargain among member states rather than enjoying widespread popular support, however, the rights of the common citizenship remain endangered in the same way that citizenship rights everywhere remain contingent upon continued support from leaders and publics. Easing restrictions on the free flow of goods or services need not automatically translate into easing restrictions on the free flow of people. This book discusses why it is occurring in Europe; more work is necessary to uncover and explain the intricacies of similar processes operating in other contexts.

Citizenship and Integration

Many authors explain integration largely in terms of the economic interests of states and state leaders, positing that integration strengthens states.[28] By contrast, one of this book's arguments is that the effort to entrench and expand a set of supranational rights, thereby creating European citizens, reflects the will to create a community of people rather than simply a free market area. The origins of EU citizenship lie in the initial negotiations and treaties that established the postwar foundations of European cooperation, but it was formally introduced with the Maastricht Treaty. Though skeptics even then dismissed it as unimportant, realization quickly grew that a shared citizenship is a significant development in European integration.[29]

Though the focus of this book is on explaining the evolution of European rights and citizenship, one of its implications is that neither of the two dominant theories of European integration—intergovernmentalism and neofunctionalism—can adequately explain this development. A key problem with the voluminous theoretical work on the EU is that theories tend to focus simultaneously on the integration *process*, the resulting *structure*, and the *operation* of that structure. Seeking to explain all three at the same time is impracticable. Briefly, intergovernmentalists argue that member states continue to be the most important actors in the EU, that "domestic" and "foreign" policy can be clearly separated, and that political leaders promote their state's interests over those of other states. Integration thus results from "a series of pragmatic bargains among national governments based on concrete national interests, relative power, and carefully crafted transfers of sovereignty."[30] By contrast, neofunctionalists argue that integration is self-reinforcing, creating ever-more-powerful supranational institutions that are autonomous from member states. Integration results from functional spillovers of supranational authority from one policy area to adjoining policy areas, shifts in national preferences, path dependence, and unintended consequences—the idea that states are unable to control supranational institutions once these have been established. Intergovernmentalism captures important truths about the process by which European rights and citizenship developed (namely, with the active support of *national* as well as European political leaders) but cannot explain why it would be in the interest of national political leaders to erase the distinction between domestic and foreign by extending rights to "foreigners" and creating a new political community of EU citizens that could ultimately subsume the states. Neofunctionalism tends to overemphasize the role of supranational institutions and cannot explain the episodic (rather than consistent or stable) growth of European rights. It does, however, forecast the consequence: the "end result of a process of political integration is a new political community, superimposed upon the preexisting ones."[31]

States are not, of course, unitary actors: they are composed of innumerable actors and interests, and the relative importance of any given set of interests or actors differs from time to time and from issue to issue. This is even truer for policy formulation at the European level, which resembles national policymaking though the EU lacks the traditional central actor, an elected government whose leaders are capable of imposing policy solutions against the wishes of opposing coalitions. Even without a strong European government, however, the familiar institutional paraphernalia of the modern state have emerged in a multilevel, highly fragmented system where policy develops beyond the firm control of any single political authority.[32] Since European regulations emanate from several institutions and represent a patchwork of policy styles and approaches, some argue that member states will seek to limit EU citizenship because it threatens to introduce supranational welfare rights, thereby putatively weakening the domestic legitimacy of the member states.[33] The process of creating European citizens contributes to building a system in which policies develop beyond the control of any single member state. Introducing citizenship reduces the power of member states if citizenship rights are both substantially important and cannot easily be revoked. This is because new actors (European citizens) have been created who can invoke rights and act autonomously, thus changing the dynamic of the integration process away from one controlled exclusively by states.

Citizenship and European Political Development

European citizenship developed through a continuing series of political junctures spanning the entire history of integration, coupled with an ongoing political and institutional commitment to safeguarding and promoting the development of European rights. This commitment to rights did not originate in material interests but from devotion to the "European idea"—shared guilt at the nationalism that had produced so much bloodshed and inhumanity and a conviction that only a "genuine European political community" would safeguard the European values of life, freedom, dignity, social justice, and above all, peace.[34] Subsequent chapters demonstrate that the "European idea" was strong in Italy, and similar arguments could be made about the Benelux countries. But others claim that it was particularly pronounced in France and Germany: some of the most fervent prointegrationists were French *paysans* who regarded themselves as "citizens of a future Europe," and the first annual conference (1947) of the German nongovernmental organization (NGO) Europa-Union noted that because the internecine wars that had destroyed so much of Europe were Germany's "fault," Germany, more than any other state, "should be ready and determined to make its contribution to the unification of Europe and thereby to lasting peace for all."[35]

One commentator minimizes the impact of the European idea, arguing that European integration was always "more about commercial gains and less about peace and liberty than politicians have admitted publicly."[36] In fact, the reasons for supporting European integration differ, and it is probably unwise to attempt to isolate only one.[37] Some prointegrationists were indeed likely motivated solely by commercial and economic interests. Others by the geopolitical demands of containing German nationalism, Soviet expansionism, or more recently, U.S. hegemony. But there also exists a third reason for supporting (or rejecting, in the case of Euroskeptics) European integration: the dream that Europe could be transformed, in the most profound way possible, into a new political entity. Whether driven purely by economic goals or also inspired by versions of the European idea, European leaders decided to establish institutions to safeguard the rights they were introducing. For one of the protagonists, it was clear that they viewed the common market as simply a means to create a genuine European political community: "Full well did they measure the importance of the economic transformations they had just decided, but in their minds, those transformations, for all their greatness, were merely accessory to, or, at the very least, the first stage of a yet greater political revolution."[38]

As this book elucidates, the story of Europe's political development is complex. European rights—and ultimately citizenship—developed through a combination of the "high politics" of intergovernmental conferences with the "low politics" of interpretation by the Court and implementation by the Commission.[39] The first critical high politics moment was the Italian insistence that free movement of labor be included in the 1951 treaty, establishing the European Coal and Steel Community (ECSC), the Treaty of Paris. Next came the expansion of this freedom to all workers and its enshrinement as an individual right in the 1957 treaty, establishing the European Economic Community, the Treaty of Rome. For the next decade and a half, member states and the supranational institutions they had established—the Commission, the Court, and the Parliament—were occupied with the implementation of free movement rights for workers and their families, a task that was accompanied by the invocation of European citizenship in the 1960s and early 1970s. The citizenship rhetoric of representatives of some member states—primarily Italy, but also Germany, Belgium, and France—was counterbalanced by opposition from Luxembourg and new member states Denmark and the UK. This opposition started to wane in the 1980s in light of Court rulings and as a result of the entry into the Community of Greece, Portugal, and especially Spain. The Mediterranean countries—supported by the French and German "motor of integration," by a post–Cold War climate in which citizenship quickly came to be seen as one way of combating the democratic deficit, and by the institutional background of years of agitation in the Parliament and the Commission—succeeded in finally passing citizenship at Maastricht. The treaty did not go far enough for some but went too far for others, particularly Luxembourg—which obtained a phase-in period for the voting rights—and the public in France and Denmark, where citizenship was a major issue in the Maastricht referendums. In light of this opposition, the 1997 Amsterdam treaty introduced only minor additions to the rights of European citizenship and specified that it would remain a supplement to national citizenship, which it would not replace. Subsequent years have witnessed continuing incremental additions to and clarifications of the rights of European citizenship, though the focus has increasingly shifted to encouraging citizens to utilize their rights, primarily the right to live and work anywhere within EU territory. Continued popular opposition to some European rights, coupled with the Union's continuing enlargement, underlines the fluid and evolving nature of European citizenship.

CHAPTER ONE

Introducing European Rights

> Resolved to substitute for age old rivalries the merging of their essential interests; to create, by establishing an economic community, the basis for a broader and deeper community among peoples long divided by bloody conflicts; and to lay the foundations for institutions which will give direction to a destiny henceforward shared.
>
> —ECSC Treaty, 1951

> The [migrant] worker must everywhere feel his European citizenship to be a source of strength and pride. For this . . . will be the most important political and social result of the liberalization of the labour market: to the extent to which it is attained, we shall all be made to appreciate the effective range of European solidarity and the progress of the idea of unity.[1]
>
> —Commissioner Lionello Levi Sandri

The individual rights at the heart of European citizenship date from the free movement provisions of the Treaty of Paris (1951), with which France, Germany, Italy, the Netherlands, Belgium, and Luxembourg established the European Coal and Steel Community (ECSC). Free movement did not figure prominently in the treaty negotiations, but its promise provided the key incentive for Italian participation. Worker mobility rights took years to negotiate and implement, ultimately being outpaced by the much wider category of free movement rights contained in the Treaty of Rome (1957). These rights—alongside free movement of goods, services, and capital, one of the four freedoms encompassing the internal market—built upon the ECSC's framework of politically negotiated free movement. The new rights—to move freely within Community territory in order to accept employment, to reside in another member state for the purpose of employment, and to continue residing there after having been employed—were implemented in three transition phases between 1958 and 1968. They differentiated the Community from the states east of the Iron Curtain: as western European states were encouraging free movement, the USSR and the European states under Communist government were raising barriers. Meanwhile the European Court of Justice (ECJ) developed the legal doctrines of supremacy—that European law would take precedence over national law, including national constitutions—and direct effect—that the subjects of European law (and those entitled to appeal to the Court) would be not only member states, as might be expected from the court of a treaty organization, but also individuals.

1.1. The European Coal and Steel Community

The idea of European unity is very old, but the political push for European rights accelerated during the Second World War, the continent's (and the world's) most destructive war. In Italy in 1943, the *Movimento Federalista Europeo* (European Federalist Movement, MFE) envisaged the creation of a European continental citizenship alongside national citizenship, consisting of direct political and legal relationships with a European federation.[2] Similarly, plans drawn up by Giovanni Gronchi (later president of Italy), Count Stefano Jacini (senator and later president of the United Nations Educational, Scientific and Cultural Organization), and labor union leader Achille Grandi called for the "option to take out European citizenship in addition to national citizenship."[3] After the war, British prime minister Winston Churchill advocated "a European group which could give a sense of enlarged patriotism and common citizenship to the distracted peoples of this turbulent and mighty continent."[4] Likewise, the European Action group in the Netherlands called for a European citizenship besides that of nationality, and the May 1948 Hague Congress resolved that direct access for citizens to redress before a European Court of any violation of their rights under a common charter was to be an essential ingredient of the European political and economic union they advocated. Organized by the International Committee of the Movements for European Unity and chaired by Churchill, The Hague Congress assembled hundreds of Europe's leaders—including Churchill,

Konrad Adenauer, Richard de Coudenhove-Kalergi, Anthony Eden, Walter Hallstein, Alcide De Gasperi, Harold Macmillan, François Mitterrand, Paul-Henri Spaak, and Altiero Spinelli—and declared the "urgent duty of the nations of Europe to create an economic and political union."[5]

In this context, the first concrete steps to European integration began with the announcement by French foreign minister Robert Schuman on 9 May 1950—the tenth anniversary of the German invasion of France, the Netherlands, Belgium, and Luxembourg—of a plan for a European coal and steel community. The symbolism of the date was not accidental. Three wars between France and Germany over the preceding three generations had exacted their toll: western Europe in 1950 was rebuilding from war, the government of the Federal Republic of Germany was still under Allied tutelage, and the Cold War was well under way. In this political and economic context, the potential benefits of closer cooperation among the western European states appeared clear. Schuman announced his plan unilaterally, but representatives from France, Germany, Italy, and the Benelux countries rapidly began earnest negotiations. British representatives observed the proceedings, but the UK ultimately decided not to participate, not wishing to jeopardize its sovereignty.[6] Potential treaty provisions were discussed during the summer and fall, and a draft treaty was ready by December. Following final negotiations, the treaty establishing the ECSC was signed in Paris on 18 April 1951, entering into force on 25 July 1952.

Though the negotiations focused almost exclusively on economic issues, some believed that the Community would narrow the scope for independent state action and herald the eventual demise of state sovereignty.[7] Free movement of workers played a minor role in the bargaining for all states but Italy. Millions of Italians had for decades been emigrating to find work elsewhere in Europe, and the promise of free movement motivated Italian participation in the ECSC: though political support for the European idea and the economic desire to acquire raw materials cheaply also figured, guaranteed rights for Italian workers to emigrate was more important—indeed, for at least fifteen years after the war, the primary interest of most Italians in European integration was the hope of finding an outlet for emigration.[8]

The issue of labor migration was broached by Paolo Taviani, the Italian negotiator, who later wrote that free movement rights for workers constituted a fundamental principle of the Community. Free movement was the key condition for Italian participation, and Taviani even envisioned creating a European ministry of labor.[9] During the negotiations, Taviani pushed for a better deal on migration by raising the specter of a High Authority with the power to set and enforce wage levels across the Community, unacceptable to other potential member states.[10] Fearing that a powerful High Authority would overturn delicate political compromises within their countries, Dutch and German negotiators capitulated to the Italian demand for worker mobility: like Italy, the Netherlands and Germany were labor-exporting countries in the early 1950s, so they did not foresee any problems, and the Italians successfully used the wage level issue as a bargaining chip to secure free movement of workers.[11]

Opposition might have come from the only potential member states with significant numbers of foreign coal workers: Belgium and France. In Belgium, two out of every five coal workers were non-Belgian, primarily Italian. In France, one out of every five coal workers was foreign, but these were mostly Polish and thus unaffected by any potential ECSC treaty provisions: in 1951 there were over seventy thousand foreign coal workers in Belgium, just under fifty-seven thousand in France, less than four thousand each in the Netherlands and Germany, few in Luxembourg, and almost none in Italy.[12] Bolstered by strong public support (French public opinion favored the Schuman Plan by a margin of two to one, despite being rather ill informed about its contents) and intent on forging a deal, the French delegation led by Jean Monnet granted concessions despite some French leaders' worries that "the Italians would export their unemployment."[13] Meanwhile, the Belgian position was pragmatic, more concerned with the fate of their ailing coal and steel industries than the prospect of even more immigration of workers.[14] Indeed, if coal mines were to close, it seemed likely that foreign workers would return to their countries of origin. By December 1947, all the German prisoners of war working in the Belgian mines—whose numbers had peaked at forty-six thousand in early 1946—had been freed and been replaced mainly by Italian miners: the June 1946 bilateral agreement with Italy stipulated that the Italian government would send to Belgium two thousand miners per week.[15]

The Italian delegation was keen to promote the free movement of its nationals elsewhere in Europe. In the earlier Organization of European Economic Cooperation negotiations, established in 1948 to distribute Marshall Plan funds, and likewise in the Franco-Italian Customs Union negotiations, Italy had presented emigration requests for large numbers of unskilled workers but received only limited offers for skilled workers. Since there were already between seventy and eighty thousand Italian coal and steel workers in the other five prospective ECSC member states, the Italian negotiators argued that it should surely be possible to achieve a sectoral arrangement if general labor mobility was unattainable.[16] In the absence of opposition from other member states, the Italian delegation was successful in its effort to include free movement rights, and the first steps to free movement rights for workers in the future Community were enshrined in the ECSC treaty, which announced that member states would "remove any restriction based on nationality upon the employment in the coal and steel industries of workers who are nationals of Member States and have recognised qualifications in a coalmining or steelmaking occupation, subject to the limitations imposed by the basic requirements of health and public policy" (Art. 69). The Italian success at including free movement for labor was limited: here in nascent form were the restrictions on free movement for the purposes of health and public policy that until the introduction of European Union (EU) citizenship allowed member states to curtail free movement rights. Another potential source of restriction was the ambiguous definition of "recognized qualifications." The treaty specified that member states would establish common definitions of skilled trades and qualifications, which left significant room for restrictive interpretation. Finally, a key institutional barrier was that the High Authority's role was limited to coordinating and advising: member states remained responsible for drafting and implementing the free movement provisions.

Mirroring its modest role in the negotiations—where only the Italian delegation placed much emphasis on labor mobility—the question of the free movement of workers remained a minor one during the various national ratification debates. Still, French and Belgian Communist parliamentarians charged that workers would "become nothing more than simple merchandise."[17] Indeed, Communist parties in all the prospective member states opposed the proposed treaty, with French Communists describing it as a tool of American foreign policy that would equate workers with goods and capital, increasing their exploitation.[18] Dutch Christian Democrats added that free movement of workers would create moral problems as families were uprooted, while German Socialists wondered whether coal and steel workers who moved to other member states would be authorized to search alternative employment in the host state if their employment was disrupted by strikes.[19] In the end, though, these concerns did not prevent the Treaty of Paris from being ratified in all the member states.

Ratification did not automatically mean that workers could freely move about Community territory: coal and steel workers were immediately subject to free movement, but worker mobility would be implemented only by unanimous agreement among the six member states. The Social Affairs Commission spearheaded efforts to achieve this agreement. One of High Authority's four general commissions, Social Affairs was responsible for raising the standard of living in Europe, which it felt could be achieved by enhancing free movement. It worked with national employment ministries to reach agreement on "a first step towards the creation of a 'common market' for labour."[20] The Council approved the agreement in December 1954, and administrative details were settled in the months that followed. Thus, the final agreement on free movement for coal and steel workers took more than twice the time it had taken to negotiate the treaty itself. The High Authority reassured anyone worried about potential mass migrations that "comparatively few workers [would] immediately avail themselves" of the international work permits that would allow them to move freely, as any significant labor migration would have to be preceded by major labor market changes.[21]

Though Italy and the High Authority had strongly urged that the definition of worker qualifications be interpreted broadly, other governments succeeded in limiting free movement to certain skilled workers: only approximately three hundred thousand of the Community's 1.4 million coal and steel workers qualified for the permits that allowed these workers to seek employment in other member states free of the red tape generally governing labor immigration.[22] An American observer reported enthusiastically on early efforts made to "enable these workers to enjoy all the social security benefits of the receiving country, thus preventing the discriminations that have frequently been practised against aliens in the past" and "to improve coordination between the various employment organizations in the member states so that workers in one country may know more easily whether jobs are available elsewhere."[23]

Despite such optimistic assessments immediately following the agreement on free movement, full implementation was delayed until after all the member states had ratified it.[24] Italy, Belgium, France, and the Netherlands did so by the end of 1955, but the German Bundestag delayed ratification until May 1956, and Luxembourg stymied the entire process by postponing its ratification until June 1957. The agreement on free movement of workers thus finally took effect in September 1957, four and a half years after work on it had begun. This sluggishness proved a constant irritant to the Italians between 1952 and 1957: most of the speeches by Italian members of the Common Assembly concerned the delay on implementing free movement.[25] Their preoccupation was understandable: the only significant migrants within the Community were the thousands of Italian agricultural workers employed in the Belgian coal mines. Though some Italian economists discouraged the idea that "opening the frontiers could free a massive emigration of Italian workers and eliminate unemployment in a flash," the political interest shown during the ECSC negotiations persisted.[26]

The delayed introduction of free movement raised such ire that the Common Assembly included the issue in its constitutional proposals for rewriting the ECSC treaty as a result of the Treaty of Rome negotiations. Free movement was the *only* policy issue to appear in a document otherwise entirely about the relationship between the High Authority and the proposed new institutions. Dissatisfied with the application of free movement, the Common Assembly concluded that the member states were too slow to implement these rights for coal and steel workers. It therefore proposed that the High Authority should take over from the member states the responsibility to establish common definitions of worker qualifications, propose immigration rules, and ensure that social security arrangements did not inhibit worker mobility. The Common Assembly further proposed giving the High Authority the power to address disparities between labor supply and demand.[27]

The High Authority focused on reducing unemployment and constructing adequate housing for coal miners and steelworkers, which prompted some parliamentarians to call for extending the "international passports for workers" to other fields.[28] President of the High Authority Jean Monnet saw free movement of workers as "one of the ways in which will be accomplished the harmonization of standards of living and of work promised by the Treaty."[29] Free movement fit with Monnet's belief in the necessity of uniting Europeans: famously, he claimed that Europe's circumstances required "that we unite Europeans and that we do not keep them separated. We are not joining states, we are unifying men."[30] With some observers claiming that the High Authority developed a "European spirit" of cooperation based on a common European interest, the Social Affairs Commission persistently pushed for free movement in the face of member state intransigence and delay, and its efforts were favorably reported in the Common Assembly's updates.[31]

1.2. From Paris (ECSC) to Rome (EEC)

Despite the slow progress on eliminating restrictions on the movement of workers, most policy makers supported the ECSC's goal of efficiently distributing workers among the member states in order to achieve a "sound economy based on a rational distribution of labour in a free market."[32] In 1954, the governments of the six member states began to consider a new economic initiative that would complement the ECSC. The Dutch pressed for a general economic common market. The Belgians—supported by French ministers, Jean Monnet, and others—countered that further cooperation should occur by economic sector, extending the ECSC into transport and forms of energy other than coal and steel. The Benelux governments presented a joint proposal combining the sectoral and common market approaches that was considered at a special meeting of the Council of Ministers at Messina on 2 and 3 June 1955. The ministers established a committee headed by Belgian foreign minister Paul-Henri Spaak to prepare a report on the feasibility of a common customs union and a common atomic energy agency. They further agreed to adopt the Benelux program, modified for more gradual implementation.

Even as the free movement provisions for coal and steel workers continued to be stymied, proponents of greater European integration pushed instead for giving rights to many more categories of workers. The impetus for extending free movement can be found in the Spaak committee's 1956 report, which viewed a common market as leading to monetary stability, economic expansion, social protection, a higher standard of living and better quality of life, economic and social cohesion, and solidarity among the member states.[33] Achieving this long list of goals depended, in the committee's view, on undistorted market competition, of which free movement for workers formed an integral part. In the Spaak committee's recommendations is the genesis of the concept of a "market citizen," who bears rights as an economic rather than political actor.[34] Just as member states—led by Italy—favored extending free movement of workers, so too did the ECSC institutions. For example, the Common Assembly noted with satisfaction that the Treaty of Rome offered the chance to correct the restrictive interpretation of the Treaty of Paris that had constrained free movement of workers.[35]

In contrast with the restrictiveness of the Treaty of Paris, the Treaty of Rome extended the scope of free movement rights to all workers, with the exception of those employed in the public service. The Treaty of Rome gave workers the right to move freely within Community territory to accept employment, to reside in any member state to work, and to continue residing there after having been employed. Though member state governments could avoid having to implement mobility rights based on public policy, health, or security concerns, these rights went much further than those of existing bilateral agreements. Bilateral agreements were important in the early years, but the difficult experience of enacting the Treaty of Paris provisions demonstrated the need to simplify decision making in the Treaty of Rome.[36] In a key difference from the Treaty of Paris, which had left the member states responsible for drafting and implementing free movement provisions, the Treaty of Rome empowered the Commission to make proposals to achieve free movement for workers. Those in favor of broadening free movement rights had learned from earlier difficulties. The Treaty of Rome thus contained a new version of the employment provisions originally announced in the Treaty of Paris half a dozen years previously, defining these employment provisions as rights.

The new mobility rights were implemented in three stages. Whereas the Treaty of Paris had required member states to agree before workers could use their new rights, the Treaty of Rome provisions were subject to a transition period scheduled to end by 1 January 1970. Parliament advocated immediately introducing free movement, claiming that delay would risk "provoking a dangerous disequilibrium between the economic and the social measures being undertaken by the EEC [European Economic Community], which would harm the move to speed up economic recovery."[37] The economic climate was propitious. Unemployment in the six member states decreased from 2.8 million to 1.5 million between 1958 and 1964 despite a substantial inflow of non-Community workers, allowing full implementation of free movement for Community workers by 1968, ahead of schedule.[38]

Despite the introduction of free movement rights, only a small portion of all migration—that of the Italian emigrants after the mid-1960s—was actually governed by the new supranational procedures.[39] The rest were governed by bilateral agreements. Indeed, within the Community, "the only important movement beyond the phenomenon of frontier workers was that of Italian labor."[40] As a 1960 parliamentary report noted, high economic growth across most of the Community was leading most member states to rely on foreign workers. Since Italy was the only member state with "sufficient reserves of labour to satisfy both its domestic as well as foreign needs . . . it is in the interest of the Community as a whole to adopt measures that would facilitate the employment of Italian labour in the other Community members."[41]

The first of the three transition phases occurred with a 1961 regulation that protected national markets and maintained the requirement for workers to obtain a work document.[42] Community workers had to wait three weeks from the notice of vacancy in order to ensure that there was no worker available within the member state in question and to give priority to workers from that state.[43] Once these conditions were met, any Community worker could take up employment within another member state. Furthermore, the regulation abolished quotas on Community workers employed within a member state: no member state could henceforth limit access to its labor market to only some Community workers. The regulation did not apply to frontier and seasonal workers, artists, and musicians, who were covered under separate provisions. The regulation was accompanied by a directive that abolished entry and exit visas for all intra-Community movement. Those crossing borders within the Community had henceforth only to show an identity card or passport to enjoy the right of entry and exit.

As these measures were being drafted, the Commission's vice president called for "the creation of a Community conscience, a common enthusiasm for

Europe; not for any abstract idea of Europe, but for a Europe which can find its justification in the improvement of the living conditions of its inhabitants."[44] One of his Italian colleagues was confident that completely equal treatment of all community workers would soon cause Europeans to think of them not as emigrants but as European workers.[45] European workers continued to migrate, and by 1963 roughly one million salaried workers were employed in a member state other than that of their citizenship.[46] Free movement rights enjoyed widespread popular support: majorities in all member states favored being allowed to work and set up firms wherever they wished in Europe, while allowing workers and firms from other countries to do the same. The highest support was in Italy (78 percent), while the most opposition was in France (32 percent). Among workers, support for such rights ranged from a high in Italy (82 percent in favor, 7 percent against, 11 percent did not know) to a low in France (50 percent in favor, 35 percent against, 15 percent did not know). Germany (72 percent, 9 percent, 18 percent), Belgium (69 percent, 18 percent, 13 percent), and the Netherlands (69 percent, 21 percent, 10 percent) were in the middle, while Luxembourg was not surveyed.[47]

The second transition phase for the full implementation of free movement was accomplished with 1964 legislation that replaced the national preference of the 1961 rules with a European preference: henceforth, no discrimination between Community workers was allowed, as all Community workers had the same right to seek employment anywhere within Community territory. Furthermore, Community workers were no longer subject to the three-week waiting period; they could accept employment as soon as a vacancy opened.[48] Unlike the 1961 Regulation, its 1964 replacement applied also to frontier workers, seasonal workers, artists, and musicians. Significantly, it accorded to migrant workers the right to bring their families, who would then have the right to education and employment in the member state of residence. A safeguard clause allowed member states to suspend free movement for Community workers (but not cross-border commuter workers, whose free movement rights could not be suspended) if there was a serious disequilibrium in a regional or sectoral labor market. Also in 1964, the member states agreed to restrict the conditions under which they could limit the entry of Community nationals under the public policy, security, or health exemptions: limiting entry would be based exclusively on the personal conduct of the individual concerned, previous criminal convictions would not in themselves constitute grounds for such measures, and member states would not introduce new provisions more restrictive than those already in force.[49]

The final provisions were settled at a Council of Ministers meeting in July 1968. Employers' organizations and the European federation of labor unions favored free movement and had successfully lobbied the member states for its enactment. These groups thus exercised "effective pressure" on the Council, while the Commission "was not aware of its own limitations and did not fully realize that it was not in a position to carry out its plans."[50] The third transition phase thus concluded with the full legal implementation of the free movement provisions announced ten years earlier in the Treaty of Rome. Contemporaries recognized that this was a "significant legal and normative development in Community relations."[51] Free movement for workers had become a fundamental right, as the 1968 Regulation elucidates: "Any national of a Member State, shall, irrespective of his place of residence, have the right to take up an activity as an employed person, and to pursue such activity, within the territory of another Member State in accordance with the provisions laid down by law, regulation or administrative action governing the employment of nationals of that State . . . [and] with the same priority as nationals of that State."[52] The accompanying directive stipulated that member states would "abolish restrictions on the movement and residence of nationals of [other member] States and of members of their families."[53] The right of Community workers to move and take up residence was thus fully achieved.

This achievement caused one observer to assert that Community workers were now no longer "foreigners," nor even "*Gastarbeiter*" (guest workers), but had rights to work, which would lead to a new form of citizenship.[54] Indeed, even before full implementation, another observer had made the same point: free movement was "a field in which the citizens of the Six will progressively be treated as if they had not French or Italian, but Community citizenship."[55] Sharing this hope, the Parliament and the Commission were enthusiastic proponents of prompt implementation. As early as 1960, free movement was described as a "fundamental right" of workers, and in 1961 the Commission presented it as "the first aspect of a European citizenship."[56] Walter Hallstein, the Commission's first president, called the achievement of free movement for workers one of "the most spectacular points in the programme which is to lead to the integration of Europe." He continued, "On the basis of this success alone, the Community could claim the right to call itself the 'European Economic and Social Community.' The consequences in terms of constitutional policy are incalculable. Do they point to the beginning of a common European 'citizenship'?"[57] Hallstein echoed his vice president, the Italian socialist Lionello Levi Sandri, who had earlier maintained that free movement of persons "represents something more important and more exacting than the free movement of a factor of production. It represents rather an incipient form—still embryonic and imperfect—of European citizenship."[58] By the mid-1960s, the idea of a common European citizenship had thus been firmly entrenched in the imaginations of Europe's political leaders.

As the genesis of a common European citizenship, free movement of workers satisfied both economic and political rationales for integration. Altiero Spinelli explained that the achievement of free movement rights within Europe had been possible because there was such high demand for workers "in the other five countries and in northern Italy as soon to make the flow of Italian workers from the south insufficient and to induce the various countries to open their gates to the immigration of workers from the Iberian peninsula, from Greece, Turkey, and the Maghreb."[59] Indeed, the level of Italian emigration to the other member states fell following the introduction of free movement rights, never regaining anything approaching its 1965 level.[60] As Italian emigration declined, so did immigration in the other member states: the total volume of Community workers entering each member state had been declining since 1956, except in Italy—where the numbers were negligible but rising—and Germany, which replaced France and Belgium as the main destination of Italian emigrants.[61] With stable or falling numbers of migrants, proponents of integration could turn their attention to the political project of bringing migrants in from the social and administrative margins. The foundation of so-called European civic rights, or a European citizenship that would enable citizens to fully integrate into the fabric of their host societies, thus lay in the free movement rights of workers. European rights were necessary to fully achieve the goal of opening Europe's borders not simply to goods, services, and capital but also to people.

1.3. Demographics, Migration, and Economic Growth

When they signed the Treaty of Paris in 1951, and even more so when they signed the Treaty of Rome in 1957, the political leaders of the six member states faced a wide range of free movement regimes devoted to facilitating worker migration. Even before the Second World War, a convention on migrant workers had been signed under the sponsorship of the Bureau International du Travail, the precursor of the International Labor Organization. This "Migration for Employment Convention" was revised in 1949: signatory governments agreed to treat migrant workers no differently than their own citizens, and to facilitate the departure, journey, and reception of migrants for employment. Seven west European states promptly ratified the Convention, including all the future member states except Luxembourg.[62]

No Communist state ratified the Convention. The contrast between west European encouragement of free movement and the states under Soviet influence was stark. In the USSR, freedom to choose one's residence was limited by passport restrictions and the requirement to obtain a *propiska*, or permit issued by the police, for residence in a particular city or town; meeting these requirements was difficult for urban residents, and rural residents could obtain *propiski* only in exceptional cases. Even in the post-Soviet period, a number of regions (most notably Moscow) continued to restrict access to legal residence despite constitutional and legislative guarantees of free movement for all citizens.[63] During the Communist period, there were similar impediments to free movement elsewhere in central and eastern Europe, particularly for interstate migrations.[64] By contrast, western European states started in the immediate postwar period to generate a host of plans to facilitate international migration.

The five member states of the Western European Union—France, the Netherlands, Belgium, Luxembourg, and the UK—had also launched several initiatives to enable free movement of labor. They adopted the following initiatives: a convention on frontier workers to facilitate free movement and define the principles of regulating salaries and working conditions (1950); a convention (1949) and administrative arrangement (1950) on social and medical assistance, obliging each member state to admit patients of any of the four other signatories under the same conditions as its own nationals; a system of cooperation among the employment offices of the five countries, encouraging exchanges of workers (1951); a convention (1949) and implementing arrangement (1954) to extend and coordinate social security provisions to workers from other WEU members, establishing the principle by which eligibility for social security would not depend on citizenship but rather would be open without discrimination to workers from any of the five signatories; a convention on social security (1953); and removed application costs for entry visas for foreign workers (1953).[65]

Similar moves were also underway in the Benelux. Five years after the signing of the 1948 economic union, ministers from Belgium, the Netherlands, and Luxembourg met in The Hague in July 1953 to sign a protocol on coordinating their economic and social policies. The protocol stated that the goal of economic union was the free movement of persons, goods, services, and capital—the famous four freedoms that would later form the core of the Community's internal market program. Though the Benelux had had a common market in labor since the end of the war, no treaty had been signed to formalize this arrangement by the time the ECSC foreign ministers met in Messina in 1955. Though the number of workers making use of the common labor market remained relatively small, the Benelux social affairs commission proposed eliminating the need for workers and employers to have a permit, regulating labor shortages and surpluses, and introducing the principle of equal treatment for nationals of any Benelux country.[66] This proposal acquired legal force in 1957, thereby establishing the first coordinated system for the free movement of workers within the future Community.

Meanwhile, in 1954 Denmark, Finland, Norway, and Sweden agreed to form a Nordic Common Labor Market. The four states abolished work permit requirements and established administrative cooperation on labor market issues. The agreement was accompanied by a protocol that exempted citizens of the four states from needing passports or residence permits when traveling or taking up residence within any of the other states.[67] Finally, passport-free movement between the UK and Ireland continued after Irish independence in 1922, maintaining the status quo. Within the Common Travel Area, citizens of the UK, Ireland, the Channel Islands, and the Isle of Man generally travel without a passport.[68] The UK continued to attract Irish workers and between 1945 and 1975 also received some three hundred thousand migrants from continental Europe—especially Poles, Germans, Italians, and Greeks.[69]

By agreeing to free movement of workers, states hoped to foster economic growth and reduce unemployment. As discussed above, one way in which the Italian governments of the 1950s and 1960s tried to reduce unemployment was by encouraging Italian workers to emigrate. Yet Italy's approach was not unique: the Netherlands also actively promoted emigration until the 1960s, even providing emigrants with stipends to encourage them to leave. While the Italian motivation for promoting emigration was high unemployment, the Dutch motivation for pursuing similar policies was its high population growth rate. Indeed, the highest net population growth rates among the member states in the postwar period were in the Netherlands and West Germany, with France in the midrange and the populations of Luxembourg, Italy, and Belgium growing more slowly. Until the erection of the Berlin Wall in 1961, West Germany received a constant flow of East German refugees, totaling approximately 2.7 million.[70] The explosive growth in the Dutch population was due to a high birth rate coupled with return migration and immigration from the colonies. For France, too, immigration was a significant source of population growth. By the mid-1950s, the Maghreb, especially Algeria, and other French colonies in Africa and overseas, had replaced Poland, Italy, and Spain as the most important sources of newcomers to France. In addition, approximately one million so-called *pieds-noirs*, white settlers born in Africa, moved to France following Algerian independence in 1962.[71]

These immigrants were generally not regarded as a burden. Indeed, free movement of labor was treated as a central element of the general economic recovery of Europe. Policy makers believed that mobility would lower unemployment in regions of emigration and foster economic growth in regions of immigration, and this is largely what occurred: between 1954 and 1959, 2.5 million new jobs were created in Italy, 2.3 million were created in Germany, and employment growth was, proportionately, only slightly lower in the Netherlands and Luxembourg.[72] Since Belgium and France were already near full employment, there was no employment growth in France, and little in Belgium. As a result of the economic boom, unemployment dropped across the Community, though it remained high in Italy. There were 1.96 million unemployed in Italy in 1954, a number that by 1959 had dropped only slightly to 1.69 million, or roughly 8 percent unemployment.[73] The new jobs were mainly taken up by workers entering the labor market for the first time, many of them women, as well as young men from rural areas. Furthermore, emigration reduced Italian unemployment considerably: in the six years from 1954 to 1959, some nine hundred thousand people—three quarters of them workers—emigrated from Italy.[74] The phenomenon of full employment—long-standing in Belgium, France, and Luxembourg—extended to Germany. There, low population growth and a booming economy soon created a shortage of workers. Meanwhile, the Netherlands continued to encourage emigration, which reduced the pool of potential workers. Not until the 1960s did the Dutch economy grow sufficiently for the emigration flood to abate.[75]

The labor shortages in France, Germany, Belgium, and Luxembourg could be met mainly by Italian emigration. The other significant intra-Community labor movement concerned cross-border commuter workers, especially between the Netherlands and Belgium, the Netherlands and Germany, and Belgium and France; in 1958, for example, there were some seventy thousand such workers.[76] Meanwhile, the member states were starting to demand more workers, leading to relatively open national policies on the admission of foreign labor. There was significant immigration into France, Belgium, and Germany of workers from Spain and Greece as well as Italy. In Germany the main non-Italian sources of workers were Austria, Yugoslavia, and refugees from Eastern Europe.[77]

Belgium typifies the evolution of worker migrations within the Community. Starting in 1946, Belgium had engaged Italy to send two thousand Italian coal workers per week to Belgium, in return for which Belgium sold Italy a guaranteed amount of coal.[78] Many workers finished their contracts and returned home to Italy, but others stayed. Though seventy-seven thousand Italians had moved permanently to Belgium between 1946 and 1949, there was still a significant labor shortage in the Belgian coal mines in the mid-1950s, lessened somewhat by the 1958 recession.[79] The work was dangerous: between

1946 and 1955, one thousand Italian workers died in work-related accidents in Belgium.[80] The 1956 accident at Marcinelle that killed 262 miners—including 136 Italians—finally spurred Italy to demand safer working conditions. As a result, Belgium reoriented its recruitment efforts toward Spain and Greece, then Morocco and Turkey. Nevertheless, the influx of Italians did not abate entirely. The 1970 census counted three hundred thousand Italians living in Belgium, not including those who had naturalized or children who had been born in Belgium, making the influx from Italy the single biggest immigration in Belgian history.[81] The free movement regimes initiated by the Western European Union, the Benelux, the Nordic Common Labor Market, and the Common Travel Area were models for the member states to follow as they cooperated to foster economic growth.

1.4. The European Court of Justice and Direct Effect

The freedoms first announced in the Treaty of Paris, expanded in the Treaty of Rome, and implemented over the course of the ensuing decade could be interpreted as simply establishing reciprocal obligations among member states, rather than creating new individual rights. The Treaty of Paris had placed the onus on member states to remove any nationality restrictions on the employment in the coal and steel industries of workers with the requisite qualifications. With the Treaty of Rome, free movement became a right—though member states could continue to plead for exceptions. Yet despite its promulgation of rights, and despite its preamble's reference to the purpose of achieving an "ever closer union among the peoples of Europe," the Treaty of Rome focused almost entirely on economic coordination among the member states. It thus remained unclear whether the treaty provided any rights directly to citizens of member states, or whether it was concerned exclusively with governments.

The task of clarifying the treaty's meaning fell to the European Court of Justice, which had been established to ensure that the treaties were interpreted and applied correctly. The Court was originally composed of nine judges: two each from France, Germany, and Italy and one each from the Netherlands, Belgium, and Luxembourg. It was successively expanded when new member states joined, and though politically weak in its early years, the Court followed common judicial practice in expanding its jurisdictional authority by establishing legal principles while not applying the principles to the cases at hand.[82] Because member states were arguably more concerned with the material outcomes of cases than the legal principles established by jurisprudence, the Court could be "doctrinally activist, building legal doctrine based on unconventional legal interpretations and expanding its own authority, without provoking a political response."[83] Overturning the Court's jurisprudence would require the states to agree on new legislation, while limiting the Court's jurisdiction would require changing the treaties, both of which were difficult. For example, though French president General de Gaulle attempted in 1968 to reduce the Court's power and competences, other member states did not agree to the reform.[84]

Some member states initially balked at the suggestion that citizens might have independent rights under the Treaty of Rome. They argued that it should instead be regarded as other international treaties in which states were the only recognized legal entities; the treaty was simply a contract among fully sovereign entities and did not apply to individual citizens. In 1963, the Court rejected this position, arguing that because the Treaty of Rome established a common market that impacted citizens as well as states, the Community itself could enact laws that were directly applicable to citizens.[85] It cited the Treaty of Rome's preamble, whereby the heads of state and government had determined "to lay the foundations of an ever closer union among the peoples of Europe," resolved "to ensure the economic and social progress of their countries by common action to eliminate the barriers which divide Europe," and affirmed "as the essential objective of their efforts the constant improvements of the living and working conditions of their peoples." The Court concluded that the Community constituted a new legal order, the subjects of which were not only states but also citizens. It followed that Community law "not only imposes obligations on individuals but is also intended to confer upon them rights."[86] The resulting principle of direct effect meant that Community law could grant individuals rights, which needed to be respected by governments (vertical direct effect) and by other persons (horizontal direct effect).

If the Court had not ruled that the treaty applied to individuals, then the drive to "eliminate the barriers which divide Europe" could have become more an economic project than a social and political one. Despite the Treaty of Rome's invocation of eliminating *social* as well as economic barriers, however, the treaty's focus was economics. Indeed it prohibits impediments to intra-Community trade much more strongly than the U.S. Constitution's interstate commerce clause, which helps determine the relationship between American states and the federal government, leading some to argue that the European Court constructed an "economic constitution."[87] But the Court rejected a strict economic logic to focus also on citizens' rights, a move that represents "an incipient form of European citizenship."[88] The rights-based approach to freedom of movement has created an extensive case law of directly effective individual rights. On the basis of the treaties, the Court helped transform the Community into an area of freedom and mobility for Community workers and their families, professionals, service providers, and now citizens.[89] National courts and private litigants did not always support the expansion of European law, but they used rulings that served their interests.[90] Direct effect was thus fundamental to the development of European rights because the enforcement and evolution of rights depend greatly on their assertion by individual beneficiaries.[91]

Direct effect would be much less powerful if Community law had remained subservient to national laws. In 1964, however, the Court ruled that the Treaty of Rome had "created its own legal system," which "became an integral part of the legal systems of the Member States and which their courts are bound to apply": the member states had "limited their sovereign rights . . . [and] created a body of law which binds both their nationals and themselves."[92] The doctrines of direct effect and supremacy became constitutional pillars of European law, and national courts were brought into the process with the preliminary reference procedure, according to which lower courts may (and supreme courts must) ask the ECJ for a preliminary ruling on issues of European law.[93] The preliminary reference procedure and the doctrines of direct effect and supremacy are important, but the legal bases of the judicial decisions are even more significant: had the treaties not extended rights, there would be nothing for the Court to decide. Indeed, integration and rights have had a mutually reinforcing impact, and the EU became more integrated because it protected the rights granted in the treaties and European law.[94]

The Treaty of Rome expanded the rights contained in the Treaty of Paris, and charged the Commission with enforcing them and the Court with interpreting them. Already in 1969, former Commission president Walter Hallstein could write that individual European citizens were affected by European rights "more strongly and more directly with every day that passes": because the Community confers both rights and duties, every European citizen was already "subject to two legal systems—as a citizen of one of the Community's member-states to his national legal system, and as a member of the Community to the Community's legal system."[95] Hallstein thus highlighted the use of law and the legal system to integrate European citizens, a protracted process by which new rights were added to the original free movement rights to construct European citizenship.

CHAPTER TWO

From Rights to Citizenship

> We could as of now decide to establish a European citizenship, which would be in addition to the citizenship which the inhabitants of our countries now possess.[1]
>
> —Italian prime minister Giulio Andreotti

> Complete assimilation with nationals as regards political rights is desirable in the long term from the point of view of a European Union.[2]
>
> —European Commission, "Towards European Citizenship"

The transformation of free movement rights from being defined and promoted in economic terms to being placed at the core of a new European citizenship was gradual. Free movement rights for workers were first justified in terms of enabling the free movement of labor, and then as a measure to complete the single market. But they were extended and expanded even after the worker movement sufficient to support the common market had been achieved. This broadening of individual rights coincided with the introduction of European Union (EU) citizenship, which took over two decades to reach fruition—from discussions in the late 1960s and early 1970s to the Maastricht Treaty. Despite substantial support in the 1970s for introducing European citizenship, the Community's first enlargement (the UK, Ireland, and Denmark in 1973) stymied the process, leading to gridlock in the Council. But the two subsequent enlargements (Greece in 1981 and Spain and Portugal in 1986) reinvigorated it. The eventual adoption of EU citizenship resulted not from Commission pressure but rather from bargaining among member states—including the three new Mediterranean members—and between member states and the European Parliament. With the Single European Act (SEA) in 1987, Parliament had gained the power of codecision, which helps explain why the member states could afford to ignore Parliament's citizenship proposals before the SEA but accepted them in the discussions preceding Maastricht.

2.1. Introducing Citizenship

By the early 1970s, it was clear that the millions of migrant workers who had emigrated from Mediterranean countries to work in more industrialized countries were there to stay. Given the large numbers of Italian, as well as Greek, Portuguese, Spanish, and other immigrants in the Community, a decision was needed on whether the Community should simply guarantee a right of residence and related social entitlements or go further to include political rights, such as the right to vote and stand as a candidate in local elections. Such rights would be extended only to citizens of other member states, thus not yet including citizens of Greece (which joined in 1981), or Spain or Portugal (which joined in 1986). The Community's first enlargement occurred on 1 January 1973 as the six founding member states were joined by Denmark, Ireland, and the UK.

At the first joint summit with the government leaders of the new member states, held in Paris in October 1972, the Belgian and Italian prime ministers suggested granting all Community citizens, regardless of their place of residence, the right to vote and run for office in local elections. The Cold War context helps explain their position: western European leaders wanted to differentiate themselves from the states on the other side of the Iron Curtain. The first point of the Council declaration pointedly reaffirmed their resolve "to base their Community's development on democracy, freedom of opinion, free movement of men and ideas and participation by the people through their freely elected representatives," thus explicitly linking free movement and democracy.[3] Several individual leaders offered their own ideas. Thus, German chancellor Willy Brandt suggested putting "social policy into a European perspective" so that "our citizens will find it easier to identify themselves with the Community."[4] Besides their common promotion of political rights in local elections, Belgian prime minister Gaston Eyskens called for "practical steps to encourage the movement of youngsters within the Community" by recognizing their academic credentials throughout the Community, while Italian prime minister Giulio Andreotti advocated establishing "a

European citizenship, which would be in addition to the citizenship which the inhabitants of our countries now possess."[5]

Commission president Sicco Mansholt warmly welcomed these proposals. He urged the member states to add "obvious content to the fact of belonging to the European Community. This Community, which has achieved the opening of frontiers for trade in industrial and agricultural goods, must now open the frontiers which still keep its citizens apart from one another," adding that "checks at the Community's internal frontiers should be done away with, and nationals of Member States progressively integrated into the social, administrative and political fabric of their host countries, with the aim of gradually conferring upon them 'European civic rights.'"[6] Yet integrating Community citizens into the social and political fabric of their host countries would become more difficult as a result of the enlargement. The original six member states had shared a continental model of social welfare; the states that joined in the 1970s and 1980s did not.[7] The goal of encouraging citizens to identify themselves with the Community became one of the challenges of adding new member states.

At the 1973 Copenhagen European Council, the nine member states of the newly expanded Community adopted a report on European identity that, they argued, was based on representative democracy, rule of law, social justice, and respect for human rights, and which would evolve as a result of the "political will to succeed in the construction of a United Europe."[8] One year later, at the 1974 Paris European Council, the member states resolved both to examine ways to give their citizens "special rights as members of the Community" and to consider "establishing a passport union," meaning a "stage-by-stage harmonization of legislation affecting aliens" and an "abolition of passport control within the Community."[9] The Italian delegation further asked "under what conditions and according to what timetable European citizenship could be granted to the citizens of the nine Member States."[10] The government leaders assigned Belgian prime minister Leo Tindemans the task of studying these proposals.

As Tindemans was working, the Commission presented a report entitled "Towards European Citizenship," which examined the idea of a passport union and the conditions under which member states could grant the right to vote and eligibility for public office to citizens of other member states. The Commission presented these rights as "the logical goal of the principle of national treatment and integration into the host country."[11] The rest of the report examined the design and timing of political rights, concluding that equal treatment for European citizens in terms of economic and social rights was politically acceptable because it had "long been a subject for frequent negotiation between States," but that public opinion might not support "equal treatment for foreigners in the political field. This is a new idea and the public will have to be given an opportunity to get used to it."[12] The Commission emphasized that European citizenship implied that citizens of any member state should automatically be treated in another member state as if they were citizens of that state. Though member states could consider facilitating naturalization, simply exchanging nationality seemed "less promising than the idea of equality with the nationals of the host State," because the emphasis should remain on residence rather than nationality.[13] The Commission further noted that, though "complete assimilation with nationals as regards political rights" was desirable, eligibility for election at national level and access to high political office could not be immediately introduced.[14] This thinking—including explicit references to the Community as approaching a commonwealth or federation type of citizenship—thus went quite far. But imagining Europeans changing citizenship as easily as, say, Americans switching from California to New York "citizenship" or Canadians from Ontario to Alberta "citizenship" seemed outlandish even to the Commission.

The idea of complete assimilation with nationals found more pragmatic expression in the Tindemans report, released at the end of December 1975, which included a chapter on a "People's Europe."[15] The report promoted freedom, equality, and social justice and argued that an "unfinished structure does not weather well: it must be completed, otherwise it collapses."[16] Since common European rights constituted a goal of a "people's Europe," it was necessary to make continual progress toward common rights. Tindemans also argued that "Europe must be close to its citizens," raising the specter of a democratic deficit if European decisions were perceived as distant or undemocratic.[17] Furthermore, he opined, the gradually increasing powers of the supranational institutions made it "imperative to ensure that rights and fundamental freedoms, including economic and social rights, are both recognised and protected."[18] The Tindemans report was controversial, though it was more cautious than the Commission report's plans for completely integrating European citizens into their host societies. Most contentious was the suggestion that a "two-speed Europe" might aid European integration, as core member states moved ahead of less eager members. The smaller member states rejected the prospect of first- and second-class Community membership, while Britain and France feared a further loss of sovereignty. French president Valéry Giscard d'Estaing "took the lead and stifled the report with the kind of bureaucratic asphyxiation that Tindemans had so bitterly complained about."[19]

Meanwhile, the Commission proposed more policies for protecting migrant workers, and the Economic and Social Committee concluded that Europeans "aspire to the abolition of frontiers."[20] With discussions about new rights at an impasse, the Court ensured the application of existing rights. The Treaty of Rome distinguished among workers (Art. 48), the self-employed who benefit from freedom of establishment (Art. 52), and those who provide cross-border services (Art. 59). The Court determined in 1976 that all three articles were "based on the same principles in so far as they concern the entry into and residence in the territory of Member States of persons covered by Community law and the prohibition of all discrimination between them on the grounds of nationality."[21] This was significant because the Court had earlier ruled that the three articles had direct effect since 1970, the end of the transitional period.[22] In other words, Community citizens could enforce their European rights not only against states—their own as well as other member states—but also against private persons and organizations. European law was thus deemed to prohibit discrimination on the grounds of nationality not only by states but also by any person or entity.[23] The Court ruled that the member states must have understood that the legislation they had passed, while not creating new rights, determined the scope of existing rights. Community legislation would thus "prohibit the introduction by a member state of new restrictions on the establishment of nationals of other member states" and would "prevent the member states from reverting to less liberal provisions or practices."[24]

Between 1976 and 1979, the committee of permanent representatives—the regular meetings of the ambassadors of the member states, commonly known by its French acronym Coreper—discussed the Tindemans Report and a preliminary draft resolution on European rights but failed to reach agreement. Part of the reason for the stalemate was that the UK was still divided on Community membership, and the other states had become frustrated with British stalling. In June 1975, just before the release of the "Towards European Citizenship" report and the broader Tindemans report, British Labour prime minister Harold Wilson had held a referendum on whether or not the UK should leave the Community. Though British voters decided 67 percent to 33 percent to remain in, this was only after difficult negotiations over the size of the UK's contribution to the Community budget, which added to the growing irritation and impatience with Britain. The UK's first Council presidency in spring 1977 was lackluster, partly because of the sometimes Euroskeptic UK ministers chairing Council meetings.[25] In November 1977 the European Parliament issued a resolution supporting European citizenship.[26] Germany favored gradually granting further rights, but the Council as a whole did not agree to give citizens of other member states the right to vote in local elections.[27]

In 1979, the European Parliament changed from being a dual mandate institution—in which all members of the European Parliament (MEPs) were simultaneously members of their national parliaments—to an institution whose members were elected directly by citizens. Henceforth, MEPs could concentrate more on European affairs. Direct elections to Parliament were intended to bolster the Community's democratic legitimacy: the idea of electing MEPs by universal suffrage had long been touted as a way "to inject some democracy into European mechanisms."[28] According to the Parliament's president, direct elections marked "a new phase in the efforts to turn a commercial Community into a citizen's Community."[29]

In July 1979, the Commission finally published a draft directive on a right of residence for member state citizens in the territory of other member states that proposed abolishing all remaining restrictions on movement and residence but specified that member states could require citizens not covered by other legislation—anyone other than workers, the self-employed, and those who wished to stay after retirement—to "provide proof of sufficient resources to provide for their own needs and the dependent members of their family."[30] Allowing states to require nonworkers to provide proof of sufficient resources was included to discourage "population movements being undertaken with the sole aim of obtaining the most favourable social benefits."[31] The European Parliament welcomed the proposed directive but argued that it should go even further, for example, with respect to students: "Students are like birds: they come, they fly away and should not be hindered to do so."[32]

Though Parliament supported the proposed directive, the Council's positive attitude soured. This was partially due to the increased immigration of third-country nationals—citizens neither of the host state (first country) nor of another EU member state (second country) but of a state outside the EU—into the Community but also to the election in May 1979 of the stridently Euroskeptic Margaret Thatcher as British prime minister, leading to a further hardening of the UK position on European integration: the draft directive did not cover third-country nationals, but Council discussions broke down.[33] The next few years were punctuated by debates in the deadlocked Council about requiring applicants to possess sufficient resources and medical insurance and about whether this was a matter of Community competence at all.[34] Other reasons for the lack of progress on citizenship were that Greece joined the Community in 1981 and that accession negotiations had started with Portugal in June 1978 and Spain in February 1979. Europe was experiencing low economic growth coupled with high unemployment and inflation, hardly propitious to granting new rights to "foreigners" from other member states, particularly given the large Greek, Spanish, and Portuguese communities within the Community. Yet the member states agreed in 1981 to introduce uniform format passports: they were "anxious to promote any measures which might strengthen the feeling among nationals of the Member States that they belong to the same Community," and considered that "the establishment of such a passport is likely to facilitate the movement of nationals of the Member States."[35] But no other significant steps toward enhancing European rights or promoting European identity were made until the Draft Treaty establishing European Union (DTEU) and SEA.

2.2. Relaunching Citizenship: DTEU and SEA

In the early 1980s, proponents of further integration reintroduced the concept of citizenship. A 1983 European Parliament report advocated extending to citizens of member states residing in a member state other than their own the right to vote and stand as a candidate in local elections.[36] Renewed discussions about Community citizenship accompanied changes in national citizenship laws. When the UK revised its Citizenship Act in 1981, for example, there were 250,000 British citizens living elsewhere in western Europe, many of whom were concerned about passing on their citizenship: the new measures to deprive their children of British citizenship roused British expatriates in Europe to "an indignation rarely seen among people who, imagining their citizenship was secure enough to pass to their children, [had] come to live and work on the continent."[37]

The European Parliament made several recommendations concerning citizenship in its 1984 DTEU, which was largely the work of Altiero Spinelli. The DTEU announced that "citizens of the Member States shall ipso facto be citizens of the Union. Citizenship of the Union shall be dependent upon citizenship of a Member State; it may not be independently acquired or forfeited. Citizens of the Union shall take part in the political life of the Union in the forms laid down by the Treaty, enjoy the rights granted to them by the legal system of the Union and be subject to its laws."[38] While only Belgium and Italy called for the DTEU to be ratified, there was widespread interest in European citizenship among other European leaders. At the June 1984 Fontainebleau European Council, the Council formed two ad hoc committees—the Committee for a People's Europe, chaired by Italian MEP Pietro Adonnino, and the Committee on Institutional Affairs, chaired by Irish senator James Dooge—thereby placing citizenship and European Union on the agenda of future European Councils. The Fontainebleau presidency conclusions specified that the Community should "respond to the expectations of the people of Europe by adopting measures to strengthen and promote its identity and its image both for its citizens and for the rest of the world"—significant because it referred to a single people (instead of multiple peoples) of Europe and to the Community's citizens (rather than those of the member states).[39] On 12 December 1984, the newly elected European Parliament passed a resolution supporting the DTEU.

In January 1985, Italy took over the presidency from Ireland, the first European format passports were issued, and a new Commission led by former French finance minister Jacques Delors took office. Of these three events, the most important development for European citizenship was undoubtedly the Delors Commission's inauguration. Delors was a dynamic leader whom some later compared to Jean Monnet, and the Commission immediately launched an ambitious project to revitalize integration.[40] Meanwhile, in February the Court rendered its judgment in the case involving Françoise Gravier, a French citizen who had moved in 1982 to Liège, Belgium, to study.[41] She applied for but was denied an exemption of the enrollment fee demanded of foreign students. When she refused to pay, her school refused to enroll her and Belgium revoked her residence permit, prompting Gravier to file suit, citing discrimination on the grounds of nationality. Belgium argued that Community students who did not normally pay Belgian taxes should pay the fee and that since 1976 there had been more Community students in Belgium than Belgian students studying elsewhere in the Community, which burdened the Belgian budget. The Commission agreed that while student mobility within the Community was limited, Belgium was indeed the member state with the highest proportion of students from other member states. Supporting Belgium, Denmark and the UK argued that the nondiscrimination clause ought not prevent a member state from favoring its own nationals for access to education, scholarships and grants, social facilities, and tuition fees. Every member state, they argued, had special responsibilities toward its own citizens. The Court disagreed, reasoning that common vocational training was indispensable to free movement of persons and that imposing on Community students a fee not imposed on domestic students discriminated on the grounds of nationality, contrary to the nondiscrimination clause.[42] By striking down discrimination against Community students, the *Gravier* outcome may have influenced the Institutional Affairs and the People's Europe committees that had been working since the Fontainebleau European Council the previous June.

In March 1985, the Institutional Affairs report called for a homogeneous internal market, replacing unanimous voting with qualified majority voting in the Council, and greater powers for the Commission and Parliament.[43] Not all member states supported these ambitious aims. The UK, Denmark, and Greece disagreed with the report's central recommendation: that the member states should negotiate a treaty on European union guided by the spirit and method of the DTEU. Despite their reluctance, progress toward greater integration continued on other fronts. The accession treaties of Spain and Portugal, which would become effective 1 January 1986, were signed on 12 June. Two days later, the Commission issued a White Paper on Completing the Internal Market, which devoted a section to free movement, subtitled "A New Initiative in Favour of Community Citizens," arguing that it was "crucial that the obstacles which still exist within the Community to free movement for the self-employed and employees be removed by 1992."[44] Citing the preliminary findings of the People's Europe report, it continued that "measures to ensure the free movement of individuals must not be restricted to the workforce only."[45] This idea, coupled with the Court's expansive interpretation of freedom of movement, provided the basis for the Maastricht Treaty's citizenship provisions.[46] The White Paper's aim of ensuring free movement for all individuals, regardless of their position in the economy, would form the core of European citizenship.

On the same day that the White Paper appeared, 14 June 1985, representatives of Germany, France, Belgium, Luxembourg, and the Netherlands signed an agreement in the Luxembourg town of Schengen to eliminate border controls. In a symbolic gesture, the signing ceremony occurred on a ship anchored on the Moselle river at the point where the borders of Germany, France, and Luxembourg meet, and the boat sailed through the waters of the three countries following the signing.[47] The Belgian secretary of state for European affairs said that the agreement's ultimate goal was "to abolish completely the physical borders between our countries," while Luxembourg's minister of foreign affairs called it "a major step forward on the road toward European unity," directly benefiting signatory state citizens and "moving them a step closer to what is sometimes referred to as 'European citizenship.'"[48] Schengen exemplified the "two-speed Europe" that the Tindemans report had proposed a decade earlier. Faced with resistance on the part of the newer member states—Denmark, the UK, and Greece—five of the original six member states pushed ahead with plans to eliminate border controls. Italy was not invited to join due to inadequate policing along its coastline, while Ireland preferred to stay in the Common Travel Area that it shared with the UK.[49]

The People's Europe committee submitted its final report on 20 June 1985, recommending the right to vote in local elections but stressing that the matter was within member state rather than Community competence.[50] It also addressed the mobility of students, a common policy on third-country nationals, and the mutual recognition of qualifications for professionals.

Stressing the value of symbols, the committee proposed a European flag and the adoption of Ode to Joy from Beethoven's ninth symphony as a European anthem.[51] It also proposed a general right of residence for all Community citizens, the creation of a European Ombudsman, consular assistance outside the Community, and the recognition of voting rights in local and European elections—proposals that would later be enacted almost verbatim in the Maastricht Treaty.[52] The impetus for enacting these changes, however, had to come from national political leaders.

The 28 and 29 June 1985 meeting of the European Council in Milan set the terms of debate for the rest of the year, though it was unclear whether the UK, Denmark, and Greece would participate in an intergovernmental conference that would result in a new treaty. The deadlock at Milan was broken by the unprecedented action of the outgoing Italian presidency in calling a vote: the proposal to convene a conference was adopted seven to three. The incoming Luxembourg presidency duly proposed revising the treaty on the basis of the Institutional Affairs and People's Europe reports and the Commission's proposals on the free movement of persons.[53] Support for expanding individual rights came even from the British House of Lords, which recommended widening the scope for individuals to challenge actions of Community institutions.[54]

The final decisions on the text that would become the Single European Act (SEA) were left to the Luxembourg meetings of December 1985, where the internal market was the dominant issue. The European Parliament called for specific deadlines for free movement: the treaties of Paris and Rome had prioritized the free movement of goods over that of persons, but Parliament gave equal importance to goods and persons (two-year proposed deadline for implementation), ahead of services (five years) and capital (ten years).[55] Meanwhile, the Commission proposed a single deadline of 31 December 1992 (the end of term of the next Commission) for establishing an area without borders, in which persons, goods, services, and capital would move freely. The Commission further proposed that free movement issues should be decided by qualified majority voting, not unanimity, and that the Commission's implementing measures should be adopted unless the Council unanimously adopted its own ones.[56] But the member states wished to retain their vetoes over free movement, and also failed to agree on Denmark's proposals for voting rights for EC citizens.[57] In the final stages of negotiations, despite extensive parliamentary lobbying, the DTEU's citizenship proposals and the idea of including a treaty article on fundamental rights were scuttled.[58] The member states agreed only to mention in the treaty's preamble the promotion of democracy, human rights, and the European Social Charter, thus excluding citizenship rights from the Court's competence. Though the SEA turned into law much of the Commission's 1985 White Paper, European citizenship policies had proceeded far enough for some member states.

Despite the SEA's preference for the internal market rather than citizenship, the Commission's directorate general (DG) for Social Affairs undertook a series of initiatives to facilitate mobility. Under the leadership of Commission vice president Manuel Marín, a Spanish Socialist, DG Social Affairs produced a report detailing the ways in which the "social dimension of the internal market" was to be realized.[59] The report mentioned mutual recognition of academic and professional qualifications and removing discriminatory practices as ways to improve free movement. It also advocated promoting social cohesion through antipoverty programs and reforming the structural funds, which were intended to reduce socioeconomic disparities among the member states. Other topics covered were employment and retraining and the Erasmus and Lingua programs, discussed below. The report also considered ways of improving living and working conditions through occupational health and safety measures, standardized contracts, and rights for part-time and temporary workers.

British prime minister Margaret Thatcher promptly asserted that these proposals would introduce "socialism by the back door."[60] Despite Thatcher's skepticism, however, the other member states doubled the structural funds to one-quarter of the Community's budget, and reformed the funds by strengthening multiyear programming and establishing priority objectives and closer cooperation with the economic and social actors. The structural funds thus became an increasingly important means of redistributing resources not only within states but also from richer European states to poorer ones. These changes added to a sense of common purpose and fostered a sense that Community membership implied a commitment to advancing existing rights.

The growing sense of common purpose also motivated action on student mobility. In 1987, the Council enacted the European Community Action Scheme for the Mobility of University Students, a program better known under the acronym Erasmus, fostering student exchanges and mobility within Europe by funding three to twelve months of study elsewhere in Europe.[61] Building on Erasmus, education ministers agreed to the Lingua program during Spain's presidency of the Council in spring 1989 and approved it that summer.[62] Neither the Economic and Social Committee (which had suggested extending European funding for foreign language training to primary and secondary schools) nor the European Parliament (which had made a number of proposals, including asking for a three hundred million ECU budget; the final budget was two hundred million) had much effect on the bargaining among the member states. Spain, Italy, Portugal, the Netherlands, Belgium, Ireland, and Greece were favorable, while Germany, the UK, and France had reservations. Though the latter three states were the largest contributors to the Community budget and thus had considerable bargaining power, Spain successfully pushed the Lingua proposal through the Council.[63] As discussed further in §6.4, these education programs would grow to become key means of creating a sense of European identity, thus helping to promote and entrench the shift from market rights to individual rights and citizenship.

2.3. From Market Rights to Individual Rights

The SEA disappointed those backing free movement rights for all Europeans. Provisions facilitating free movement of workers and the self-employed had been enhanced during the 1980s. For example, social security benefits were extended in 1982 to cover the self-employed rather than simply employees. But there were no new rights, and existing rights continued to be justified not in political terms but simply as good economic policy. An observer at the time noted that unfilled proposals to shift rights from an economic focus toward political and social goals pointed to the persistent "difficulties in the incremental approach toward European Citizenship and what might be termed a European Welfare State."[64] Lacking unanimous support from the member states, advocates of change were forced to settle for piecemeal progress.

Yet there was progress, and it intensified after the Greek, Spanish, and Portuguese accessions ended the objection that extending free movement rights would lead to chaos. Greece (1981) and Spain and Portugal (1986) joined the Community with special provisions phasing in free movement of workers, provisions that parallel the later transition arrangements for workers from the 2004 enlargement countries, discussed in §5.1. The reason for the phase-in was existing member states' fear of massive immigration from the new member states, a concern that remained even when the transition period ended.[65] The perceived injustice of the phase-in helps explain the Mediterranean states' subsequent support for EU citizenship. The existing member states did not much change their positions between the SEA and Maastricht negotiations, but the addition of new member states that had not had the right to vote on the SEA altered the outcome of the Maastricht negotiations, where Spain and, to a lesser extent, Portugal were key actors promoting the notion of European citizenship.[66] The European Councils at The Hague in June 1986, London in December 1986, and Hanover in June 1988 all concluded with agreement that a general right of residence should be extended to all European citizens in order to create a citizens' Europe.[67] Despite these agreements, the member states failed to approve the Commission's proposal on the general right of residence—now many times amended from the original 1979 version. Some were reluctant to agree because they were concerned that extending residence rights to all citizens would prove costly to states with more generous welfare rights. Thus, Denmark argued that a treaty change rather than normal legislation was needed because the treaty provided only for free movement of workers and the self-employed, while the UK also remained wary of extending residence rights beyond these two groups, arguing that "students, pensioners, and the self-supporting should not become a burden on the host state's social security or health services."[68]

After years of inaction following the early 1970s discussions of individual rights and the resulting 1979 draft directive, the Commission in May 1989 finally changed its approach. Multiple amendments had made the draft directive more restrictive than existing policies, thus the Commission decided that the draft directive was "no longer the appropriate framework to enable the Council to reach positive conclusions regarding the various categories of persons covered by the proposal for a Directive."[69] Instead of a single directive, the Commission proposed three: for students, retired persons, and economically inactive citizens. Each was tailored to the target group and justified on the basis of a different treaty article. It matters greatly which article is used as the legal basis of legislation because different articles are subject to different voting procedures, affecting how easily the legislation can be amended. The Commission proposed basing the directives concerning students and retired persons on treaty articles requiring qualified majority voting rather than unanimity; the directive on economically inactive citizens would continue to require unanimity. Concerned at the prospect of qualified majority voting rather than unanimous voting, the Council in December 1989 decided to dispense with the separate legal bases of the three proposed directives and have them once again all be covered under the treaty provision on which it had been impossible to reach agreement over the preceding decade.[70]

In response, the Parliament attempted to restore the legal basis of the proposed student directive by suing the Council.[71] It argued that the original basis reflected more closely than the Council's amended basis the Community's competence concerning the free movement of students and the principle of nondiscrimination on the basis of nationality. The Commission did not join the Parliament's action. After eleven years of legislative haggling, it was unwilling to jeopardize the agreement that had finally been achieved, though the agreement simply adopted the rhetoric of a citizens' Europe while actually insulating the member states from the "welfare tourism" they feared.[72] The Parliament won its case against the Council, and the legal basis of the student directive was changed back to the nondiscrimination article from the Council measures article, though the directive's provisions remained unchanged. Parliament may have wanted to leave open the possibility of launching future challenges of the directive's provisions—which would be easier if it was based on the nondiscrimination article rather than the Council measures article, because the latter required unanimous agreement while the former simply required a qualified majority. The Parliament may also have been simply asserting its right to intervene, choosing free movement rights for students as an easy case with which to strengthen its role in the legislative process.[73] Regardless, Parliament played a major role in reintroducing the goal of European citizenship in the discussions leading to the Maastricht Treaty.

2.4. The Charter on the Fundamental Social Rights of Workers

A salient development in the push to include citizenship in the Maastricht Treaty was the debate over workers' rights that preceded the Maastricht negotiations. Following the June 1988 Hanover European Council, at which the government leaders affirmed the importance of the internal market's social aspects, the Commission asked the Economic and Social Committee to consider a Community Charter of Fundamental Social Rights of Workers. The December 1988 Rhodes European Council reaffirmed that completing the single market was not an end in itself but aimed to "ensure the maximum well-being of all, in line with the tradition of social progress which is part of Europe's history. This tradition of social progress should be a guarantee that all citizens, whatever their occupation, will have effective access to the direct benefits expected from the Single Market."[74] On 22 February 1989, the Economic and Social Committee adopted the Charter by 135 to 22 votes. Three weeks later, the European Parliament resolved that the pressures of competition should not jeopardize the adoption of European social rights.[75] At the Madrid European Council in June, the member states agreed and stressed that the single market should weigh social concerns as much as economic ones. In response, Parliament resolved that the Community's social dimension required implementing all the fundamental social rights enshrined in Community law and that these rights created new scope for actions before the Court.

Following the Marín Report, the Commission presented the Strasbourg European Council of December 1989 with a Community Charter of the Fundamental Social Rights of Workers, more commonly known as the Social Charter. Eleven leaders signed, with only Thatcher refusing. Soon afterward, the UK vetoed fourteen of seventeen draft employment-related directives. The British would stay outside the Social Charter until Tony Blair's Labour Party defeated John Major's Conservative government in 1997. The Charter established the major principles of European labor law; its preamble affirmed that "the same importance must be attached to the social aspects as to the economic aspects" of the single market. Incorporated into the Maastricht Treaty as the Social Protocol, it expressed the determination of all signatories to advance social policy. Four days after his Labour Party's 1997 election, new UK foreign secretary Robin Cook confirmed that Britain would finally accede, explicitly invoking the Charter's rights: "We do not accept that the British people should be second-class citizens with less rights than employees on the Continent."[76] Though the Charter's rights are restricted to workers rather than all persons, it is noteworthy that the language Cook chose to promote it is that of citizenship.

The process of extending European rights from workers to new categories of people was gradual. Building on earlier ideas about constructing a common political community—rather than simply an economic one—some European leaders in the early 1970s wanted to transform the free movement rights into an authentic common citizenship. They were restrained primarily by the exigencies of the first enlargement (1973), particularly the opposition of Denmark and the UK. After an unsuccessful attempt to reintroduce citizenship in the DTEU, the project of building European citizenship gained renewed vigor with the SEA and the single market program. At the same time, adding social rights to the economic freedoms of the internal market was at first limited to workers, with the Charter on the Fundamental Social Rights of Workers.

CHAPTER THREE

Maastricht's Constitutional Moment

A European citizen is developing even before actions by States shape Europe.[1]

—Italian memorandum to the other member states

Citizenship of the Union is hereby established. Every person holding the nationality of a Member State shall be a citizen of the Union.

—Maastricht Treaty, 1991

Citizenship returned fully to the agenda with the fall of the Berlin Wall, as the member states decided in 1990 to shape the future political union by including and extending European citizenship rights. With the SEA, the European Parliament had gained the power of codecision, which helps explain why the member states could afford to ignore the Parliament's citizenship proposals in the run-up to the SEA but generally accepted them in the discussions preceding Maastricht. In contrast with traditional state citizenship, which generally evolved from centuries of political consolidation and social and economic transformation, European Union (EU) citizenship was simply introduced by a treaty concluded by national executives. Because it consolidated and transformed preexisting rights into the new legal category of citizenship, the Maastricht Treaty was the "constitutional moment" that created European citizens.[2] The creation of the EU required defining "the rights and duties of the affected individuals as happens in national States."[3] Nevertheless, member state concerns about the potential for unchecked growth in citizenship rights helps explain why the Maastricht Treaty refused to grant the Court jurisdiction over "third pillar" issues, those relating to justice and home affairs. Indeed, the treaty does not depart from the principle that member state nationality remains primary while EU citizenship is derivative and secondary. By specifying that European citizenship would remain dependent on member state citizenship, European policy makers were able to avoid confronting the long-standing traditional body of rights already extant in each of the member states.

3.1. Bargaining over Citizenship

The fall of the Berlin Wall provoked intense efforts to advance European integration, culminating in the Maastricht Treaty. In the changed geopolitical context, a key concern of the Dublin European Council of April 1990 was to shape future political union by introducing European citizenship rights. The political leaders of the member states asked how the new treaty would "include and extend the notion of Community citizenship carrying with it specific rights (human, political, social, the right of complete free movement and residence, etc.)."[4] This interest was supported by earlier work, such as a parliamentary report that argued that the SEA encouraged developing the Community but did not allow adequate action in a range of fields, including citizenship.[5] On the basis of the report, a parliamentary committee chaired by David Martin—British Labour member of the European Parliament (MEP) and Parliament's vice president—met from November 1989 to February 1990 to draft a resolution asking the member states to hold an intergovernmental conference not simply on economic and monetary union (EMU) but also on incorporating fundamental rights into the treaties, increasing social and environmental provisions, and reforming Community institutions.[6]

The Commission had previously taken the view that the conference should focus solely on EMU. In the parliamentary debates, however, Commission president Delors came out strongly in favor of expanding its scope to include the other issues proposed by Parliament. Italy, Belgium, Greece, Germany, and France agreed. The Italian Parliament passed a resolution supporting the European Parliament's resolution, while the Italian delegation to the conference argued that "a European citizen is developing even before actions by States shape Europe" and that a "legal framework [must] be provided to this new situation."[7] Meanwhile, Belgium again raised the issue of the democratic deficit.[8] To remedy the deficit, the Belgians suggested empowering the Parliament and expanding citizens' rights by removing border controls, writing human rights into the treaty, joining the European Convention on Human Rights (ECHR), and allowing Europeans residing outside their state of citizenship to vote in local and European Parliament elections.[9]

Greece similarly favored including European citizenship and basic human rights in the treaty, extending the right to vote in local and European Parliament elections to citizens living in other member states, and simplifying citizens' access to the Court.[10] The point of these reforms was to remedy the democratic deficit and engender constitutional patriotism: the Community should "strengthen its citizens' feelings of belonging to one legal community."[11] The German and French governments agreed: Chancellor Helmut Kohl and President François Mitterrand called for a second conference on political union to be held parallel to the conference on economic and monetary union. Kohl and Mitterrand urged the Union to integrate and extend the notion of Community citizenship and its specific rights (human rights, social and political rights, complete freedom of movement) in favor of citizens of the Union.[12]

With France and Germany urging the introduction of European citizenship, the other member states could not ignore the issue. At the Dublin European Council of 28 April 1990, the government leaders asked their foreign ministers to decide whether a second conference parallel to the one on EMU would be necessary. The British opposed such a parallel meeting, but there was growing support from other governments. For example, in a letter of 4 May 1990, Spanish prime minister Felipé Gonzalez urged the other governments to address European citizenship, arguing that it should be based on the legal framework of Schengen and the free movement of persons.[13]

To prepare for the new treaty, Parliament meanwhile requested a series of interinstitutional preparatory conferences to bring together representatives from the Parliament, Commission, Council, and the member states. There were three conferences with the foreign ministers to discuss political union and one with the finance ministers to discuss EMU. At the first, the Spanish delegation argued that political union required "real content" and could be based on "three pillars: an integrated economic space, a common foreign and security policy, and a common citizenship."[14] The idea of three pillars would later be adopted in the treaty, though the third pillar of citizenship would be broadened to include a range of issues relating to justice and home affairs. When the heads of government returned to Dublin in June, they agreed to convene a conference on political union parallel to the one on EMU. Parliament responded quickly and passed a second report that sought to shape the agenda.[15] It defined "European Union" as including a common citizenship and a common framework for protecting basic rights. It also advocated entrenching basic human rights in the treaty and granting voting rights in local and European elections in the member state of residence.

At the end of September 1990, Spain sought to define the proposed European citizenship in a memorandum entitled "Towards a European Citizenship," which argued that the idea of European Union required creating an integrated space in which European citizens play a central and fundamental role.[16] Spain thus proposed "a qualitative jump which allows an area of essentially economic character to be transformed into an integrated area which would be at the direct service of the citizen."[17] Meanwhile, Denmark proposed creating a European Ombudsman, and the Commission favored introducing Community citizenship—defined as free movement and voting rights in local and European elections—and incorporating a reference to the ECHR in order to "encourage a feeling of involvement in European integration."[18] In a strategic move, the Commission linked European citizenship with increasing the powers of the Parliament as two ways to reduce the now widely acknowledged democratic deficit.[19] Meanwhile, the November 1990 parliamentary assizes were an innovation: never before had treaty negotiations been preceded by a conference of the parliaments—representatives of the European Parliament and the twelve national parliaments—that would later have to approve the outcome of the negotiations. The assizes met in Rome, and its concluding declaration, which supported adding European citizenship and fundamental rights to the treaties, was overwhelmingly approved.[20]

The December 1990 Rome European Council proposed including four sets of citizenship rights in the treaty. The first, civil rights, included "participation in elections to the European Parliament in the country of residence [and] possible participation in municipal elections." The second, social and economic rights, consisted of "freedom of movement and residence irrespective of engagement in economic activity, [and] equality of opportunity and of treatment for all Community citizens." The third was joint diplomatic and consular protection of Community citizens, and the fourth was "a mechanism for the defence of citizens' rights as regards Community matters ('ombudsman')."[21]

The Gulf War influenced the early months of the negotiations, which lasted from the Rome European Council until the final negotiations in Maastricht in December 1991. Reaching firm policy positions was difficult, because where the EMU conference dealt with one subject, the political union one comprised many more issues. Against this background, the intergovernmental conference on Political Union and European Citizenship commenced on 21 February 1991, promptly followed by the Commission's report on European citizenship.[22] Meanwhile, the Luxembourg presidency prepared a "nonpaper" or comprehensive draft on political union and submitted it to the foreign ministers on 15 April. This nonpaper narrowed the content of European citizenship from the earlier proposals made by Parliament, some of the national delegations, and the Commission. Indeed, the Commission's updated proposals for citizenship included the familiar catalog of rights as well as "every Union citizen's obligation to display solidarity with other Union citizens and with nationals of non-member countries resident in the Union"—a duty that was later dropped.[23] In May, three issues on which government leaders' personal representatives were unable to agree—citizenship, social policy, and economic policy—were discussed by the leaders themselves. The citizenship discussions focused on whether it should have direct effect: Denmark and, to a lesser extent, the UK opposed creating a European citizenship that would entitle individuals to force member states to respect their rights as EU citizens.[24] Meanwhile, Parliament passed a resolution in June stipulating that EU citizenship should be additional to national citizenship, that it should be placed within the framework of human rights contained in the ECHR, and that third-country nationals should also enjoy rights.[25]

During the summer of 1991, the Yugoslav crisis drew attention away from the negotiations. Following Luxembourg's example, the new Dutch presidency also prepared a global draft in September, over two months into its presidency. In a major embarrassment for Dutch diplomats, the foreign ministers of the other member states who met on 30 September 1991 rejected the text as a basis for future negotiations. The Dutch draft did not appease the traditionally reluctant member states and alienated France with its foreign policy provisions and Luxembourg by ignoring the April draft. Even those who thought that the Luxembourg text should have been more detailed felt it was now too late to regain lost ground. Negotiations thus proceeded with the Dutch submitting issue-by-issue modifications of the Luxembourg text, culminating in a new working draft on 8 November. Parliament had meanwhile submitted another report on European citizenship on 6 November, proposing a system of European social rights within the framework of European citizenship.[26]

The Maastricht European Council was held on 9 and 10 December 1991, and the text finalized only in the early hours of 11 December. In the negotiations, "France and Germany focused on foreign policy and security, Spain on citizenship and cohesion, Italy and Belgium on the powers of the Parliament and majority voting, Denmark on the environment."[27] Consistent with their traditional role as the "motors of integration," support from the French and German delegations was key to passing the citizenship provisions. The proposed right of EU citizens to vote in municipal and European elections in their state of residence rather than state of origin posed constitutional problems for France and would become a major focus of its ratification debate, but President Mitterrand had a strong political stake in supporting it: besides being committed to the European idea, he had long backed extending suffrage. Though Mitterrand realized that the citizenship provisions would require amending the French Constitution, he also calculated that they would force the opposition to choose between relaxing French sovereignty and appearing anti-European.[28] Dividing his political opponents was a powerful reason for Mitterrand to support European citizenship, but doing so also furthered what he called his *grand projet*, to "turn the whole of Europe into one space."[29] As the example of France shows, Maastricht represented not only a process of supranational institution building and integration but also the outcome of national politics of the member states and the intergovernmental conflicts and bargaining among them.[30]

3.2. Maastricht's Citizenship Provisions

Amending the Treaty of Rome, the Maastricht Treaty granted all EU citizens four sets of rights: free movement rights, political rights, the right to common diplomatic and consular protection abroad, and the right to petition Parliament and appeal to the newly established European Ombudsman. First, Maastricht consolidated and expanded free movement by decoupling it from employment status and giving it direct effect, meaning that the right to move and to reside anywhere within EU territory became an individual right for all EU citizens. This was a key move because free movement is the fundamental right of European citizenship.

Second, all European citizens gained the right to vote and to stand as candidates in European Parliament and local elections in their state of residence, under the same conditions as citizens of that state. Member states themselves remained responsible for the voting rights of their citizens residing abroad.[31] Though the participation rate of Union citizens remained below the overall turnout, the principle of EU citizens voting in other member states was innovative. For some, however, there can be no federal Europe and no truly meaningful European citizenship unless the Parliament becomes truly European in its mode of selection and campaigning.[32]

The right to participate in local politics is arguably more important than the right to participate in European Parliament elections. Participation rates for European elections are far lower than national elections, while turnout in local elections tends to be only slightly lower than national elections. Indeed, local politics may be more relevant than European politics to Europeans residing abroad, and it is generally easier to be elected to city councils than to the European Parliament. When arrangements to implement the right to vote and run for local office were introduced in December 1994, these rights had already been extended to Union residents in Ireland, Denmark, the Netherlands, Spain, Sweden, Finland, and the UK.[33] Except in Ireland, these rights had been subject to minimum residence periods or reciprocity agreements. Member states were given two years to adapt their electoral laws, but some were slow to react. By January 1997, only eight of the fifteen member states had fully implemented the rights, and the Commission began legal action to force the others to comply. Luxembourg and Belgium initially resisted. In Luxembourg, the issue was the sheer number of Union residents: over one-third of Luxembourg residents were citizens of other member states (primarily Portugal, France, and Italy), and the established parties worried that giving these people the right to vote would radically alter Luxembourg politics. The fear in Belgium was primarily that enfranchising non-Belgians would upset the linguistic balance of Brussels, since far more of the non-Belgian Union citizens living in the city spoke French than Dutch. In its July 1998 resolution on the second Commission report on citizenship, the European Parliament called on Belgium to comply, which it finally did; indeed, the application of the new right of citizenship took a while to be finally settled everywhere.[34]

The third set of rights comprising EU citizenship—the right to consular and diplomatic protection by the foreign service of other member states—was not at all controversial in the Maastricht negotiations. Yet it was an innovation in international law that went far beyond the Vienna Conventions of 1961 and 1963 on diplomatic and consular relations.[35] The member states expected that introducing common protection arrangements for Union citizens in third countries would also "strengthen the idea of European solidarity as perceived by the citizens in question."[36] They restricted the right to natural persons—thereby excluding companies and other legal persons—and limited it to basic consular services: assistance in cases of death, serious accident or serious illness, arrest or detention; assistance to victims of violent crime; and the relief and repatriation of distressed citizens. Though diplomats and consular officials could choose to offer assistance in other situations, the member states did not include standard diplomatic (as opposed to consular) protections, such as a state's demands (on behalf of its citizens) for reparations for a violation of international law.[37] The member states nevertheless did agree to establish an emergency travel document, which they hoped would "provide a clear demonstration of the practical benefits of being a citizen of the Union."[38]

Finally, the right to petition the European Parliament enhanced democratic legitimacy by creating a direct political link between the Parliament and EU citizens. Individually, or in groups, citizens participate directly in European politics by submitting petitions. Parliament responds to petitions, and its members can use them in agenda-setting ways. Over one thousand petitions were received annually, and several—such as those against testing cosmetics on animals—were signed by over one million EU citizens.[39] Meanwhile, the right to appeal to the Ombudsman represents a direct and legally binding relationship between individual citizens and Union institutions—one that aids citizens in safeguarding their European rights, which in many cases have become more extensive than national ones.[40] In 1995, the Parliament elected Jacob Söderman, previously Ombudsman of Finland, to be the first European Ombudsman and investigate complaints about bad administration in EU institutions and bodies. Most complaints came from individual citizens and concerned access to documents and information, as well as staff recruitment issues. Others involved infringements of human or fundamental rights, or contractual disputes. Söderman worked to define bad administration, foster transparency, and manage a caseload of over two thousand complaints annually, in order to help "the European Union [turn] into Citizen's Europe."[41]

3.3. Ratifying Maastricht

The importance of Maastricht's citizenship provisions during the ratification debates differed from state to state. Some thought that creating European citizenship had little practical importance and doubted whether it could function effectively.[42] With ideals of legal or political theory in mind, it is perhaps tempting to castigate the leaders who were enthusiastic about European citizenship for not giving it more content, but such assessments miss the political realities they faced. Though the treaty ultimately passed with relative ease in most member states, the introduction of some aspects of EU citizenship aroused deeply negative sentiments. In a survey in spring 1993 that asked respondents seventeen propositions, ranging from whether the national currency should be replaced by a European one to whether there should be a common European foreign and security policy, "any citizen of another EC country who resides in (our country) should have the right to vote in local elections" was the third least popular. Overall, 48 percent of respondents favored extending the right to vote, while 41 percent opposed it. There was more opposition than support in five of the twelve member states: Denmark (36 percent of respondents in favor, compared to 60 percent opposed),

Greece (35 percent to 54 percent), Luxembourg (41 percent to 50 percent), France (45 percent to 48 percent), and Germany (42 percent to 43 percent).[43] The least popular proposition of all, however, was allowing EU citizens to run for office: only 38 percent of respondents agreed that "any citizen of another member state who resides in (our country) should have the right to be a candidate in local elections," while 48 percent opposed it. In only four member states were more respondents favorable than opposed: Ireland (55 percent to 28 percent), the Netherlands (50 percent to 40 percent), Spain (49 percent to 31 percent), and Italy (41 percent to 37 percent). There was strong opposition in the eight other member states, most notably in Denmark (30 percent to 66 percent), France (29 percent to 64 percent), Greece (24 percent to 63 percent), Luxembourg (28 percent to 57 percent), and the UK (39 percent to 52 percent). The extensive popular opposition to EU citizenship's political rights helps explain the politics of ratification within many member states.

Denmark was the first member state to attempt ratification, and its initial failure to do so, despite support from most of its political parties, came as a shock. In the referendum on 2 June 1992, Danish voters rejected the treaty by the narrow margin of 50.7 percent to 49.3 percent. When the governments of the eleven other member states decided to continue with the ratification process while leaving open the possibility of Danish participation, the opposition parties and the government joined to draft a "national compromise." The Danish parties interpreted the referendum as a "no" to a United States of Europe rather than to Community membership or European cooperation. In the "national compromise" document, Denmark asked the other member states for special provisions in four areas: defense policy, EMU and the euro, justice and police affairs, and citizenship. The section on citizenship specified that Denmark would "have no obligations in connection with citizenship of the Union," though it would allow Union citizens to vote and run for office in European and municipal elections.[44] Following a flurry of diplomatic activities, the European Council meeting in Edinburgh in December 1992 confirmed that Denmark could opt out of EMU, that it would not be required to participate in joint defense, and that justice and police affairs decisions would be taken intergovernmentally. The Council also clarified that Maastricht's citizenship provisions "give nationals of the Member States additional rights and protection," that they "do not in any way take the place of national citizenship," and that the "question whether an individual possesses the nationality of a Member State will be settled solely by reference to the national law of the Member State concerned."[45] Secure in the knowledge that they were saying no to common defense, justice and police affairs, currency, and European citizenship, 56.7 percent of Danish voters approved the Maastricht Treaty, with the Edinburgh declarations, in a second referendum on 18 May 1993.[46]

Free movement became a crucial issue in the Irish referendum because of the question of abortion. Citing a 1988 Irish Supreme Court decision (based on a 1983 constitutional amendment) that the fetus's right to life was fundamental, a private group called the Society for the Protection of Unborn Children had sued three student groups for publishing contact information for British abortion providers. The Irish High Court referred the case to the European Court of Justice (ECJ), which ruled in October 1991 that, though abortion was a service (thus implying freedom of movement), it was not against Community law for member states that forbid abortion to prohibit groups from distributing information about abortion providers in other member states unless these providers themselves were involved in the distribution.[47] Worried that the ECJ decision might nevertheless block its abortion policy in light of Maastricht's free movement provisions, Ireland insisted on adding a protocol specifying that nothing in the treaty would affect the Irish abortion prohibition. Two months later, however, the country was convulsed by the case of X, a fourteen-year-old girl who had become pregnant as a result of rape. The Irish High Court ruled that X could not travel to England for an abortion, provoking widespread protests that prompted the Irish Supreme Court to reverse the ruling, but only on the grounds that the girl was suicidal.[48] Facing growing criticism that the protocol it had negotiated made Irish women "second rank citizens," the government hurriedly attempted to secure the right to travel and to information.[49] The other member states obligingly clarified that "the Protocol shall not limit freedom to travel between Member States," or freedom "to obtain or make available in Ireland information relating to services lawfully available in Member States."[50] Ireland further promised a separate referendum on abortion, thereby helping secure the treaty's approval with 69 percent of the votes. Turnout was 57 percent in the referendum of 18 June 1992, a mere two weeks after the Danish rejection had thrown the entire treaty into doubt. For Jacques Delors, the Irish result was "the happiest day of his Presidency," because it meant that the process of ratification could continue in the other member states.[51]

In Belgium, most political leaders agreed that Maastricht was not ambitious enough, particularly on social policy issues. However, a key aid to ratification was the government's decision to postpone amending the Belgian Constitution, which limited to Belgian citizens the right to vote and to stand for election and thus conflicted with the treaty's extension of voting rights to all EU citizens. The governing coalition of Christian Democrats and Socialists argued that it was unnecessary to amend the Constitution before ratifying the treaty and invoked Luxembourg's decision to postpone constitutional amendments until after ratification. Despite Belgium's constitutional court ruling that the Constitution had to be amended before Parliament could ratify the Maastricht Treaty, the government stood firm because a constitutional amendment would have required calling new elections, and opinion polls predicted disastrous results for the coalition parties.[52] In contrast with most Belgian political parties, the nationalist Vlaams Blok opposed the treaty, primarily because of the voting rights issue. The party feared that EU citizens living in Brussels would vote for French-speaking rather than Dutch-speaking candidates and that Maastricht would soon lead to voting rights for all foreign residents in Belgium.

In France, as in Belgium, the proposed voting rights were controversial. The constitutional Council considered three proposed treaty articles unconstitutional because they infringed national sovereignty: the articles on visa policy, the European Central Bank, and voting rights for EU citizens.[53] The ruling meant that the French Constitution had to be amended before France could ratify Maastricht. President Mitterrand decided to see if both the National Assembly and the Senate could agree on proposed revisions, failing which there would be a referendum. The government introduced a bill to amend the Constitution on 22 April 1992. Mitterrand's view that the issue would split the political right reflected statements by Alain Juppé, secretary general (later foreign minister, then prime minister) of the Gaullist *Rassemblement pour la République* (RPR), who in mid-February had called it "completely out of the question to give foreigners the possibility of having municipal councillors, who could then endorse a candidate for the presidency, elect senators or become mayor."[54] The proposed bill acknowledged this concern by specifying that EU citizens could not serve as mayor or take part in the election of senators. This did not ease RPR members' worries, forcing party leader Jacques Chirac to choose between supporting the Maastricht Treaty—including its citizenship provisions—and agreeing with those in his party who opposed it. The National Assembly first discussed the draft bill for amending the Constitution on 5 May. During the following week, ninety-seven amendments were tabled. One specified that the voting rights provisions of European citizenship would be spelled out in a separate law. The amended bill was passed on 13 May and went directly to the Senate, where some senators—mainly Gaullists led by RPR senator Charles Pasqua—demanded input on the forthcoming law on the voting rights of European citizens.[55] As early as the 1988 presidential campaign, Mitterrand had suggested giving the vote to foreigners residing in France, and his reputation as "the most European of the European leaders" was not undeserved: the idea of

European political union was the cornerstone of Mitterrand's political commitments.[56] His efforts helped result in the narrow approval—51 percent to 49 percent—for the treaty in the 20 September 1992 referendum.

The ratification process in Italy was smooth, and the treaty was ratified in approximately one-third the time normally taken to transform a bill into law.[57] The treaty enjoyed the unanimous support of Italian political parties, and ratification would have been even faster had Italy not been recovering from the turmoil of the first elections following the start of the anticorruption *mani pulite* or "clean hands" inquest.

In the Netherlands, too, the ratification debate was uncontentious. Dutch political leaders were relieved that a treaty had been agreed upon during their presidency, and the government made it clear that it expected its carefully constructed text to be passed easily, as indeed it was with an overwhelming majority vote in Parliament. None of the political parties supported calls for the treaty to be put to referendum, and all lamented the initial failed referendum result in Denmark. Given the lack of interest among any of the main parties to oppose the treaty, there was little parliamentary debate and virtually no public debate.[58] Frits Bolkestein, the new leader of the conservative People's Party for Freedom and Democracy (VVD), and later European commissioner from 1999 to 2004, did write an essay provocatively entitled "A Union-Citizen One Finds Only at McDonald's," which echoed British prime minister Margaret Thatcher's October 1988 speech in Bruges: there should be no central regulation by "Eurocrats," least of all in the fields of social policy and foreign policy, but rather a return to market forces and free trade among sovereign states.[59] In the end, however, the VVD joined the consensus position and approved ratification.

In Greece there was wide support for European citizenship, though the Greek Communist Party feared the loss of national identity, and other members of Parliament were concerned about EU citizens running in local and European Parliament elections. Konstantine Mitsotakis's New Democracy government, supported by the Panhellenic Socialist Movement (PASOK) opposition party of Andreas Papandreou, stressed that European citizenship would run parallel to Greek citizenship and that loyalty to Greece would not be sacrificed.[60] The most important reason for Greece's ratification, despite these concerns, was its acceptance into the Western European Union (WEU). Mitsotakis had threatened to veto the entire Maastricht package if Greece was not admitted, though PASOK preferred bolstering Greek defense within NATO rather than the WEU.[61]

Luxembourg was the most opposed of any member state to Maastricht's citizenship provisions. As discussed above, this was because almost one-third of Luxembourg's residents were not Luxembourg citizens: most were EU citizens, and the ratification debate focused on the issue of voting rights. Opposition to extending voting rights to EU citizens was so strong that some government deputies wanted to veto the entire treaty unless it allowed stringent criteria for voting rights, including strict voter registration; relinquishing the right to vote in the country of origin; having resided in Luxembourg for at least ten years to vote and twelve to run for office; limiting the allowable proportion of non-Luxembourg candidates on any party list to half (precluding a "Portuguese" party, for example); preventing EU citizens from becoming mayor or alderman; limiting EU citizens to no more than 25 percent of city councillors; and requiring all city council debates to take place in the Letzeburgesch language, against the long-standing tradition of allowing French and German. Prime Minister (later Commission president from 1995 to 1999) Jacques Santer's government successfully defused the opposition, using the treaty "as a pretext for making an autochthonous population accept a series of unavoidable measures more easily."[62] In a concession to Luxembourg, however, the 1993 directive laying down conditions for the right to vote provided that, if the proportion of voting-age EU citizens who reside in but are not citizens of a member state exceeds 20 percent of the total voting-age population, the member state may restrict the vote to EU voters who have resided there for a minimum period.[63] Luxembourg remains the only member state to meet this condition.

Given the many Portuguese citizens resident in other member states, the Portuguese Parliament welcomed Maastricht's citizenship provisions. Prime Minister Aníbal Cavaco Silva's Social Democratic government "welcomed the benefits to Portuguese emigrants arising from Citizenship of the Union."[64] Ratification proceeded smoothly.

Spain had been a chief proponent of entrenching EU citizenship in the treaty. This required amending the Spanish Constitution, which had previously provided that only Spanish citizens could stand for election in municipal elections.[65] The Congress of Deputies and the Senate passed the constitutional requirement unanimously (partly due to the widespread notion that EU citizenship was a "Spanish" proposal) and, though some parties had in vain advocated holding a referendum on the treaty, later overwhelmingly approved the treaty itself.[66]

The UK had opted out of both monetary union and Maastricht's social policy agenda, an anathema to its Conservative government—indeed, Prime Minister John Major argued that "Britain used the Maastricht negotiations to reassert the authority of national governments"—and European citizenship was therefore not a major issue in the UK's ratification process, though the Liberal Democrats favored a comprehensive immigration policy "as an indispensable adjunct to European citizenship."[67] Yet Major's intervention did not convince everyone. His predecessor as prime minister, Margaret Thatcher, vigorously disagreed, stating, "I don't think it does anyone any good to try to dissolve twelve countries, twelve different languages, into something called European citizenship"—and asking, in the House of Lords, "If there is a citizenship, you would all owe a duty of allegiance to the new Union. What else is citizenship about? There will be a duty to uphold its laws. What will happen if the allegiance to the Union comes into conflict with the allegiance to our own country?"[68] The first vote on Maastricht in the House of Lords concerned removing parts of EU citizenship from the ratification bill, but this failed narrowly, paving the way for Maastricht to be approved in the UK.

Many had expected German unification to cause East Germans to enter the EU labor market, and hundreds of thousands of East Germans did seek employment in the former West Germany. Though this could have caused higher unemployment in the West, the opposite occurred: unemployment declined in the West and rose in the East as many East German companies went out of business, unable to compete with their western counterparts.[69] The accession treaties for Greece, Spain, and Portugal had all provided for transition periods before the application of certain Community laws, including provisions for free movement of persons. German reunification, however, did not involve an accession treaty. Instead, the former German Democratic Republic was absorbed by the Federal Republic of Germany, and Community law automatically applied to the former East Germany. Though the Maastricht Treaty did not achieve as much political integration as many Germans had hoped, all the parties with the exception of the Party of Democratic Socialism (PDS), the former East German Communists, supported ratification.[70] But ratification would wait until a ruling from the German Federal Constitutional Court. Though the voluminous judgment rejected the claim that Maastricht was unconstitutional, it did establish limits to European law. For example, the judges declared that Maastricht established "a union of countries in order to create an ever closer union among the peoples of Europe (organized as states), rather than a state based on a European people."[71] The German Court also clarified the nature of EU citizenship. "With the establishment of union citizenship by the Maastricht Treaty," wrote the judges, "a lasting legal tie is knotted between the nationals of the individual Member States which, though not as strong as the common nationality of a single state, provides a legally binding expression of the degree of de facto community already in existence."[72] With the Court's blessing on 12 October 1993, Germany ratified Maastricht, the last member state to do so.

The fall of the Berlin Wall in 1989 led to intense efforts to advance European integration, resulting in the Maastricht Treaty. Proposals to expand the focus of the treaty discussions beyond economic affairs to include a political component quickly gained support from the Delors Commission and a number of member states. Proponents of adding political elements to European integration advocated returning to the notion of citizenship that had been discussed in the past but never entrenched in Community law. German chancellor Helmut Kohl and French president François Mitterrand favored integrating and extending the notion of a Community citizenship. They and other leaders suggested that European citizenship should signify respect for human rights, social and political rights, and complete free movement. The bargaining resulted in four sets of rights: free movement, the right to vote and run as a candidate in local and European elections, the right to common diplomatic protection abroad, and the right to petition Parliament and appeal to the Ombudsman. Of these, the right to vote and run as a candidate in one's place of residence were the most controversial. Strong majorities of the public in Denmark, France, Greece, Luxembourg, and the UK were opposed. There was less strident opposition in Germany, Belgium, and Portugal. Only in Ireland, the Netherlands, Spain, and Italy did a majority of the public support both rights. Those who criticized the political leaders for not strengthening the notion of Union citizenship should recall this popular opposition and the difficulties encountered in implementing the treaty. On balance, Maastricht achieved less than some had hoped, but more than many had thought possible.

CHAPTER FOUR

Europe's Homogeneous Space

It is not a question of eliminating ethnic and political borders. They are a historical given: we do not pretend to correct history, or to invent a rationalized and managed geography. What we want is to take away from borders their rigidity and what I call their intransigent hostility.[1]

—Robert Schuman

We propose to put the finishing touches to the formation in Europe of a homogeneous space, where freedom of movement will be guaranteed by a common approach.[2]

—Helmut Kohl and Jacques Chirac

The formal introduction of citizenship at Maastricht accomplished what had been a goal since even before the earliest days of the European Coal and Steel Community in the 1950s: turning "the whole of Europe into one space."[3] Far from being a final constitutional settlement, however, the introduction of European Union (EU) citizenship in the Maastricht Treaty unleashed a further flurry of debates and decisions in the ongoing process of creating European citizens. While Robert Schuman in 1963 had claimed that European integration would not eliminate borders, German chancellor Helmut Kohl and French president Jacques Chirac in 1995 sought to complete "the formation in Europe of a homogeneous space." This work continued with the Treaty of Amsterdam and the Treaty of Nice, followed by enlargement of the Union and the drive to transform the treaties into a constitution, discussed in the next chapter. The bargains struck at Amsterdam and Nice further consolidated European rights, leading the European Parliament to correctly describe EU citizenship as "a dynamic institution, a key to the process of European integration" that was "expected gradually to supplement and extend the rights" of national citizenship.[4] In order for citizens to truly feel at home in the "homogeneous" space, however, they needed European social rights.

4.1. European Social Rights

EU citizenship's enactment at Maastricht sparked debates about a pan-European welfare state because shared citizenship can justify redistribution between citizens.[5] This discussion was not new: as early as the Spaak report of 1956 there had been a conscious drive to add "thick" social rights to the "thin" rights of freedom of movement. The Treaty of Rome negotiations concerning social policy were more difficult than those concerning free movement, but the new Community in 1958 adopted detailed social security provisions for migrant workers. Five years later, there followed regulations concerning social security for frontier workers, temporary and other nonresident workers, and health and maternity benefits and family allowances for family members residing in a member state other than the one in which the worker was employed. Intended to foster mobility within the Community, these regulations also influenced the bilateral accords between member states and worker recruitment countries such as Spain, Portugal, Greece, and Turkey.[6] Though the early provisions covered only some employment rights, the number and scope of social policy decisions continued to increase, supporting former Commission president Hallstein's 1972 description of the growth of European social policy as an irresistible flow: though the treaty provided only modest scope for launching a common social policy, "the European ground-swell, slowly but irresistibly, washes over the national sandbanks."[7]

Yet the growth of European social rights was sporadic. Even as early as the 1960s, the Commission attempted to advance European social rights in order to make member state citizens "actually feel that they are citizens of the one Community" and "be aware that their common fortune is attributable to the Community."[8] But the tension between this goal and the wishes of the member states erupted at a Council meeting in 1964: the national ministers responsible for social affairs stated unanimously that social security fell within the sole jurisdiction of national governments, and that Community institutions therefore had no competence in this area. There followed a complete breakdown in communications, and for two years, social affairs ministers simply did not meet as a council. They finally met again in December 1966, agreeing that Community social policy rules would not be passed unless they had the unanimous support of the member states. This was not only an institutional defeat for the Commission but also the end of the Community's efforts to increase benefits for workers, which was replaced by the goal of controlling social security costs.[9] The emphasis would for a long time remain not on the citizens but on the market. Invariably, European social rights were justified in terms of facilitating mobility: coordinating social security systems, mutual recognition of qualifications, a European role in family policy, ensuring equal access to social benefits, and even EU efforts to combat poverty were all intended to reduce or eliminate barriers to free movement.[10]

Market forces both generate and limit the spread of rights, and the aim of creating an EU-wide labor market facilitated the passage of EU rules.[11] Comparative examples abound of social rights that originated in markets. In the age of the welfare state, a key impediment to migration has been the risk of being cut off from social support in one's country of origin while not being admitted to social support in the destination country. Social rights thus represent a key to full citizenship: by virtue of social citizenship rights, individuals are entitled to equal or equitable access to a range of primary goods, such as education, health, and welfare. If these benefits fall under noncentral jurisdiction then issues of redistribution become important. This is a familiar concern in federal states, where the central government must work to limit impediments to citizen mobility. Similarly, only by ensuring that social entitlements apply regardless of the jurisdiction of residence does unproblematic migration among European states become viable. Just as social rights within federal states require coordination between the federal government and the constituent jurisdictions, so too European rights require coordination between European institutions and the member states. In order to safeguard the content of EU citizenship, supranational institutions such as the Commission and the Court have attempted to limit residence requirements for program access while promoting portability and mutual recognition. In national states, unlike in the EU, social welfare programs are generally centrally designed rather than regional or local in nature. Granted, regional governments in federal systems often exercise significant discretion in program design and delivery (think of the role of Canadian provinces in health insurance, or the variation among U.S. states' rules for welfare benefits for poor families), but the central government tends to hold the purse strings. By contrast, the EU funds very few direct social programs.

The primary constraint on the growth of EU social rights is the limited size of the EU budget, which accounts for barely 1 percent of Europe's gross domestic product (GDP), far less than member state spending. (By contrast, the U.S. federal budget accounts for approximately 19 percent of American GDP, while U.S. state and local governments spend another 9 percent of GDP.) Because of its small budget, the EU provides minimal direct financial support for social welfare. But in the field of social *regulation*, the progress has been so remarkable that some EU rules exceed the most advanced national measures in the level of protection they afford, causing social rights activists to pursue a European rather than national strategy because they expect European citizenship to enhance social rights.[12] European regulations have indeed caused member states to adapt their social policies, benefiting domestic citizens. But perhaps the most significant beneficiaries of EU citizenship have been people who move between or among member states. Indeed, if they never cross member state borders, EU citizenship may contribute little to the social status and day-to-day experience of citizens of the member states.[13]

Two European Court of Justice (ECJ) decisions illustrate the growing importance of EU citizenship in promoting European social rights, particularly for Union migrants. The first concerns María Martínez Sala, a Spanish citizen who had lived in Germany since 1968 and applied in 1993 for a child-raising allowance. Her application was rejected because she did not have German citizenship, a residence entitlement, or a residence permit. When she appealed, the German court requested a preliminary opinion from the ECJ, which responded that Martínez Sala was entitled to the allowance because nationals of any member state can rely on their European citizenship for protection against discrimination on grounds of nationality.[14] The second case concerns Rudy Grzelczyk, a French citizen who had moved to Belgium for university studies and applied for the same financial allowance granted to Belgian students.[15] The allowance was initially granted but then withdrawn because Grzelczyk was a student rather than a worker. Requesting a preliminary opinion, the Belgian court asked the ECJ whether, in light of the *Martínez Sala* ruling, the principles of European citizenship and nondiscrimination allowed the Belgian government to refuse assistance to EU citizens. The case drew a long list of interveners. The social services authority argued that EU citizens were not entitled to claim social benefits because existing legislation required individuals to possess sufficient social security protection. Belgium and Denmark concurred, submitting that EU citizenship did not give citizens new or more extensive rights to social security. Belgium added that its student assistance grant was an instrument of social policy, unlinked to vocational training, and hence outside EU competence. France argued that extending the principle of equal treatment to all EU citizens, rather than simply workers, would establish total equality among all EU citizens, which would be difficult to reconcile with national citizenship rights. Portugal argued that, because of EU citizenship, Europeans were no longer simply economic actors in an economic community, and the distinction between workers and others was thus no longer valid. The UK countered that, though Grzelczyk suffered discrimination on the grounds of his nationality, EU law allowed such discrimination in matters of social rights. In its decision, the Court held that discrimination solely on grounds of nationality is prohibited and that states' social security rules must be read in conjunction with EU citizenship provisions. "Union citizenship is destined to be the fundamental status of nationals of the Member States," it ruled, "conferring on them, in the fields covered by Community law, equality under the law irrespective of their nationality."[16]

In both *Martínez Sala* and *Grzelczyk*, then, the Court upheld the right to equal access to social benefits on the basis of EU citizenship. This was an important shift from earlier restrictions of such rights to workers (and other economic actors) exercising free movement. That the change came only several years after the member states had included citizenship in the treaty should restrain worries that the Court might overstep its authority by legislating against member state wishes. Indeed, the Court in the mid-1970s accepted more restrictive national eligibility requirements for social security payments for migrant workers in the wake of the first social security coordination regulation, though it never abrogated the treaty's defense of free movement.[17]

Many EU initiatives promote intra-European movement. Consider the push to introduce a European health insurance card to replace the paper forms previously needed to access health treatment during a temporary stay in another country. Introducing the card, Irish prime minister Bertie Ahern called it "a very tangible manifestation of an initiative by the European Union with real, practical benefits for its citizens," while Commission president Romano Prodi labeled it "another piece of Europe in your pocket."[18] As these statements indicate, the symbolism of a *European* health card is not accidental: it was intended to reinforce the portability of benefits throughout EU territory, and it achieves one of the hopes of the Tindemans report: the "day that Europeans can move about within the Union, can communicate among themselves and when necessary receive medical care without national frontiers adding to the problems of distance, European Union will become for them a discernible reality."[19]

In the hope of bringing "American-style mobility to the European employment market," the Commission constantly works to facilitate mobility by attempting to coordinate social security systems, harmonize taxation systems, and increase information about employment opportunities.[20] The disparities in social entitlements in the various member states make those systems difficult to reconcile. Attempting to minimize impediments to free movement, the Commission urged member states in 2006 to update the social security benefit policies, noting that "coordination of national security systems is meaningful only at Community level: its basis lies in the free movement of persons in the EU and it is justified by this free movement. These rules concern all European citizens moving within the Union for any reason whatsoever."[21] The updated rules apply to all EU citizens, rather than simply the various categories of people (employees, the self-employed, civil servants, students, and pensioners) gradually covered since the first coordination legislation was implemented in 1972.[22] They cover all branches of social security: sickness, maternity, accidents at work, occupational diseases, invalidity benefits, unemployment benefits, family benefits, retirement and preretirement benefits, and death grants. The new rules reinforce the right to export social security benefits, introduce the principle of good administration, and strengthen the principle of aggregation, meaning that national authorities must consider employment or residence anywhere within the EU when calculating eligibility for social security.

The updated rules go some way toward ameliorating the fragmentation of European social rights. As a consequence of their gradual development, these rights categorize individuals by personal attributes and economic activity. Thus workers, students, retirees, and professionals are covered by different pieces of legislation, obfuscating similarities in their rights. Even within the category of free movement of workers, five different regulatory frameworks apply: self-employed workers exercise freedom of establishment when they move to another country to work; they are covered under cross-border provision of services when they continue to reside in their home country while providing services abroad. Employees are frontier workers if they work for a company that is not located in the same country as their residence; they are migrant workers if they move to another country to work for a foreign company; and they are posted workers if their home-country company sends them to work abroad. This division of rights into different categories has struck some as odd and in need of change, particularly since the introduction of EU citizenship. Thus, a 1998 Commission panel argued that the piecemeal development of EU rights was "no longer consistent with the all-embracing status of European citizen."[23]

4.2. The Amsterdam Treaty

The Amsterdam Treaty resulted from the longest intergovernmental conference to date, sixteen months of negotiations from March 1996 to June 1997. It came about because the Maastricht Treaty specified that a treaty revision had to occur. Preparations started in spring 1995. The Cannes European Council in June 1995 stressed that treaty revisions should aim to "strengthen public support for the process of European integration by meeting the need for a form of democracy which is closer to the citizens of Europe," a sentiment reiterated at the Madrid European Council that December: the conference should make Europe more relevant to its citizens (as well as preparing for enlargement, and strengthening EU foreign policy).[24]

Just as German chancellor Helmut Kohl and French president François Mitterrand had written to the other government leaders in 1990 at the start of the Maastricht negotiations, so too Kohl and new French president Jacques Chirac issued a letter in December 1995 laying out their vision for the new treaty. Though the Kohl-Chirac letter mentioned a number of goals, including enhancing EU citizenship, there was no clear overall Franco-German position, despite another Kohl-Chirac letter and joint meetings between the Germans and the French. In previous treaty negotiations a common Franco-German approach had often acted as a "motor" for the EU's development, but the defeat of Alain Juppé's center-right coalition by Lionel Jospin's center-left coalition in France on 1 June 1997 ruined the usual Franco-German joint formulation of positions before meetings of the European Council.[25] Jospin's unexpected election in France followed exactly one month after the 1 May 1997 election in the UK of the Labour Party under Tony Blair, ending eighteen years of Conservative rule under Margaret Thatcher and John Major. The transition to new governments in both the UK and France complicated the final weeks of treaty negotiations.

The negotiations had not started well either, due to political turmoil in Italy, which held the presidency in the first half of 1996. The coalition formed after the December 1994 downfall of Silvio Berlusconi's first government had gone from crisis to crisis and finally collapsed on 12 January 1996, twelve days into the Italian presidency. After a failed attempt to form yet another government from within Parliament, general elections were called for 21 April. Despite the chaotic handling of meetings, sudden changes in dates, and a general lack of political leadership, bureaucrats at the ministry of foreign affairs attempted to salvage the Italian presidency by circulating notes to the other member states. In the areas of citizenship and fundamental rights, they even attempted to produce a draft treaty text.[26]

The elections resulted in a center-left government headed by Romano Prodi (later Commission president from 1999 to 2004). During the final two months of their presidency, the Italians tried to make up for lost time by presenting summary notes on the three priority areas, collected in a progress report—rather than a draft treaty, as some had hoped—to the Florence European Council of 21 and 22 June.

The Danish objections to Maastricht's citizenship provisions weighed heavily during the first months of negotiations. Echoing these objections, the UK government of John Major in March issued a White Paper entitled "A Partnership of Nations": it rejected new rights, arguing that human rights were already sufficiently protected in Europe and that extending the rights of EU citizenship might ultimately transform the Union into a sovereign state.[27] Together with Denmark, the UK argued that fundamental rights should apply to everyone within EU territory rather than depending on EU citizenship, that any new EU citizenship rights should not be directly effective (so that citizens could not bring them to the European Court of Justice), and that the financial consequences of any new rights would require careful assessment.[28]

Ireland assumed the presidency from Italy on 1 July and, ignoring British and Danish intransigence, suggested expanding EU citizenship by granting EU citizens the right to vote in referendums and nonmunicipal elections, establishing an EU volunteer service, and introducing a right to petition the Commission. On 3 October, the Italian and Austrian governments jointly proposed introducing a right of petition, a right of association in European trade unions, and a right to education in at least one second language, as well as suggesting that the EU should sign the European Convention on Human Rights (ECHR) and that European political parties should be strengthened.[29] In Austria, the opposition Liberals suggested going even further by extending EU citizenship to third-country nationals who had resided legally within the EU for five years, but this proposal lacked government support and was not included in the joint proposal.[30] Italy later suggested giving the Commission the exclusive right of initiative on issues of immigration, asylum, and external borders (meaning that EU legislation in these areas would have to originate with the Commission), giving the Court full competence to review legislation and hear appeals and ultimately giving Parliament codecision power over these areas rather than having them remain the exclusive competence of member states.[31] Similarly, France suggested that free movement issues—including visas, asylum, and immigration—should be decided by qualified majority voting rather than unanimity, which would also make it easier to pass coordinated European legislation. Meanwhile, Finland proposed extending "the social rights and duties of European citizens" by adding new rights to EU citizenship, having the EU sign the ECHR, and possibly enacting an EU Bill of Rights.[32] In the same vein, Portugal even drafted a European Citizens Charter, which listed all the rights of European citizenship, including social and economic rights, and was intended "to provide citizens a clear picture of the advantages and added value of European citizenship."[33]

None of these proposals were adopted in the Amsterdam Treaty, which postponed the hardest issues, including citizenship, instead focusing on monetary union: indeed, the member states excluded half of the bargaining issues in order to secure ratification.[34] In terms of citizenship, Amsterdam accomplished little more than granting citizens the right to communicate with EU institutions in any treaty language, the result of a last-minute Belgian proposal. Though many had expected that citizenship would become a key part of Amsterdam, it did not: the shadow of the Danish rejection of Maastricht had made states wary, lest strengthening Union citizenship be interpreted as weakening national citizenship. To ease such fears, the member states added a new clause—"Citizenship of the Union shall complement and not replace national citizenship"—that went well beyond the declaration attached to the Maastricht Treaty, which stated that the question whether an individual had the nationality of a member state would be settled solely by reference to the national law. With the "complement and not replace" clause, the Danish government could claim that its reservation on citizenship had been incorporated, helping to pass the Amsterdam Treaty in Denmark despite strong opposition linking enlargement and EU citizenship to fears of uncontrolled immigration.[35] The May 1998 referendum resulted in a yes vote of 55.1 percent in favor of Amsterdam—not quite as wide a margin as the 56.8 percent that had passed the revised Maastricht Treaty in May 1993 but better than the 50.7 percent rejection in the first Maastricht referendum of June 1992.

In the end, Danish and British intransigence blocked the wider conception of citizenship rights supported by the other member states, meaning that the EU would have to rely on instrumental benefits rather than new rights as the primary source of legitimacy.[36] Instead of granting EU citizens new rights, Amsterdam empowered EU institutions to introduce new policies in such areas as employment, public health, the environment, consumer protection, education, sports, and culture. Significantly, it gave the ECJ the authority to more strictly enforce nondiscrimination principles and to address gender inequality, public health, and consumer protection. Member states agreed to work toward "an area of freedom, security, and justice," which meant among other things bringing into the treaty the Schengen arrangements. The treaty promised greater coordination on immigration and asylum policy, though

Germany, which was absorbing the bulk of refugees and asylum seekers, insisted on restrictions because responsibility for immigration and asylum was shared between the German Länder and the federal government. Nevertheless, some observers expected that the ECJ would promptly gain control over immigration policy.[37]

4.3. The Charter of Fundamental Rights

Pressure to codify European rights continued after Amsterdam. At the Cologne European Council in June 1999 the heads of state and government identified the "need, at the present stage of the Union's development, to establish a Charter of fundamental rights in order to make their overriding importance and relevance more visible to the Union's citizens."[38] They agreed that this Charter should contain the rights and freedoms guaranteed by the ECHR, the European Social Charter, the Community Charter of the Fundamental Social Rights of Workers, and member state constitutional traditions. But they furthermore specified that the proposed Charter should also include the "rights that pertain only to the Union's citizens."[39] Identifying rights that would pertain only to EU citizens—rather than all EU residents or everyone subject to EU law—was seen as a way of increasing EU legitimacy by strengthening and giving more substance to EU citizenship.[40] Echoing this desire, Parliament in September 1999 resolved that "the creation of an ever closer union among the peoples of Europe is inseparably linked with the task of increasing, in addition to fundamental rights, citizens' rights, namely the political, economic and social rights associated with Union citizenship."[41] Thus Parliament repeated the distinction between fundamental or human rights and rights specifically for EU citizens, claiming that increasing EU citizens' rights would reinforce European integration.

The Cologne European Council specified the Convention's composition: fifteen representatives (one for each member state) of the heads of state and government, thirty representatives of the national parliaments, sixteen representatives of the European Parliament, and Justice and Home Affairs Commissioner António Vitorino, representing the Commission. Bringing together European and national representatives was not entirely novel, because the 1990 parliamentary assizes had done so preceding the Maastricht Treaty negotiations, but this was the first time that any group other than an intergovernmental conference would write such a fundamental EU document.

The Tampere European Council of October 1999 further detailed the procedures that the Convention would use. In a crucial difference with previous treaty processes using intergovernmental conferences, the heads of state and government recommended that the Convention's hearings, and documents submitted at those hearings, should be public rather than hidden behind the traditional veil of diplomatic negotiations. Tampere furthermore gave the Convention's leadership the power to forward the draft Charter when they deemed it would eventually be approved, a major innovation because it led the Convention's members to decide that votes should be avoided in favor of consensus, which in turn shaped the style and content of debates.[42] The Convention's cooperative spirit made its deliberations transparent, accountable, and legitimate—and led some to argue that the "Convention method" should replace intergovernmental conferences, because traditional diplomatic negotiations did not produce results.[43]

The Convention held its inaugural meeting in December 1999. It immediately received submissions from many nongovernmental organizations (NGOs) and interest groups. For example, the European Movement—the umbrella organization of national prointegration movements formed at the 1948 Hague Congress—submitted its European Citizens' Charter, originally proclaimed in 1997 on the fortieth anniversary of the Treaty of Rome. This Charter affirms that all European "residents have the right to obtain the citizenship of the state where they reside," that "the Union shall ensure the harmonization of rights of access to national citizenship," and that EU institutions will strengthen European citizenship, which "resides on a European model of society which includes respect for the individual and for fundamental rights and a commitment to solidarity amongst its members," thereby making Europe "the avant-garde of the future democracy without frontiers that will become a reality in the 21st century."[44] Here citizenship would become available to everyone moving within and into the EU, with harmonized access to national citizenship. But it would also become a proselytizing force for a worldwide democracy without frontiers.

The preamble to the Charter that the Convention ultimately drafted affirms that the EU "places the individual at the heart of its activities, by establishing the citizenship of the Union and by creating an area of freedom, security and justice." The Charter itself contains an exhaustive listing of rights covered in six chapters: dignity, freedoms, equality, solidarity, citizens' rights, and justice. The catalog of rights is so extensive that some questioned whether it was sufficiently "mature" to be legally enforceable.[45] The Charter deviates from earlier lists of EU rights by expanding the social rights extended to EU citizens and, in some cases, any individual—regardless of citizenship status—resident within EU territory. The tension between rights for EU citizens and rights for others remained and is evident, for example, in the Charter's article on the freedom to choose an occupation and the right to work: everyone has the right to engage in work and to pursue a freely chosen or accepted occupation; only EU citizens have the freedom to seek employment, to work, to exercise the right of establishment, and to provide services in any member state; and third-country nationals authorized to work in the member states are entitled to working conditions equivalent to those of EU citizens. This makes three separate categories of rights holders within a single Charter article. In October 2000, the Convention forwarded the final text of the draft Charter of Fundamental Rights to the Council, in the hope that it would become part of the Nice Treaty.

4.4. The Nice Treaty

The Amsterdam Treaty had not resolved the institutional issues that needed to be addressed before enlargement, particularly voting in the Council and Parliament and the size and composition of the Commission. These issues were important due to fears that the decision-making process, already difficult with fifteen member states, would break down entirely with twenty-five or more. As a result, the member states had started yet another intergovernmental conference in February 2000 to, in the words of the eventual Nice Treaty, "complete the process started by the Treaty of Amsterdam of preparing the institutions of the European Union to function in an enlarged Union."[46] The conclusions were adopted at the Nice European Council that December and signed in February 2001. After ratification by all the member states, the treaty came into force on 1 February 2003.[47]

The Nice European Council was far from the EU's finest hour but was not an unmitigated disaster: most of the negotiations concerned the way in which decisions would be made after enlargement, and the resulting changes were technical and limited.[48] In terms of citizenship rights, however, Nice extended qualified majority voting to free movement: henceforth, decisions about the right to move and reside freely within EU territory would no longer require the unanimous support of all member states. The member states did exempt provisions on passports, identity cards, residence permits, social security, and social protection from qualified majority voting. Provisions in those areas would continue to require unanimity. Nevertheless, decisions about free movement provisions could now more easily be made.

The change of free movement issues from unanimity voting to qualified majority voting prompted the Commission, even before Nice came into force, to draft a directive on the right of EU citizens and their family members to move and reside freely within EU territory.[49] The Commission proposed lengthening from three to six months the period in which EU citizens and their families could reside without conditions in other member states, to combat sometimes lengthy administrative procedures and ambiguity about the rights of family members. After six months, an optional system of registration would replace the necessary residence card. For employed or self-employed people, the only condition on the right of residence would be engaging in gainful activity, which could be proved by a simple declaration. For people not in work and students, the right of residence would, for the first four years of residence in the host member state, continue to be subject to the individual having sufficient resources and health insurance. Rather than having to provide proof, however, EU citizens would be allowed to simply declare that they had sufficient resources and insurance. Finally, after four years of continuous residence, EU citizens would automatically acquire the right of permanent residence, without conditions and with full access to social welfare and immunity from expulsion. In addition to these changes, the proposed directive also broadened the definition of "family member" and strengthened their rights. It included in the category of "family member" unmarried partners if national legislation recognized them, and parents and children whether or not they were dependent or minor. Family members who were third-country nationals would also enjoy greater legal protection, for example, in the event of death of the EU citizen on whom they depended or the dissolution of the marriage under certain circumstances. Finally, the directive clarified the limitations to the right of residence on grounds of public policy, public security, and public health. Its impact would thus be significant. Once Nice entered into force, approval required only a qualified majority vote rather than unanimity, as the Commission informed the Parliament and Council.[50]

After extensive negotiations, the member states adopted the directive in 2004, affirming that "Union citizenship should be the fundamental status of nationals of the Member States when they exercise their right of free movement and residence," and that it was thus necessary to revise the existing legislation that dealt separately with workers, the self-employed, and students and other inactive persons "in order to simplify and strengthen the right of free movement and residence of all Union citizens."[51] But this was not all. The directive furthermore asserted that guaranteeing "permanent residence by Union citizens who have chosen to settle long term in the host Member State would strengthen the feeling of Union citizenship and is a key element in promoting social cohesion, which is one of the fundamental objectives of the Union."[52] Though employed and self-employed persons and their families would have access to social assistance, host states retained the discretion to grant such assistance to students and people not in work until they had resided in the host state for five years, when they acquired permanent residence.[53]

With the directive, the member states specified the impact of two Court decisions: the *Grzelczyk* decision concerning student maintenance grants and a 2002 decision that EU citizens (and members of their families, even if they were third-country nationals) who did not have residence rights as workers still had such rights through EU citizenship.[54] Students and individuals who had not worked in their host state did have a right of residence, but social assistance was at the host state's discretion for the first five years.

Because most of the people moving from one EU member state to another were employed or self-employed, and hence already covered prior to the directive, it was most beneficial to third-country nationals who were family members of EU citizens, as well as students and the unemployed or retired. As the directive was being negotiated, the Commission proposed that "tangible expression be given to the legal content of European citizenship" and that the EU's "priority objectives be better defined in the Treaty, focusing on the development of the idea of European citizenship and ensuring respect of the fundamental rights and freedoms recognised by the Union's Charter of Fundamental Rights."[55] Finally, the Nice Treaty also launched a debate about the EU's future—including issues such as the division of competencies between the EU and the member states, simplification of the treaties, and the legal status of the Charter—that would ultimately lead to the Convention and the draft Constitution.

A large part of the impetus for this debate was continually growing concern about the "democratic deficit." Governments often pool authority at the international or supranational level in order to maintain their influence in the face of globalization. Yet the paucity of democratic oversight of supranational decision making creates a democratic deficit to the extent that popular control over these decisions is absent. For example, most international organizations have no directly elected Parliament. The EU is an exception to this rule. But the European Parliament's authority is restricted by the Commission (over which it has limited control), the Council (over which it has no control), and the Court (over which it likewise has no control). Some commentators claim that there is actually no democratic deficit in Europe because *national* parliaments scrutinize the operation of their ministers and diplomats as well as of "their" commissioners and judges. In practice, however, national parliaments lack sufficient resources for effective scrutiny. Even national *governments*—which presumably enjoy parliamentary support, even if they reflect public opinion only imperfectly—often have inadequate means of control over European decisions.

A broader meaning of the democratic deficit is that individual citizens do not understand the complexity of European decisions and do not identify themselves with Europe. The democratic deficit, in this view, flows from the fact that Europe is not only undemocratic but also seems distant. This was Belgian prime minister Leo Tindemans's view when he argued in 1975 that "Europe must be close to its citizens" and was shared by the governments that argued during the Maastricht negotiations that the EU should "strengthen its citizens' feelings of belonging to one legal community."[56] But concern with the democratic deficit dates back even earlier. Altiero Spinelli, for example, wanted European institutions to derive their legitimacy from the direct consent of European citizens and to exercise their powers directly on the citizens, without interference from the member states: he lamented the construction of a technocratic "Europe of offices" and bureaucrats rather than a Europe of citizens.[57] Introducing direct elections to the European Parliament and subsequently strengthening it was one way of addressing this concern. Encouraging Europeans to utilize their European rights is another. Rather than viewing the polity in national terms, however, these solutions involve reconceiving the relevant political community in European terms. The initiatives described in this book for creating European citizens become necessary in order to create a sense of European identity and, ultimately, a European people.[58] Enhancing European democracy does mean introducing more transparency and efficiency. But full European democracy, rule by the people, will remain unattainable until a European public exists. This explains the push for a European Constitution and what the chair of the constitutional Convention termed *affectio societatis*—a feeling of identification with the Union as a whole rather than simply with the member states.

Rather than resolving matters, the official introduction of EU citizenship at Maastricht provoked efforts to determine the meaning of this new status. Most notably, European social rights—already present since the origins of integration, but generally phrased in economic terms—started being justified on the basis of citizenship rather than the market. The Amsterdam and Nice treaties further specified the position of Union citizenship, and a convention of Europe's political leaders drafted a European Charter of Fundamental Rights that consolidated the panoply of European rights into a single document. Finally, efforts continued to combat the democratic deficit by enhancing European citizenship.

CHAPTER FIVE

Toward a Constitution

> At present, the European Union has no competence to regulate matters relating to nationality. These remain at the level of the Member States. Nevertheless, I feel that we have to start reflecting together also on questions relating to nationality.[1]
>
> —Commissioner António Vitorino

> Until now, Europe was mainly associated with a common market. Now Europe will be more and more a place of citizenship.[2]
>
> —Spanish foreign minister Ana Palacio

At the Laeken European Council of December 2001, the heads of state and government declared that EU "institutions must be brought closer to its citizens. Citizens undoubtedly support the Union's broad aims, but they do not always see a connection between those goals and the Union's everyday action."[3] What was needed, they agreed, was more transparency and democracy at the European Union (EU) level. These are not priorities for most international organizations, and those who believe that EU policies are subordinate to the effective scrutiny and control of national governments do not believe that democratic legitimacy should concern the EU.[4] But if Europeans are Union *citizens*, in a similar relationship with the Union as with the member states of which they are also citizens, then absent or weak democratic legitimacy is a serious problem. At Laeken, the member state leaders determined that EU citizens wanted better democratic scrutiny at all levels of government, concluding that "citizens [were] calling for a clear, open, effective, democratically controlled Community approach."[5] They further questioned whether the Charter of Fundamental Rights should be included in the treaty, whether the EU should finally accede to the European Convention on Human Rights (ECHR), and whether these issues should be settled in a European Constitution that specified the relationship between member states, the values of the EU, and "the fundamental rights and obligations of its citizens."[6] Though not new, these questions were intended to provoke discussion within the constitutional Convention, which worked in the shadow of the Union's most dramatic enlargement ever: ten new member states in a first wave, with more to follow. Indeed, the Convention included representatives from the ten countries that would join in 2004 plus Romania, Bulgaria, and Turkey. The rights of EU citizenship conflicted with the reality of accession negotiations that led to transition arrangements for free movement of workers, made in order to render enlargement more politically palatable within the existing member states. The entry of new member states with citizenship traditions different from those of existing ones also affected the future development of EU citizenship. Both the place of third-country nationals and the issue of who would defend European rights remained salient.

5.1. The 2004 Enlargement

The EU's most significant enlargement admitted ten states in 2004: Cyprus, the Czech Republic, Estonia, Hungary, Latvia, Lithuania, Malta, Poland, Slovakia, and Slovenia. In all but Malta and Cyprus, policies similar to the Soviet *propiska* (residence permits) system—which limited the right to move even between different cities within the Soviet Union, let alone between different Republics—had for many years restricted mobility.[7] For individual citizens in these post-Communist states, freedom of movement symbolized the "return to Europe" of EU accession: EU citizenship promised a right to reside and work anywhere within Union territory. As discussed in §2.3, the perceived injustice of the delay in granting free movement to Greek, Spanish, and Portuguese citizens helps explain these states' subsequent support for European citizenship. Experience with these earlier accessions quashed objections that extending mobility rights to citizens of countries with lower average income and higher unemployment would lead to chaos. Once the concept of European citizenship had become widely accepted, it became politically more difficult to distinguish free movement of persons from free movement of goods, services, or capital. Yet negotiations with the central and eastern European states witnessed a renewal of similar objections.

Those who hoped that European integration would shift from a focus on economic integration toward an increasing emphasis on individual rights were disappointed. Because of largely unfounded fears of mass migration from accession countries to existing member states, full free movement rights were once again phased in. Citizenship had not yet been formally introduced at the time of the Mediterranean enlargements in the 1980s, but it did immediately apply to citizens of Sweden, Austria, and Finland when those states joined in 1995—indeed, most Swedish, Austrian, and Finnish citizens had previously enjoyed free movement rights under European Economic Area agreements. Because EU citizenship grants individual rights of residence and employment, citizens of acceding countries should gain these rights throughout the EU, and citizenship of existing member states should gain them in the new ones, but this did not immediately occur with the 2004 enlargement. Official documents about this accession scrupulously avoided mentioning EU citizenship as such, focusing instead on the four freedoms: free movement of goods, capital, services, and persons, with the last generating the most contention.

Negotiations concerning free movement of goods proceeded smoothly compared with the politically sensitive discussions regarding free movement of persons. Similarly, free movement of goods had been immediately guaranteed in the Treaty of Rome, while free movement of all persons (rather than simply of workers) was fully achieved only after years of debate. Though free movement of goods had also taken years to fully achieve, free movement of persons was guaranteed for all EU citizens only in 1993 as a right of EU citizenship. During the accession negotiations, free movement of capital was more contested than free movement of goods, due to the question of investment land and secondary residences. Recognizing the "high political sensitivity" of this issue, certain candidate countries were granted a seven-year transitional period for purchases by citizens of other EU member states of agricultural and forestry land, and a five-year transitional period for purchases of secondary residences.[8] The phase-in would not apply to certain individuals, such as self-employed farmers wishing to establish themselves and reside in the new member states. But rather than declaring the right of establishment and the freedom to provide services to be fundamental freedoms for EU citizens, the Commission simply asserted that the exemptions would protect "integrity of the single market."[9] Under the right of establishment, any self-employed individual, along with his or her family, can move anywhere in the Union to establish a business. Thus, citizens of accession states could move to existing member states as independent contractors or service providers, bringing their families with them. Unlike free movement of workers, the right of establishment and the freedom to provide services have always been effective immediately upon accession. Indeed, the freedom to provide services has even been invoked to strike down national residency requirements for third-country nationals.[10]

Free movement of persons was one of the last issues to be negotiated. The negotiators relied on economic arguments, and offered transitional arrangements to assuage those worried about too many workers from accession states migrating to existing member states. The Commission proposed phasing in free movement of workers from all acceding states other than Cyprus and Malta, acknowledging that only a delayed introduction would "ensure the widest possible public acceptance of enlargement."[11] During a general transition period of five years, member states would continue to enforce their own laws on accepting workers from accession states, though the phase-in would be reviewed after the first two years. After the five-year period, any member state experiencing serious disturbances in its labor market could maintain its national provisions for a further two years, meaning that full free movement rights for workers could be delayed as long as seven years.

The perceived necessity of these transition periods was not supported by existing migration patterns. Before the 2004 enlargement, approximately three hundred thousand accession state citizens were legally employed in the EU, accounting for only 6 percent of the 5.3 million EU workers who were not EU citizens. Seven out of every ten of these accession state workers lived in Germany and Austria, but even in these two countries they represented only about 10 percent of all non-EU workers. There were also an estimated six hundred thousand accession state citizens living without authorization in the EU, but granting them the rights to which EU citizenship should have immediately entitled them would simply have legalized their status, ameliorating their situation.[12] Most studies predicted that few people would move from accession states to existing member states after enlargement, and the bilateral migration arrangements between candidate and existing member states were underutilized: there were already more spaces for workers from accession states to move to existing member states than there were workers willing to move.[13] Thus, Internal Market commissioner Frits Bolkestein had argued that "in a healthy economy it is better to prepare for competition than to erect new barriers. After all, the freedom of people to move is a central pillar of the single market."[14]

Rather than justifying freedom of movement in terms of European citizenship, Bolkestein, like most opponents of transition arrangements, relied on economic arguments. Yet, despite the existence of EU citizenship, domestic political concerns trumped European rights: upon accession, twelve of the fifteen existing member states—the exceptions were Ireland, Sweden, and the UK—decided to restrict access to their labor markets, and Poland, Slovenia, and Hungary adopted reciprocal restrictions. The phase-in was incomplete because the transition arrangements covered only workers seeking employment with a company based in an existing member state. Workers posted abroad, independent contractors seeking to relocate, and independent contractors wishing to provide services were not covered. Indeed, anyone not seeking employment from an existing member state company gained residence rights immediately upon accession. Nevertheless, the European Parliament supported transition periods in "regions where workers are likely to commute across borders," in order to "secure an urgently needed socially sustainable integration process."[15] This was not accidental: in Austria, Euroskeptic and anti-immigration rhetoric was linked to arguments against EU enlargement, and other member states also witnessed growing fears of economically disadvantaged easterners flooding over the borders once they were lowered. For example, the Danish People's Party, a populist party with an anti-immigration platform that had become the third largest party in the Danish Parliament in 2001, campaigned against free movement. In Germany, some businesses and unions opposed admitting workers from accession states because they feared competition from lower wage workers. These fears were overblown: the first review of the transition arrangements showed that migration flows from the new to the old member states were "very limited," while flows from the old to the new and among the new member states were "generally negligible": the proportion of new member state citizens grew significantly only in Ireland, Austria, and the UK, and even there they had positive economic effects.[16] As a result, Finland, Greece, Portugal, and Spain decided to lift restrictions in 2006, while Belgium, Denmark, France, Italy, Luxembourg, and the Netherlands decided to loosen them, leaving only Austria and Germany with full restrictions.[17]

Though most attention focused on movement from accession states to established member states, movement among accession states also deserves scrutiny. Consider, for example, the potential impact of granting Slovak or Romanian citizens the right to live and work in Hungary, and vice versa. Though movements within the Austro-Hungarian empire had not been particularly restricted, the period between its collapse after the First World War and the fall of the Berlin Wall seven decades later was characterized by ever-increasing enforcement of borders. New states were keen to control their boundaries as part of the process of nation building, and they were generally also eager to minimize the political impact of ethnic minorities on their territories. The continued existence of minority populations across the region implies that becoming part of borderless Europe may have unpredictable consequences. Borders that had been established and enforced since the end of the Austro-Hungarian, Russian, and Ottoman empires—those between the new member states—were slated to fade in importance. After decades of restrictive border controls, central and eastern Europe would again become a space in which migrations may occur with little hindrance from political authority; the demographic and political repercussions of this development remain unclear. The debate in Hungary about extending citizenship to ethnic Hungarians who are citizens of surrounding states such as Romania and Slovakia, for example, takes on added significance if both they and their (nonethnic Hungarian) compatriots share EU citizenship. EU citizenship means the end of allowable nationality-based discrimination between Hungarian citizens, Romanian (or Slovak) citizens who are ethnically Hungarian, and Romanian (or Slovak) citizens who are not ethnically Hungarian. In such a context, it is unclear why the project to extend Hungarian citizenship to the roughly three million ethnic Hungarians from surrounding countries should proceed. Indeed, the 2001 Law concerning Hungarians Living in Neighboring Countries may have been motivated more by partisan efforts to build a stronger conservative party than by renewed nationalism or "ethnic activism" for the individuals the law covered.[18]

Historical parallels can illuminate the relationship between citizenship and enlarging a political community. Consider U.S. president Thomas Jefferson's 1803 acquisition of territory from France, doubling the size of the United States. Though the Louisiana Purchase treaty stipulated that the territory's inhabitants would be incorporated into the Union and promptly admitted "to the enjoyment of all the rights, advantages, and immunities of citizens of the United States," Congress debated whether the treaty could grant U.S. citizenship: when it was noted that bestowing citizenship by treaty contravened the U.S. Constitution, Senator John Quincy Adams proposed a constitutional amendment giving Congress the authority to incorporate new territories into the Union and bestow citizenship on their inhabitants.[19] The underlying dynamic of EU enlargement is the same: the extension of the polity to new territory, and the granting of citizenship to the inhabitants of those territories. Yet, unlike the lengthy debates concerning the Louisiana Purchase territories, there was little debate about whether the EU had the authority to bestow Union citizenship with enlargement treaties. But enlargement did underscore many questions relating to citizenship, including the variation in national rules for admission to citizenship.[20] To address opposition, enlargement and the consequent bestowal of citizenship rights was not a single event, as with most previous historical cases of unification or annexation, but rather a gradual process. Though it is difficult to conceive of citizenship rights being bestowed in stages, the extension of EU citizenship rights to citizens of accession states did proceed gradually.

Most analyses of EU enlargement center on the economic consequences, but focusing on citizenship reveals the politics behind what has been termed the "technical, depoliticized process of exporting the Union's *acquis communautaire*"—the body of EU law.[21] Enlargement forces a new examination of the content and meaning of European integration. The question of whether there are core rights and auxiliary ones is raised when EU citizenship's key rights—to move and take up residence—are denied to at least one important category of individuals: migrant workers from accession countries. Though this right was scheduled to be phased in, citizens in the new member states perceived restrictions to free movement as a denial of the Union's basic freedoms.[22] At this writing, this question will continue to loom large in the EU's scheduled enlargements to Romania and Bulgaria, followed by Turkey, Croatia, the remaining non-EU states of the western Balkans, and possibly beyond.

5.2. The Convention and the Constitution

The Convention on the Future of Europe met from February 2002 until July 2003. In addition to its chairman (former French president Valéry Giscard d'Estaing) and two vice chairmen (former Italian prime minister Giuliano Amato and former Belgian prime minister Jean-Luc Dehaene), the Convention was composed of one government representative from each of the fifteen member states and thirteen candidate states, two representatives from the parliaments of each of the member states and candidate states, sixteen members of the European Parliament, and two representatives of the European Commission—a composition almost identical to that of the Convention that had drafted the European Charter of Fundamental Rights.[23] In his introductory speech, Convention president Giscard d'Estaing laid out his hope for the Convention: "We must ensure that governments and citizens develop a strong, recognised, European 'affectio societatis,' while retaining their natural attachment to their national identity."[24] Giscard d'Estaing invoked the need to satisfy demands for participating in a strong EU, while remaining rooted in national political, social, and cultural life. He also lamented the difficulty of combining a strong feeling of belonging to the Union with a continuing sense of national identity.

Other Convention members shared the desire to build a European identity. The Dutch government representative, former foreign minister Hans van Mierlo, advocated a greater European role in education "in order to inculcate an awareness of and feeling for democracy."[25] Democracy, he added, would be strengthened by giving the European Parliament a greater say in all policy areas, simplifying the treaties, and building basic social rights into them. Though he argued that introducing European social rights would ameliorate the democratic deficit, van Mierlo believed that attempts to bring Europe closer to ordinary citizens were doomed to fail unless those citizens were made aware of Europe "through both formal and sentimental education, both facts and feelings."[26] The aim, in other words, should be to educate citizens to be both democratic and patriotic Europeans.

Former Irish prime minister John Bruton (later EU ambassador to the United States, from 2004) concurred in urging his fellow Convention members to address the issue of democratic legitimacy. For Bruton, the key problem was that Europeans felt they lacked the ability to elect and dismiss a European government that they saw as their own: "Our task in the next year is to find a way whereby Europe's people will feel that they—not the elites, they—as citizens, elect *their* government in Europe just as they elect their government in their own country."[27] Focusing on this need for Europeans to develop a sense of ownership over the European government, Bruton also emphasized the importance of distinguishing between immigration and citizenship. He envisaged an agreement on common policies on asylum and immigration but excluded the possibility of a common naturalization policy as politically infeasible: "Nations would find it difficult to agree on a common policy on National Citizenship, even though the Maastricht Treaty has already created the concept of European Citizenship and of European citizenship rights."[28] Bruton also noted that including the Charter of Fundamental Rights in the Constitution would raise the question of whether these rights would apply to all residents of the Union or only to citizens of the member states. But he shared the sense that what was most lacking was a sense of EU emotion and ritual, pride, and patriotism.[29]

For the Commission, a key task of the Constitution would be "to give European citizenship . . . its full meaning."[30] Representatives of the Committee of the Regions agreed, writing that the Constitution should "flesh out European citizenship" by incorporating the Charter of Fundamental Rights into the future constitutional text, which would "enable every national of an EU Member State to recognise European citizenship as a source of new rights and the expression of belonging to a new community."[31] Meanwhile, the Spanish Socialist members of the Convention proposed a citizen's statute to go beyond the "embryonic version" of citizenship in the Maastricht Treaty.[32]

In order to "bring citizens, and primarily the young, closer to the European design and the European institutions," as the Laeken Declaration invited, the Convention convened a European Youth Convention, gathering 210 young people from 9 to 12 July 2002. The European Youth Convention enthusiastically proclaimed that the time had come to create a true European citizenship, that social rights were part of European citizenship and that the Union should therefore develop common legislation in the fields of social policy, that there should be a common European immigration policy, and that all EU citizens should "have an EU passport, which is the same for all member states."[33]

Responding to such demands, the first comprehensive draft of the Constitution specified that each EU citizen "enjoys dual citizenship, national citizenship and European citizenship; and is free to use either, as he or she chooses; with the rights and duties attaching to each."[34] The wording suggested that the relationship between state and citizenship would be altered. Under the existing system, where EU citizenship depended on national citizenship, individuals retained their national citizenship while moving freely within the wider European territory. Dual citizenship could make the Union resemble a federal state, in which residence determines local affiliation. Opponents of a federal Europe were quick to charge that the reference to dual citizenship would accomplish exactly that. Danish Euroskeptic member of the European Parliament (MEP) Jens-Peter Bonde drew a parallel with citizenship in Bavaria, where one is a citizen under the Bavarian Constitution and simultaneously under the German federal Constitution, but in a conflict between rights and obligations under the two different constitutions, the federal Constitution prevails. Thus, claimed Bonde, the reference to dual citizenship was designed so that "EU citizenship can grow. National citizenship can be removed to the museums."[35] Reacting to such criticism, the Convention returned to the language of the Amsterdam Treaty: rather than mentioning dual citizenship, the revised constitutional draft specified again that "citizenship of the Union shall be additional to national citizenship; it shall not replace it" (Art. I-8). The mention of dual citizenship was removed from the final draft because of the opposition of a number of the larger member states; in order to assure passage, it was necessary to satisfy those most critical of a stronger EU citizenship, though some Convention members were confident that dual citizenship would be introduced in the future.[36]

Attempting to simplify the unwieldy and sometimes paralyzed decision-making process—a process that became even more complex and difficult to navigate with the accession of ten new member states in 2004—the draft Constitution proposed to change the voting procedures for issues related to citizenship. In the field of social policy, the coordination of social security provisions for migrant workers would move from unanimity to majority voting. Meanwhile, the agreement reached at Nice prevailed both for social policy and antidiscrimination, because some of the issues are addressed in member state constitutions. The fact that the Charter was included in the Constitution, the Commission affirmed, meant that the EU would have a "legal obligation to ensure that fundamental rights are not just respected, but actively promoted as well."[37]

The Constitution was neither fully what prointegrationists nor Euroskeptics would have wished.[38] Article I-8 adds to the symbols of the Union the euro and the motto "united in diversity," and confirms 9 May as "Europe Day." Yet perhaps it is unnecessary to expect new rights in order to proclaim that the Constitution represents progress, though it contained few new citizenship rights. Perhaps, given the political sensitivities of the looming enlargement, it was not realistic to expect many new rights. On the other hand, the Constitution consolidates the existing rights of European citizenship. And it is significant that the coordination of social security provisions for migrant workers would move from unanimity to majority voting, since progress on coordination has often been hampered by the resistance of one or a small number of states. This change would make it easier to reach decisions—perhaps with opt-outs for various member states, similar to the way in which the Schengen system started with five member states before gradually growing—and contribute to the mobility of workers. Given the deeply divisive nature of the debates surrounding the extension of free movement to citizens from the enlargement states, free movement and social security rights for those who move within Europe remain contentious. Because it was unclear whether the draft Constitution would be ratified, the perspective of Ana Palacio, Spanish foreign minister and Convention member, may have been premature: Palacio argued that Europe had been mainly associated with a common market but would become "more and more a place of citizenship."[39]

The constitutional treaty had been approved by the European Parliament and the parliaments of Lithuania, Hungary, Slovenia, Italy, Greece, Slovakia, Austria, and Germany, and by referendum and Parliament in Spain (76.7 percent approval on 42.3 percent turnout), when it was defeated in two referendums: in France (54.7 percent rejection on 69.3 percent turnout) on 29 May 2005 and in the Netherlands (61.6 percent rejection on 62.8 percent turnout) three days later. Its subsequent approval by referendum and Parliament in Luxembourg (56.5 percent approval on 87.8 percent turnout), and parliaments in Latvia, Cyprus, Malta, Belgium, Estonia, and Finland, did not resolve the situation, since the treaty needed to be passed by all member states.[40]

In the wake of the failed referendums in the Netherlands and France, some leaders again called for a United States of Europe, in which integration-minded states would proceed with integration while more Euroskeptic states remained behind.[41] The European Commission believed that the "crisis" could "be overcome only by creating a new consensus on the European project, anchored in citizens' expectations."[42] As a result, it promoted "Plan D," for democracy, dialogue, and debate. This was intended to be a lengthy process of democratic reform, helping to "create a citizens' ownership of EU policies."[43] Under the rubric of Plan D, the Commission increased funding for organizations to provide information about the EU and make citizens more aware of EU issues. The White Paper on Communication lamented that the public sphere within which political life occurred in Europe remained largely a national sphere, and that a "pan-European political culture" was still developing; it proposed that public discussion about the EU needed to be deepened, with national, regional, and local public authorities responsible "to put in place the forums to give this debate life."[44]

In May 2006, the Commission launched a "Citizens' Agenda for Europe," urging member states to pursue policies and projects embedded in a coherent political agenda aimed at creating "an institutional settlement which strengthens the overall political ambition of consolidating a 'projet de vie en commun.'"[45] Commission president José Manuel Barroso repeated this idea of consolidating a new *projet de vie en commun*—literally a project of living together but with the implication of a union of shared ambitions and aspirations, such as in marriage—in a June 2006 speech to the European Parliament, suggesting that the member states should seize the occasion of the fiftieth anniversary of the signing of the Treaty of Rome, in 2007, to issue a new declaration of their collective intentions to continue integration.[46] Whatever the future of the constitutional treaty, this *projet de vie en commun* would form the political agenda for pursuing integration, while the policies were detailed in the Citizens' Agenda: fostering peace, prosperity, and solidarity by promoting rights and EU citizenship; strengthening antiterrorism policy; improving external border protection; developing the common European asylum system and a common migration policy; increasing police and judicial cooperation; fully utilizing existing mechanisms to tackle threats to citizens' security in areas including food, health, and terrorism; and increasing cooperation on consular affairs to better protect EU citizens outside the EU. The Citizens' Agenda concluded with the words of Jean Monnet: "There is no future for the peoples of Europe other than in union."[47]

5.3. Europeans and Third-Country Nationals

The attribution of citizenship, particularly the question of who has the power to confer or remove it, is prior to any discussion of the rights that citizenship entails. Because citizenship's historical evolution was intimately connected with that of state sovereignty, the attribution of citizenship was traditionally viewed as flowing solely from state authority. Thus the 1930 Hague Convention specified that it "is for each State to determine under its own law who are its nationals."[48] Over the next fifteen years, however, millions of individuals were stripped of their citizenship—not only in Nazi Germany but also in France and elsewhere.[49] As a result, in Article 15 of the Universal Declaration of Human Rights, states agreed in the aftermath of the Second World War to limit their sovereignty by specifying that everyone is entitled to a nationality and that individuals cannot be arbitrarily deprived of their nationality or denied the right to change it. Within this broad framework, however, policies on the attribution of citizenship differ substantially. Individual states frequently revise their laws and policies concerning such issues as dual nationality, immigration, and naturalization, all of which impact who is a citizen and who is not. EU states differ sharply in their policies in this area, and these differences have led to the growth of a significant population of EU residents who are not EU citizens. By 2006, over fourteen million such third-country nationals resided within the EU.

During the constitutional Convention, the citizenship debate's focus extended from EU citizens to third-country nationals, with the Commission underlining the importance of civic citizenship for facilitating integration: its 2003 report on immigration, integration, and employment had argued that immigrants "should be helped to settle successfully into society through the acquisition of certain core rights, with the corresponding obligations."[50] This civic responsibility would prepare immigrants to acquire citizenship and allow for their future political participation. Incorporating the Charter of Fundamental Rights into the Constitution would confirm the rights and obligations of legally resident third-country nationals because the Charter would apply to all European residents, rather than just citizens of the member states.[51] Furthermore, the Commission promoted naturalization as an integration strategy: it welcomed the easier conditions for naturalization in some member states and promised to exchange information about best practices concerning the implementation of citizenship laws. In the Commission's view, the Constitution should provide legally resident third-country nationals with civic citizenship, which should include the right to vote and run for office at the local level. It reflected the views of MEPs such as Pervenche

Berès, chair of the French Socialist delegation in the European Parliament and alternate member to the Convention, who advocated decoupling national from EU citizenship and basing EU citizenship on residence in order to make citizenship available to everyone who had long resided within the Union.[52]

The Economic and Social Committee (ESC) also advocated using European citizenship to integrate third-country nationals. It had resolved that policies for integrating immigrants needed to be improved and that the Convention should therefore examine the possibility of granting Union citizenship to long-term resident third-country nationals.[53] ESC members anticipated many immigrants settling permanently in Europe, while mobility between member states would increase further as freedom of movement evolved. They argued that equality between all residents—EU citizens and third-country nationals—was "a *sine qua non* for integration. A community cannot have living within its midst some people who are debarred from the political and other rights enjoyed by those 'foreigners' who are Member State nationals."[54] The ESC thus highlighted the problem with a state's granting immediate rights to citizens of other EU member states (even if they had moved very recently) while denying those same rights to long-term residents (who may have resided there for decades or even have been born there). The ESC argued that third-country nationals were discriminated against. Some member states granted them the right to vote in local elections, but most did not, and the ESC argued that "such discrimination on the grounds of nationality must be eliminated."[55] This is a novel argument because it extends the nondiscrimination principle to third-country nationals. The implication is that member states must not only treat citizens of other EU member states in the same way that they treat their "own" citizens, but that they must also treat third-country nationals in the same way. At its logical limit, this would eliminate any special treatment on the basis of either national or EU citizenship.

Some commentators shared the ESC's surprise that third-country nationals did not yet enjoy rights of European citizenship.[56] The political leaders had called at the Tampere European Council in 1999 for long-term resident third-country nationals to be granted "a set of uniform rights which are as near as possible to those enjoyed by EU citizens" but faced concerns within some member states.[57] Nevertheless, in 2003 they adopted a directive on the status of long-term resident third-country nationals: all EU states now grant third-country nationals long-term resident status after five years' continuous legal residence.[58] Furthermore, long-term residents have the right of residence throughout the EU, fostering their free movement within Europe. The directive, coupled with a related one on family reunification, furthers the "stage-by-stage harmonization of legislation affecting aliens" that the political leaders discussed as long ago as 1974.[59] This legislation prepares the way for a common immigration policy, which has likewise been discussed for years, with the Commission promoting civic citizenship as a way of integrating immigrants.[60]

The fact that all EU states now grant third-country nationals the same legal status after five years is a step toward a common integration policy, even if a common immigration policy still appears distant. Rights for EU citizens have transcended borders since the first free movement provisions of the European Coal and Steel Community (ECSC), but until this directive, third-country nationals had remained largely excluded from these rights: nationality of a member state had been central to the acquisition of European rights.[61] There are of course significant differences in the first five years of integration policy, including sharp divergence among the member states concerning conditions of admission and the role of public authorities. The reaction to the July 2005 bombings in London, the response to the October and November 2005 riots in France, and the politically popular toughening of Dutch integration policy during the same period highlight the continuing challenge of integrating immigrants—as well as the differences in member state approaches. EU citizenship continues to derive from different national traditions of citizenship, though there has been a significant degree of convergence in member state naturalization policies.[62] On the other hand, although different member states' approaches to immigrant incorporation were constantly changing, there remained strong divergence in the overall philosophy: universalist states such as France refuse to sanction group rights for immigrant cultures, while more multiculturalist approaches welcoming of cultural diversity dominate in states like the Netherlands and the UK.[63] The difficulties in constructing a common integration policy indicate that a common immigration policy might be even harder to achieve. Nevertheless, calls continued for citizenship of residence and a common status for third-country nationals throughout the EU: the European Association for the Protection of Human Rights and its member associations launched a petition to deliver to the European Parliament that "any individual who resides on the territory of a member State or who is a national of a member State gains citizenship of the Union."[64]

5.4. Defending European Rights

Just as violations of human rights justify protecting individuals against their governments, so violations of European rights justify protecting Europeans.

But doing so requires institutions with not only the authority but also the power to impose obedience. The draft Constitution declares that the Union "shall promote economic, social and territorial cohesion, and solidarity among Member States" (Art. I-3) and reiterates that "any discrimination on grounds of nationality shall be prohibited" (Art. I-4). This nondiscrimination clause is categorical, wide ranging, and ambitious, but it is unclear that it can be easily enforced. Successfully prohibiting nationality-based discrimination requires an institution capable of enforcement. One of the biggest dangers to European rights is noncompliance by member state authorities with EU laws, chief among them citizenship rights and the nondiscrimination ban. In a complex legal environment in which there are multiple sources of law, the recognition of rights implies an enforcement authority. If the central authority is absent or weak, defiances of rights can arise. The dynamics by which this operates are well known. For example, some U.S. states and municipalities have at various times resisted applying federally guaranteed liberties. Yet the United States, like all federal states, possesses mechanisms to ensure the national application of federal laws, even in areas where subnational jurisdictions have shared or even had sole responsibility for applying legislation. When in 1957 the governor of Arkansas attempted to prevent the racial desegregation of schools called for by a 1954 U.S. Supreme Court case, for example, President Eisenhower sent the army to intervene. An analogous response is difficult to imagine in Europe—not least because the Commission's president has no troops to call upon.

European rights must be institutionalized in such a way that they bind member state governments. Institutional backing is a prerequisite for the successful continuation of citizenship in any context. In the case of EU citizenship, the Commission is dedicated to ensuring that the treaties are applied, the Court to ensuring their consistent interpretation, and the Parliament and Council to revising them. While these institutions have avidly defended EU citizenship since its introduction, their support could wither. Some observers claimed that the European Court of Justice (ECJ) created an economic Constitution based on free movement, and that its jurisprudence created and expanded European rights far beyond the original intentions of the member states.[65] Previous chapters demonstrate that this exaggerates the Court's role, at least in the area of citizenship rights: member states and their leaders pushed for European rights and halted their growth when some member states objected. But judicial decisions can have important legitimizing power: legislative or policy changes may appear more "just" when they receive a court's approval, explaining why the selection of judges is always political rather than neutral. But courts can only do so much. Indeed, the U.S.

experience shows that courts themselves seldom produce significant social reform without popular support. While court decisions generally do not mobilize supporters of reform, they may energize opponents, suggesting that one result of litigation intended to produce social reform may be to strengthen the opponents of such change.[66] There must be an analogous worry in Europe: if the Court is too ambitious in its rulings, it could arouse opposition to the European rights that its judgments are intended to further. Throughout the member states, there generally exists a consensus on the desirability of common European rights, but change may occur quickly. The member states always have the power collectively to revise the treaties and revoke European citizenship. While this is highly unlikely, it does underline the problem of passing common legislation: unanimity is still required in many policy areas, and member states have been reluctant to surrender authority.

The Commission has been relatively successful at eliminating discrimination on the grounds of nationality, at least in principle. For example, as a result of Commission pressure and "infringement proceedings against all the Member States concerned, nationality is no longer a condition for access to a substantial number of public-service jobs in many of the Member States."[67] But individuals may continue to face de facto discrimination in much the same way that discrimination against women or members of minorities continues within liberal democracies with nondiscrimination laws. Like the Court, the Commission can only do so much to change social norms. Its power is circumscribed by limited enforcement capabilities and organizational design. At the same time it is worth asking why, for example, despite the introduction of the euro as a common currency, there has been no attempt to build a European economic government: the regulatory powers of the European Central Bank over economic issues are arguably weaker than those of the Commission and Court over citizenship.[68]

Because free movement developed as an economic phenomenon, rather than one related to European citizenship, responsibility continues to be shared among the Commission's different branches: the Internal Market directorate general (DG) is responsible for the right of establishment and the freedom to provide services; free movement of workers and the coordination of social security regimes are handled by the Employment and Social Affairs DG; while the Justice and Home Affairs DG is responsible for issues related to the free movement of nonemployed persons and the entire citizenship portfolio.[69] The Justice and Home Affairs DG has a unit devoted to citizenship, racism and xenophobia, the Charter of Fundamental Rights, and the Daphne program (designed to combat violence against children, young people, and women), and another unit devoted to free movement of persons, visa policy, external borders, and Schengen, along with other units. In 2002, the unit devoted to free movement of persons, visa policy, external borders, and Schengen had just six officials, plus another three bureaucrats on exchange from member states. Created as a separate DG in 1999, the entire Justice and Home Affairs DG had just 180 officials, out of the 17,000 or so Commission officials. But it subsequently merged into a new DG for "Justice, Freedom, and Security" (responsible for immigration, asylum, borders; civil justice, rights, and citizenship; and internal security and criminal justice) and had grown to 320 officials by 2006. European institutions do have some power to back up their limited authority, but despite Commissioner Vitorino's sentiments, expressed in his quote at the beginning of this chapter, member states appear likely to remain the sole arbiters of who qualifies for national citizenship and thus for European citizenship.

The challenges of enlargement likely helped derail the draft constitutional treaty that was agreed by a second convention following the one that had drafted the Charter of Fundamental Rights. Indeed at this writing it is far from clear whether the most ambitious aims of European citizenship can be realized in a Europe of more than two dozen states. Those states are also, individually and collectively, facing demographic and cultural concerns about immigration, and the idea that European citizenship might act as a bridge between third-country nationals and member state citizens remains salient. It appeared to some that the EU would function more as a union of states than a union of citizens, at least partially because citizens remained unaware of the benefits of EU citizenship: "Many of the things that have a concrete impact on people's lives—such as the right to live, work and study anywhere in the Union—are taken for granted. People forget that such things are possible only because of the Union."[70]

CHAPTER SIX

The Limits of European Citizenship

It is difficult to fall in love with a common market.[1]

—Jacques Delors

Differences in national sentiment are both significant and fluid.[2]

—Max Weber

As long as it is willing to remain *one* city, it may continue to grow, but it cannot grow beyond that point.[3]

—Plato

Creating a European citizenship common to nationals of the member states reflects the steady growth of individual rights discernible throughout the entire process of European integration. Yet it also signifies a move to a new form of supranational political membership. Though previous chapters demonstrated the constant growth—admittedly episodic and sporadic, but always tending to greater rights—of European Union (EU) citizenship, there also exist countervailing forces. The attempt to add a veneer of common European rights over well-established national rights based on dissimilar ethical and moral conceptions raises challenges. This helps explain why EU citizenship did not develop faster or more fully, and why it could be weakened or even repealed. Examining the limits of European citizenship and the ways in which it could increase rather than decrease tension within the EU, there are risks to a common citizenship that require responses informed by comparative experiences of managing conflict and difference.

6.1. Opposition to European Rights

The expansion of the rights of European citizenship is reversible. This is because the process of establishing rights is not unidirectional: rights can be and often are reduced, repealed, or revoked. The idea that rights, laws, and even citizenship remain politically contested is not a novel point, but it is instructive to consider conditions that make such contestations more or less likely to succeed and to examine the causal mechanisms involved in successful transformations of rights. Though it appears that the growth of common European rights is not yet finished, it is important to identify countervailing forces that problematize the future of European citizenship. European political leaders have actively engaged in polity building by creating European citizens. The common European identity putatively flowing from common EU citizenship might advance the mutual understanding and trust that enable democratic citizenship, transforming the EU into a multinational or supranational political community in which feelings of common loyalty reflect a shared patriotism rather than a common national identity[4]—or perhaps not. Most European leaders and those who study European integration have been remarkably silent about the potential negative effects of common rights.

It is a widespread belief that European integration is irrevocable, and many view the EU as the only (or at least the best) means of resolving common problems, exhorting "nostalgic nationalists" to cease pining for the past.[5] However, any explanation of European integration that focuses on political agency and struggles for power reveals the contingency of political development: political processes can be transformed rapidly and decisively. The process of European integration has been almost exclusively unidirectional, but it need not always be so. The extension to citizens of EU member states of common rights founded on a common European citizenship could come under pressure. European rights can invoke popular opposition, which could lead to their growth being arrested or reversed.

Resistance to immigration from outside the Union exists across the member states.[6] But resistance to the rights of European citizenship remains confined to some populist parties and religious groups. Thus, the Dutch populist Pim Fortuyn campaigned to reintroduce border controls within the EU, a perspective shared by the French far-right *Front nationale* (FN), which advocates not only renouncing EU citizenship and the Schengen free movement provisions but also pulling out of the EU altogether.[7] Similarly, the Austrian Freedom Party and the Danish People's Party vigorously opposed free movement for new EU citizens from enlargement states. And the Greek Orthodox Church warned in its 1997 Easter encyclical, read out in all Greek Orthodox churches during Easter services, against the threat posed by the Schengen agreement.[8]

While these examples demonstrate that some populist and religious groups have opposed the right to free movement within Europe, it is unclear whether this concerns opposition to free movement for EU citizens rather than non-EU citizens. Would French NF voters really mind if a few thousand Belgians moved to Paris? Or would Danish People's Party voters mind if a few thousand Swedish citizens moved across the bridge into Copenhagen? While the answer is presumably negative, at least for modest migrations, posing the question raises the issue of where Europeans draw the boundary between "us" and "them." The fact that such boundaries do exist is exemplified by the disproportionate attention paid to visible minorities. In France, for example, Algerians received far greater negative attention than another group of foreigners: the Portuguese, who outnumbered the Algerians until the mid-1990s.[9] Greater opposition might arise if more use were actually made of the right to free movement.

Though the strongest opposition to the rights of European citizenship remains confined to the political margins, preceding chapters demonstrated that the expansion of these rights has been controversial. Certainly the prevailing model of EU citizenship as a simple addition to national citizenship responds to some degree to the notion that European citizenship competes with and undermines the foundations of national citizenship.[10] Some theorists contend that political objectives must be promoted by strengthening citizenship and fighting political battles at the level of the nation-state, through national movements and parties: citizenship ought to remain within the exclusive jurisdiction of national states, they argue, and "efforts to build supranationalism ought not to compete with or undermine democratic institutions within the member states."[11] Of course, there is no intrinsic reason why national states should be preferred to the EU as the site of political struggle. If national citizenship safeguards national democratic institutions, then it should not be weakened. Yet, it is unclear how democratic European institutions can be constructed if not through the concurrent creation of a European patriotism and sense, however thin, of identification as European citizens.

Rights are always contested. To survive, they require not only institutions to safeguard them but also political support. The sustainability of European rights thus depends not only upon the continued strength of European institutions but also on a shared European identity. This identity must be *European* rather than global: EU citizenship would lose significance if it simply became like human rights, or if a genuinely cosmopolitan political order arose in which the EU were simply a regional branch of a global system of governance—however unlikely the emergence of a genuinely global political order appears.[12] But this possibility underlines the fact that a shared European identity means differentiating Europeans from others and solidifying a particularistic collective identity. Instead of a *jus gentium*, what is being constructed is a *jus europæum*. To reiterate the point of the Laeken Declaration and the conventions that drew up the Constitution and the European Charter of Fundamental Rights, the rights that individuals have by virtue of EU citizenship must be more than simply human rights, or EU citizenship would have little meaning. Indeed, global human rights cannot simply replace the civic solidarity that emerged in the framework of the nation-state: civic solidarity is rooted in particular collective identities, while cosmopolitan solidarity must support itself solely on the moral universalism of human rights.[13] Of course, the civic solidarity that emerged in the framework of the nation-states in Europe is malleable, not fixed. Weber's conclusion that differences in national sentiment are both significant and fluid is the hope of those now attempting to build a common European identity.[14] But it is worth recalling Jacques Delors's observation—that it is difficult to fall in love with a common market—paired with the observation that no nation is purely civic; all are bound at least in part by shared stories of their members' particular identities.[15]

The January 2006 debate within the European Parliament about a report on citizenship reflects the tensions created by EU citizenship.[16] Prepared under the leadership of the Italian Communist member of the European Parliament (MEP) Catania, the report advocated making EU citizenship both more easily available and more meaningful. A provision calling for "creating a political area and a form of citizenship which reflect current trends within Europe's democracies [by] granting political rights to anyone residing legally and on a long-term basis in the European Union, irrespective of his or her original nationality" passed by the thinnest of margins: 305 votes in favor to 305 votes against with seven abstentions. Another, asking member states to consider "establishing a closer link between permanent legal residence over a reasonable period of time and the acquisition of national—and hence European—citizenship," passed by two votes, though a provision recommending increased coordination about the criteria and procedures for acquiring citizenship passed more easily. A series of other provisions failed, including one calling for standardized European election procedures with some

MEPs elected on transnational European lists, another asking the Commission to study the harmonization of member state citizenship rules, and a third that "EU citizenship based on residence should be the ultimate goal of the dynamic process which will make the European Union a genuine political community." The vote on that failed by 276 to 343 votes with ten abstentions. A provision advocating "a direct link between some aspects of the tax system and the financing of the European Union" failed, while another asking member states to give EU citizens a clear understanding about the proportion of their taxes going to the EU budget, passed by four votes. With all the amendments, the final report failed, with 276 votes in favor, 347 votes against, and 22 abstentions.

Euroskeptic, populist, and far-right politicians particularly welcomed the report's demise. *Front nationale* MEP Marine Le Pen, daughter of FN founder Jean-Marie Le Pen, called EU citizenship a "machine for crushing nations and national identities so that they can ultimately be replaced by a European identity." She claimed that the proposals came "straight from the upper echelons of Euro-federalist bureaucracy" and were "an integral part of the submersion and immigration/invasion process desired by the Commission." Another FN MEP characterized EU citizenship as "a device designed to destroy our national rights to identity and sovereignty." He concluded that the "nations of Europe, under threat of being flooded by immigration on a global scale, do not need European citizenship. Rather, they need to have their national rights reaffirmed." For the leader of Vlaams Belang, it was clear that state citizenship and all associated rights should remain exclusively a member state competence. An MEP from the Austrian Freedom Party argued that promoting EU citizenship would do nothing to turn EU skeptics into enthusiasts. Citing the attacks in London, the murder of filmmaker Theo van Gogh, and the street battles in France, he called for minimum standards for granting citizenship—including the "capacity for integration into the majority culture" and "the protection of our indigenous European peoples." Support was mixed even among proimmigrant parties. Thus, a Swedish Green Party MEP argued that third-country nationals should indeed have the right to participate in the democratic process but argued that the EU should not use the issue "as a lever for developing its ambitions to take control of the Member States' democratic structures and so increase its powers." Similarly, Greek Communist MEP Georgios Toussas characterized EU citizenship as "an ideological construct of no practical value" since only member states grant citizenship. The Catania report thus creates "the false impression of a non-existent 'European citizen' on a single 'political and cultural territory,' so that it looks as if there is no going back from an imperialist and reactionary

EU." For Toussas, the problem is that the report attempted to "introduce through the back door aspects of the reactionary European Constitution rejected by the peoples of the EU." He unreservedly supported immigrants' rights, but argued that the acquisition of these rights had "nothing to do with the misleading ideology of 'European citizenship.'" Taken as a whole, the debate on the report demonstrated the wide range of views concerning EU citizenship, including strong opposition to its more radical possibilities.

6.2. Nondiscrimination and National Culture

The draft Constitution states that the EU "shall respect the national identities of its Member States, inherent in their fundamental structures, political and constitutional, including for regional and local self government" (Art. I-5). Respecting the national identities of the member states while simultaneously guaranteeing common rights for all Europeans could raise potential conflicts between acknowledging individual rights and defending national culture. The principle of nondiscrimination, by virtue of which citizens of other EU member states are considered to be entirely equivalent to citizens of the state in question, raises issues of the defense of national culture.

The nondiscrimination clause highlights the tension between equality and diversity. Political theorists propose various ways in which liberal democratic states can recognize multiple forms of belonging to the political community and overlapping identities and citizenships. Several argue that equal citizenship necessitates recognizing the multiple histories, needs, and aspirations of the various communities that constitute the political community.[17] Yet any pluralistic society also possesses a shared culture, however thin, that is necessary for political stability. Though modern legal systems of rights are generally universalistic, in the sense that they assume neutral and equal individuals, they also have an ethical character to the extent that they reflect the political values of a specific community. This ethical character need not conflict with civil rights as long as constitutional principles and the ideal of achieving basic rights remain central. If the institutions uniting citizens remain "neutral" with respect to differences among ethical-cultural communities, which are grounded in their own moral conceptions, political integration can succeed. Even uncoupling universalistic law from particular ethical communities, however, "a nation of citizens can sustain the institutions of freedom only by developing a certain measure of loyalty to their own state, a loyalty that cannot be legally enforced."[18] The problem for many states is that it is difficult to forge bonds of common citizenship in a deeply diverse community.[19] It is therefore important to discover how loyalty can best be created, sustained, or destroyed.

The breakdown of Czechoslovakia, Yugoslavia, and the Soviet Union demonstrated that even seemingly secure states can decompose rather quickly. It is important to consider how the same could happen to the EU. One way in which EU citizenship could break down is if a member state refused to recognize it, perhaps ultimately leading to separation. This possibility may seem remote. If a member state were to refuse to recognize European citizenship, then the citizens of that member state would likewise cease to be European citizens—and thus lose their rights. Citizens could be expected to resist this change. Yet perhaps the secession scenario is not entirely far fetched: the draft Constitution for the first time includes provisions for leaving the EU. It may be only a matter of time until a serious anti-EU movement emerges in one or more states. Indeed, the rise of Euroskeptic parties in many member states might presage precisely that. The comparative study of secessionist movements demonstrates that they are generally driven by varieties of substate nationalism. Similarly, nationalism could arise in opposition to European integration. Of course, some varieties of nationalism might actually facilitate the development of political identification with Europe. This is the case with many instances of substate or infranationalism in Europe today: Scottish, Catalan, Basque, and Flemish nationalists often explicitly support "Europe" as a way of minimizing the political importance of the state—in these cases, the UK, Spain, or Belgium.[20]

Simply stating that nationalism could work to undermine EU citizenship is thus insufficient: it is necessary to specify what kind of nationalism would do so. Integrative and disintegrative tendencies operate simultaneously. Though it may be premature to claim that "nationalism today is historically less important than it was in the nineteenth and first half of the twentieth century," it is true that supranationalism and infranationalism frequently go together.[21] EU citizenship can thus be seen as both opposing state nationalism and supporting substate or suprastate nationalism. Lord Acton, writing in 1862, still claimed that political and national boundaries *should* diverge, so that states would always contain more than one nation.[22] Former Canadian prime minister Pierre Trudeau drew on Acton's ideas to promote his policies of bilingualism and multiculturalism, policies sometimes criticized for transforming Canada from a federation of two nations into a state based on undifferentiated individual rights.[23] European citizenship evokes the same tension: a view of the EU as a community of self-regulating communities and a competing view of a superstate composed of undifferentiated individuals possessing European rights.

For some, the United States represents an influential model of what European citizenship should aspire to be. Constitutional parallels are often invoked to suggest that, just as the various U.S. states joined together, so should European member states. Perhaps more relevant for citizenship rights are the frequent positive references to American mobility. Commission officials and others often hold up for admiration and imitation the ease and frequency with which U.S. citizens move between states. The message is that European citizens, too, should enjoy such mobility, which requires them to actually use the rights they possess. It is not mobility for its own sake; rather, those who promote "American" mobility for Europe are often driven by the desire for full employment, a more flexible labor force, or similar rationales. But there is also the argument that increased mobility within Europe will facilitate building a shared political community. The difference between barriers to migration between EU member states and between U.S. states are a matter of degree, a continuum rather than a stark distinction. Indeed, most of the rights and obligations of American citizenship were long defined at the state rather than national level.[24] With few exceptions, social and labor policies before the New Deal were enacted and implemented at the state or local level. While the national government incorporated citizens within a liberal realm of rights, where they were regarded as free and equal citizens, states made eligibility for social provisions conditional on gender, race, and other norms. The result was a "semifeudal" rather than rights-oriented welfare state, in which the institutional arrangements of federalism permitted regionally based cultural differences to thrive.[25]

Thus, the construction of a shared political community in the United States was not as simple as sometimes assumed: the early United States was a union of diverse states rather than a homogeneous body of citizens. Thomas Jefferson may have exaggerated by claiming that the United States was a "compact of independent nations," but he did not embellish much in terms of citizenship: American citizenship meant a "double allegiance" to both state and nation.[26] Americans long struggled over whether state or national citizenship should be primary, and though many thought the question settled by the American Civil War or the New Deal, it constantly resurfaced.[27] Over time, the central government's authority grew through expansive interpretations of the Fourteenth Amendment (which provided that "All persons born or naturalized in the United States, and subject to the jurisdiction thereof, are citizens of the United States and of the state wherein they reside") and the interstate commerce clause. The Fourteenth Amendment was a direct response to the U.S. Supreme Court's *Dred Scott* decision (1857), which helped spark the Civil War: the Court ruled that African Americans were not citizens and that the rights of citizenship in a state and in the Union were distinct. In response, the Fourteenth Amendment was intended to "make national citizenship paramount to state citizenship, to confer national citizenship upon the newly freed slaves, and to secure for the former slaves the equal enjoyment of certain civil rights."[28] The triumph of Union citizenship over state citizenship seemed secure, but as the federal government abdicated its responsibility to protect rights in the latter part of the nineteenth century, individual states retained the power to define most aspects of citizenship without interference from the national government.[29] The American example thus demonstrates the continuing conflict between local culture and nondiscrimination throughout the Union—whether United States or EU.

The most significant difference between Europe and the United States is that the linguistic, cultural, economic, and political differences among the states in Europe are so much more significant than those among American states. In addition, one particular reason why there has not been as much free movement in Europe as in the United States is the problem of coordinating welfare systems.[30] Member states remain reluctant to extend benefits to non-nationals. For example, in June 2002 the Dutch minister of education justified restricting the number of scholarships available to Dutch students to study outside the Netherlands by citing recent European Court of Justice (ECJ) rulings enabling non-Dutch students to temporarily move to the Netherlands, qualify as "Dutch," and then return home to study, while receiving Dutch scholarships. The government further claimed that this strategy is available not only to residents of the EU but also to residents of candidate member states such as Poland and associated states such as Morocco.[31] The logic of this example illustrates the continuing strength of a limited view of who "we" are: other EU citizens may be closer than non-EU citizens, but neither group is truly Dutch. In this context, enlargement and the addition of millions of new European citizens problematizes once again the question of the borders of the EU and even perhaps the meaning of Europe.[32] In the perceived conflict between deepening and widening, enlargement could lead not simply to the cessation of deepening but to a reversal, a making more shallow. The European ban on nationality-based discrimination may invoke particularistic reactions once there are more Europeans protected by the ban.

Of course, citizenship is not only about rights but also about duties. Here, integration is continuing, as exemplified by the proliferation of agreements on how to tax cross-border commuters. One example is that of Dutch citizens living in Belgium and commuting to work in the Netherlands. Income taxes were collected by the Dutch authorities, who long failed to forward the funds to the Belgian municipalities, which levy income-based property taxes. The dispute, which involved millions of euros in unreimbursed taxes, was finally resolved in September 2002 with an agreement between the Dutch and

Belgian ministries of finance.³³ The principle on which the taxes are collected is that workers pay taxes in the country in which they work rather than the country in which they reside, which then receives reimbursement from the country that has collected the taxes. Though small, this example is meaningful. The EU is not simply a collection of states. It is also, to borrow from E. P. Thompson, who was writing about class, "a multitude of individuals with a multitude of experiences."³⁴ Thus, the Dutch citizens resident in Belgium were incorporated into the Belgian fiscal system, and Belgian municipalities successfully imposed the same conditions on Dutch as on Belgian residents. This fits with a certain kind of "struggle for recognition," a constitutionalism based on consent, continuity, and mutual recognition.³⁵

6.3. Free Movement's Impact

As explained in earlier chapters, the first Community free movement rights were focused on economic actors. They applied first to certain categories of workers, then to most categories of workers, then to workers' families, and so on. The internal market initiative of the mid-1980s led to the extension of mobility rights to students, retired people, and other noneconomic actors. Finally, the introduction of EU citizenship in the Maastricht Treaty consolidated free movement rights for all EU citizens. Following the extension of mobility rights to the non–economically active in the early 1990s, there was initially not much change in the numbers of people choosing to reside in another member state. Since then, however, the number of EU citizens residing in a member state other than that of their citizenship started to increase, soon surpassing six million. The impact varied: Spain for example witnessed an almost fourfold increase in the number of permanent residents from the other EU member states between 1987 and 2005, while the increase in other states was less striking.³⁶ The numbers do not reveal the full extent of the increase, however, because many migrants fail to register, reside for only part of the year (such as northern Europeans spending the winter on the Mediterranean) and thus do not qualify as "permanent" residents, or naturalize to the host state's citizenship, disappearing from the statistics. Thus, in the Netherlands, the number of officially resident EU15 citizens rose only modestly from 165,465 in 1986 to 210,072 in 2005, with a decline in the mid-1990s after a change in citizenship policy made it easier to naturalize. However, during the same period some eighty thousand citizens of the other EU states were granted Dutch citizenship. If these people were instead added to the overall figures of officially resident "foreigners," the increase would be considerably higher.³⁷ The point is that the official number of EU citizens permanently resident in a state other than that of their citizenship discounts many who have disappeared from the statistics because of naturalization or dual citizenship.

Perhaps because of the seasonal (hence unreported) nature of their movements, the stereotype of northern Europeans heading south to retire may need some revision. Only 51,000 of the 295,000 non-Spanish EU citizens permanently resident in Spain in 1999 were over the age of sixty-five, a proportion (17 percent) almost exactly equal to the proportion of Spanish citizens over the age of sixty-five. There were national differences—for example, fully 26 percent of the twelve thousand Belgian citizens, 25 percent of the seventy-five thousand British citizens, and 21 percent of the sixteen thousand Dutch citizens permanently resident in Spain were over the age of sixty-five, but only 15 percent of the forty thousand French citizens and 14 percent of the fifty-eight thousand Germans, to say nothing of the very low proportions of Italian (11 percent of the twenty-seven thousand resident in Spain) and Portuguese (8 percent of the twelve thousand), citizens were over the age of sixty-five—overall, however, the age distribution of citizens of other member states resident in Spain resembled that of Spanish citizens.

In Germany, by contrast, migrants arrive to work or to study. Only 5.5 percent of the 619,000 Italian citizens, 6.7 percent of the 115,000 UK citizens, and 6.8 percent of the 365,000 Greek citizens resident in Germany in 2001 were over the age of sixty-five, compared with 18 percent of German citizens. Conversely, fully 30 percent of the Italian citizens resident in Germany in 2001 were under the age of twenty-five, compared with 26 percent of German citizens. Thus, a large number of Italian students and families with members under the age of twenty-five make their homes in Germany. These numbers may reflect the phenomenon of return migration on the part of those who had left to find work abroad: working-age individuals move to another country to work, then return to their home country to retire.[38] Of course, many of these migrations are simply international versions of forms of migration familiar in national settings, such as the movement of rural workers to urban jobs and their subsequent return home for holidays or retirement. This is likely the case for large numbers of Spanish citizens in Germany, Portuguese citizens in France, Irish citizens in the UK, and so on. The overall point is that migration within the EU, while still nowhere near the level of interstate or interprovincial mobility in federal states such as the United States or Canada, is gradually increasing. This is a positive development to the degree that movers develop a sense of European loyalty and entitlement (but a negative development to the extent that nonmovers feel threatened).

The share of EU citizens living in a member state other than that of their nationality has remained fairly stable around the turn of the millennium, at approximately 1.5 percent, slightly less than the higher proportion observed in the 1950s and 1960s. Before the 2004 enlargement—thus not yet including citizens of the new member states—Germany hosted the bulk of this population (1.9 million), followed by France (1.3 million), the UK (0.8 million), and Belgium (0.6 million). In terms of countries of origin, Italians remained the largest group: 1.2 million (more than 2 percent of the national population of Italy), most of whom lived in Germany, France, Belgium, and the UK. One million Portuguese (nearly 10 percent of the national population) resided elsewhere in the Union, mostly in France, Germany, and Luxembourg. Furthermore, the total of six million included 480,000 Irish (13 percent of the total Irish population; 92 percent of whom resided in the UK); 477,000 Spanish citizens who lived mostly in France and Germany; 455,000 British citizens who lived mostly in Germany, Spain, and Ireland; 436,000 Greek citizens who lived primarily in Germany; 395,000 French citizens; 360,000 German citizens; and smaller numbers of citizens of other member states. EU citizens who move to another member state tend to concentrate in their main neighbor member state: five out of every six Austrians residing elsewhere in the EU lived in Germany, four-fifths of the Belgians lived in the four adjacent member states, two-thirds of the Dutch citizens lived in Belgium or Germany, and so forth. Migration to other member states is often linked with employment opportunities, which explains why EU citizens residing in a member state in which they do not hold citizenship had smaller than average households: 2.1 persons compared to 2.4 for the EU as a whole, mainly because the migrants have fewer dependent children.[39] Of course none of these numbers include people who have moved and subsequently naturalized to the citizenship of their host state, nor does it include dual citizens who may shuttle back and forth and thus are not registered as "foreign" in either state. Further, there are no statistics on temporary residents such as students or retired people who spend only part of the year in another member state, nor do the numbers include those who fail to officially register their move. The figure of six million citizens residing outside their member state of nationality would be considerably larger if it included these categories of people.

Given these numbers, it is perhaps not surprising that freedom of movement is the most widely known right of EU citizenship. Indeed, the rights conferred by EU citizenship are far better known than EU citizenship itself. Though it was introduced with the Maastricht Treaty in 1992, a decade later many Europeans were not yet aware of its existence. An October 2002 survey found that about one-third of respondents knew what Union citizenship means, one-third had heard about it but were not sure about its meaning, and one-third had never heard the term Union citizenship.[40] The fact that one-third of respondents had not heard of Union citizenship pales in comparison with the level of ignorance on other issues. For example, another survey of twenty-five thousand respondents at the end of June 2003—just after the constitutional Convention had officially presented its draft Constitution after sixteen months of intense negotiations—found that 55 percent had never heard of the Convention or its work, and only one-third of respondents knew that the Convention had been working on a draft Constitution.[41]

Despite the widespread ignorance of the meaning of EU citizenship, 70 percent of those interviewed in the 2002 survey replied correctly to seven of eleven statements concerning the rights of Union citizens. The most familiar right was that of Union citizens to work in any member state, with 89 percent correct replies. However, 57 percent of respondents believed that a work permit is needed, though it is not. Next came the right to take up residence throughout the Union, with 84 percent correct replies. Fully 70 percent of respondents knew that EU citizens have the right to run for a seat in the European Parliament in their country of residence, but only half were able to correctly answer whether or not "Citizens of the European Union living in (our country) have the right to be a candidate for local elections" (they do, as a right of EU citizenship) or whether or not "Citizens of the European Union living in (our country) have the right to vote in national elections" (they do not, though such a right could be granted by a member state at its discretion).[42] The fact that half of respondents incorrectly believe that EU citizens may vote in national elections in their country of residence (mostly in Spain, Portugal, Italy, and Greece, where approximately three out of every five respondents believe this, compared to less than two out of every five respondents in Denmark, Austria, Finland, and Luxembourg) may help explain the current opposition to extending full freedom of movement rights to citizens of the new central and eastern European member states. In any case, it is significant that the rights it brings are better known than EU citizenship itself, though as I show below, many of those rights have a longer history than the formal introduction of EU citizenship in 1992. Entitlements are likewise central to the notion that "European citizenship must serve to guarantee concrete rights and duties, in particular, freedom, justice and security, and ensure access to basic public services at European level. The benefits of membership for citizens now extend beyond market freedoms, and these issues must be prioritised."[43]

The evolution of EU citizenship mirrors the political development of Europe, as integration has increasingly come to signify political rather than simply economic cooperation. Public opinion data underscores this point: in reply to a question about what the EU means to them personally, 50 percent of respondents in a 2005 survey answered the freedom to travel, study, and work anywhere in the EU. Other answers included "the euro" (38 percent of respondents in the EU as a whole), "peace" (32 percent), "stronger say in the world" (28 percent), and "cultural diversity" (28 percent). Free movement was the most important aspect of the EU for respondents in twenty-one out of the twenty-five member states; it was second most important in three member states and third most important in Austria (after the euro and an increase in crime).[44] In the 2005 survey, over half of EU citizens identified as European: 2 percent felt European only, 7 percent felt European first and then their nationality, and 48 percent felt their nationality first and European second. Meanwhile, 41 percent of respondents identified as their nationality only.[45] There has been little change in the overall picture: in 1993, 4 percent of respondents felt European only, 7 percent European and then their nationality, 44 percent their nationality and then European, and 40 percent their nationality only—but the more recent numbers include respondents from the 1995 and 2004 enlargement states, where respondents tended to feel less European than respondents in states that had been members longer.[46] Unfortunately, the surveys do not include information on migration, but those who have lived in more than one member state are more likely to identify as European than those who have not. Sociological research indeed demonstrates this, though EU citizens residing and working in EU member states other than that of their citizenship tended to be more active in the economic sphere than in the political one.[47]

Rights are ultimately only as secure as the political and institutional support they enjoy. Does sufficient support exist to maintain or expand common European rights? In this chapter I problematized the future of European citizenship by considering ways in which the process that led to its introduction is reversible. Since rights, like laws and even constitutions, are altered and reinterpreted over time, the success and permanence of European citizenship remains in question. I argued that EU citizenship minimizes difference by superimposing common European rights on national legal systems that are not always perfectly compatible. By examining the limits of European citizenship, I analyzed ways in which it might increase rather than decrease tension within the EU. I argue that there are risks to a common citizenship and that addressing these risks will require responses grounded in the comparative experience of managing conflict and difference. Though I ultimately believe that the growth of European rights is not yet finished, significant countervailing forces exist. In particular, I focused on political opposition, the relative paucity of effective guarantees for European rights, and the potential tensions between nondiscrimination and national culture. Of course, the possibility exists of overestimating the strength or depth of national affiliations. Over the past several centuries, political elites within European states have utilized nationalism to construct and sustain political institutions that, however strong they appear, ultimately remain malleable. Perhaps European citizenship will ultimately surpass national citizenship.[48] If so, the process will be neither natural nor inevitable but will occur as a result of sustained political will to make it succeed.

6.4. Educating European Citizens

In national contexts, education is a key means of promoting economic advancement and individual social mobility. But national authorities also use education to foster civic engagement and a shared sense of community. Education has played a similar dual role in the process of European integration. Indeed, education was an area of "intense interest" to European leaders from the very beginning of European integration, and promoting student mobility was intended to foster a coordinated European system of higher education.[49] European action in the field of education was first justified as a means of facilitating the free movement of workers and contributing to Europe's economic recovery. Yet, it was also intended to foster a European cultural identity and create a shared sense of European citizenship.[50] Indeed, in any context, questions of citizenship must be posed in terms of process and access: individuals are not automatically citizens but rather become citizens through one or several processes of citizenship creation.[51]

The Treaty of Rome gave the Commission the task of promoting cooperation in the field of vocational training. Acting on a proposal from the Commission, the Council would then "lay down general principles for implementing a common vocational training policy capable of contributing to the harmonious development both of the national economies and of the common market" (Art. 128). While this economic rationale predominated in the early years of European integration, it was gradually supplemented by the desire to foster common citizenship. As a Commission summary of this transformation notes, the growth of Community education and training programs coincided with the development of the "People's Europe" concept: "European citizenship is reflected in and supported by the kind of experience they offer; they are themselves instruments of free circulation and examples of the recognition of European diversity. They offer experience of the reality of European union and unity: the free movement of people, ideas, and products."[52] Education, free movement, and EU citizenship here are thus linked.

The development of European education policy has also been regarded as a way of addressing the democratic deficit. The European Parliament resolved in 1982, for example, that education "about the Community and Europe must be provided in schools, both as a nucleus of common content in the various schools curricula and as a vital body of knowledge enabling European citizens to freely exercise their political rights of control and critical participation."[53] Education about Europe would thus help close the perceived gap between individual citizens and the European institutions, to help them exercise democratic control through political participation.

The national ministers of education affirmed in 1985 that the ever-closer union among the peoples of Europe called for by the Treaty of Rome could "only be achieved on the basis of the citizens' understanding of political, social, and cultural life in other member states."[54] Education policy was not only a way to increase knowledge among European citizens, however, but also part of an effort to build "a European model of culture correlating with European integration."[55] Europeans should therefore be "well informed on the goals of European integration and the European Community's means of action. Teaching about that dimension is therefore part and parcel of the education of the future citizens of Europe."[56]

Despite such ambitions to build a European culture through education, however, with the exception of vocational policy there was little Community action in the field of education before the mid-1980s. The earliest Community program designed to foster the mobility of students was Erasmus, the European Community Action Scheme for the Mobility of University Students. It started in the 1987–1988 school year by funding 3,244 university students to study in other member states, and grew exponentially. The national ministers of education affirmed that they wished to bolster the "European dimension in education" and "strengthen in young people a sense of European identity."[57] But the question soon arose whether the Community had the authority to engage in education policy at all. The "Erasmus judgment" in 1989 defined higher education as falling under the Treaty of Rome's discussion of "vocational education," hence under the authority of the European Community.[58]

In order to clarify the extent of the Community's role in education, the member states agreed in the Maastricht Treaty that the Community would encourage cooperation between member states "by supporting and supplementing their action, while fully respecting the responsibility of the Member States for the content of teaching and the organization of education systems and their cultural and linguistic diversity" (Art. 126.1). Community action would develop the European dimension in education, particularly through the teaching of European languages; encourage mobility of students and teachers; promote cooperation between educational establishments; develop exchanges of information and experience; and develop youth exchanges and exchanges of socioeducational instructors (Art. 126.2). Though the treaty referred to the responsibility of member states for the content of education, the list of areas for Community action was lengthy.

European action intensified further with the Maastricht Treaty's enshrinement of the Community role in education. The Commission affirmed that "education lays the foundations of awareness and of European citizenship," and it called, among other measures, for a European voluntary service.[59] By 2002, over one million students had studied in another European country under the auspices of the Erasmus program, and the Commission triumphantly announced that "Erasmus students are contributing to shaping a common European identity."[60] Erasmus students did indeed seem to feel more European, and they often remained in the country where they went on exchange, but acquiring a European political identity remained a "somewhat random result" of the Erasmus program.[61] With the ultimate goal of funding 10 percent of all European students, the Commission aimed to have funded the exchange of three million Erasmus students by 2011, when the program was expected to fund almost three hundred thousand students annually.[62]

European citizenship is invariably invoked to justify common action in the field of education. In its 1995 White Paper on education policy, for example, the Commission argued that cultivating knowledge was "particularly appropriate to the building of Europe," because "education lays the foundations of awareness and of European citizenship."[63] In a related Green Paper in 1996, the Commission added that with "increasing freedom of movement should come a growing European consciousness. . . . Mobility within the Community ought to contribute to the development of solidarity between all Europeans."[64] The European institutions actively worked to ensure that education would indeed lay the foundations of European citizenship. Between 2004 and 2006, for example, the Union distributed ?72 million to organizations that promote active European citizenship.[65] Another example is a report on European programs for youth, culture, and audiovisual and civic participation, suggestively entitled *Making Citizenship Work*, which emphasized the need for European citizens to have a sense of belonging to the EU. It stated that the "growing importance of citizenship in the European order and the values it is based upon has been mirrored by an equal growth in importance at Union level of education, youth and cultural policies."[66]

The member states and the European institutions placed particular emphasis on language education. Between 1990 and 1995, the Lingua program for language education "brought mobility to almost 200,000 people: 120,000 young people through collective educational projects, 30,000 students through inter-university cooperation programmes, and 30,000 teachers through grants for in-service training."[67] Encouraging mobility and language learning was not an end in itself but rather a means of building a European identity. Thus, encouraging Europeans to develop competence in two European languages in addition to their mother tongue was described as an integral aspect of European citizenship: "Multilingualism is part and parcel of both European identity/citizenship and the learning society."[68]

Building on Erasmus and Lingua, there was an explosion of other programs (also often named after European thinkers). The "Socrates" program was launched in 1995 to "develop the European dimension in studies at all levels so as to strengthen the spirit of European citizenship, drawing on the cultural heritage of each member state"[69] Socrates regrouped all programs in education, while the parallel "Leonardo" program regrouped the Community's vocational training programs. Both were allocated ?1.15 billion between 2000 and 2006. The common element of all EU programs in the field of education is their focus on building European citizens. An assessment of the Youth in Action program, for example, notes that the "importance assigned to EU citizenship" in the treaty underlined the role that the program should play in "promoting the active citizenship of young people and strengthening their sense of belonging to Europe."[70]

In addition to Community action, cooperation among member states also dramatically increased. In 1998, at the eight hundredth anniversary of the founding of the Sorbonne university in Paris, European education ministers issued the Sorbonne Declaration, which called for a European Higher Education Area. The next year, in June 1999 at Europe's oldest university, education ministers from twenty-nine countries issued the Bologna Declaration. The "Bologna process" included a variety of goals, one of which is the introduction of a two-tier model based on the separation between bachelor's and master's degrees. Bologna's overall aim is to manage the mobility of university students, teachers, and graduates in a context in which free movement makes it "essential for national education and training systems to consider the European dimension."[71] In other words, "mobility of students and academic and administrative staff is the basis for establishing a European Higher Education Area."[72] But the free movement of persons is not only a *cause* of coordination in the field of education; it is also the *effect* of the various programs discussed here. Mobility of students and staff leads to policies favorable to mobility, which increases the numbers of students and educators making use of the opportunities for free movement, which in turn leads to calls for policies fostering even more mobility. The development of European educational policy, including references to combating the democratic deficit and fostering the free movement of students and academic staff, thus parallels the development of European citizenship more generally. European states still utilize a wide variety of educational and other mechanisms to construct and reconstruct their national identities, though they have gradually converged in terms of the content of those identities: the extent to which the Europe idea becomes part of national identities will ultimately determine how successful integration can be.[73] The political project of creating European citizens continues.

Conclusion

L'Europe n'est qu'une nation, composée de plusieurs.[1]

—Montesquieu

There are no great nations—it may almost be added that there would be no society—without the notion of rights.[2]

—Tocqueville

A state is a perfect body of free men, united together in order to enjoy common rights and advantages.[3]

—Grotius

Citizenship is a malleable institution. Like other effects of political contestation and bargaining, it can undergo both radical transformation and minute tinkering. In some states, citizenship laws and policies are deeply rooted and resistant to change. Elsewhere, they are less firmly entrenched, shifting easily as a result of partisan politics or other political conjunctures. As an institution, citizenship also shapes the terms of its own transformation by *defining* political actors and the rules within which they operate. It is precisely because citizenship delineates political membership—separating citizens from others, specifying the rights and duties of each category of people, and privileging certain public identities over alternatives—that citizenship is always contentious.[4] Decisions about the content of rights and duties, about the proper balance between them, and about which individuals should be considered citizens provide the foundation for all politics. The key point is that citizenship lacks a clear denotation and remains always open to contest.

Though citizenship is nothing novel, the start of the twenty-first century witnessed several important developments. After a slow process of solidification and crystallization from the peace of Westphalia to the First World War, and a period of hegemony of the nation-state in the twentieth century, the ties between political communities and states once again shifted. Most pertinently, the sources of rights multiplied. In addition to the traditional national sources of rights, a European Union (EU) citizen enjoys rights under the Universal Declaration of Human Rights and other United Nations (UN) conventions supported by the embryonic International Criminal Court, the Council of Europe with its Court in Strasbourg, and of course the European Union with its Court in Luxembourg. The focus of this book has been on the rights that individuals enjoy in the European Union, rights that coalesced into EU citizenship. It demonstrated that European citizenship had long been an aspiration of political leaders from throughout Europe but that translating this aspiration into policies and laws was a gradual enterprise. The expansion of entitlements from their origins in free movement for workers illustrates the transformation of European integration from an economic to a political phenomenon based on individual rights. National political leaders, generally supported by supranational actors, introduced and subsequently expanded supranational rights and citizenship because they found it in their domestic interests to do so or because they believed that doing so was desirable for European integration.

To make this assertion is to simplify a process that was profoundly complex and sometimes even arbitrary. Policymaking is rarely uniform or easy, nor does it always follow in logical steps. The political world—the real one in which we live—is messier than the theoretical world. Nevertheless, the European experience captures important truths about the political, economic, and social processes that foster integration. The development of European citizenship mirrors integration processes operating in analogous situations in other times and places: political commitment can transform free movement of workers into an individual mobility right for workers. This modifies the political environment, producing demands for further rights. With ongoing political commitment, the resulting extension and expansion of rights may culminate in a common supranational citizenship, as happened in Europe. Like rights, however, the meaning and content of citizenship are never fixed, and supranational citizenship such as that now found within the EU can be undone in the same way that it was constructed.

It remains as important as ever to take citizenship seriously, because citizenship defines who we are and how we act politically. In other words, debates about citizenship are debates about the nature of the political community. The development of European citizenship resembles in many ways the development of citizenship in traditional states, so that examining the design and operation of citizenship in states clarifies the development of European citizenship, and vice versa. For example, the rights of citizens of federal states differ from unit to unit within the federation, just as citizens of different EU member states possess different rights. Because a necessary condition for a shared political community is the ability of citizens to move about within the common political space, migrations within democracies tend to be unhindered. Likewise, the political barriers to migration between substate jurisdictions are dramatically lower than those concerning migration across international borders. This is because the individuals in question share a single citizenship, and thus a single internationally recognized legal status. Migration between EU member states, however, belongs to a different classification: movement between putatively sovereign states.

Comparative examples demonstrate that free movement rights are fundamental to citizenship: democratic citizenship invariably guarantees individuals the right to move within the state's territory, though the precise operation of that right differs from state to state. In much the same way that bureaucracies, courts, and legislatures in other states safeguard the right of citizens to move freely within the state's territory, so too the European Commission, Court, and Parliament work to safeguard the right of European citizens to move freely within Union territory. Within states, individuals who move from one jurisdiction to another (from one city or province to another, for example) lose the rights and duties associated with their status as residents of the first jurisdiction and gain new status as residents of the second, but they experience no change in the rights and duties associated with their overarching citizenship. Indeed, it generally matters little—in terms of the rights and duties of citizenship—which jurisdiction one moves from or to within the common social, economic, and political space. Within the EU, however, analogous differences remain more substantial. A (French) European citizen moving from France to Germany and a (German) European citizen moving from Germany to France experience differences both in the continuing rights and obligations to their member state of origin and those to their new member state of residence. Such differences might encourage individuals to move to particular states for particular purposes. As European borders become more malleable, understanding the changing rules and practices of citizenship in Europe is increasingly important.

In any state, it is only by ensuring that rights apply regardless of the citizen's place of residence that national citizenship possesses any power. Similarly, the European institutions attempt to implement principles such as benefit portability, prohibition of residence requirements for access to programs or rights, and mutual recognition of qualifications and credentials in order to uphold and expand EU citizenship. Such a dynamic is evident in a multitude of EU initiatives intended to reinforce the portability of benefits throughout Union territory. Rather than thinking of citizenship as flowing directly from a state to an individual, we should reconceptualize citizenship in terms of the variegated and complex relationships that individuals actually experience in their encounters with multiple jurisdictions.

History is replete with examples of barriers to international migration being established or removed in response to political pressures. Within market economies, however, free movement of workers tends to be guaranteed. In establishing a common, supranational market, Europe's political leaders opted not only to establish such free movement but also to guarantee it by means of individual rights—and then to extend those rights to other categories of people, culminating in a common, supranational citizenship. The development of rights is perhaps a function of the debate about the extent to which political authorities want to control free movement of people alongside that of goods, services, and capital. Indeed, there are parallels between debates about the constraining effects of globalization on national autonomy and arguments in the eighteenth century about the domestic effects of market integration.[5] The question then becomes why other contemporary examples of market integration have not led to the same kinds of supranational rights. Certainly it is not because of any absence of people moving: the scale of Mexican immigration to the United States, for example, belies the idea that there is no movement within the North American Free Trade Agreement (NAFTA) comparable to that of the early years of the European Community. But there is no NAFTA citizenship.

This book explained why European states relinquished their authority over borders. In other words, the process by which liberalization of trade in goods led to the liberalization of movement for people and supranational rights. Scholars of nationalism have long argued that processes of state building were linked with the rise of a national consciousness, but the exact mechanisms by which national consciousness arose is a matter of debate. Easing restrictions on free movement within the state's territory was a critical prerequisite. Just as a key development in today's EU is the reduction or elimination of internal boundaries, so too the removal of internal borders was a crucial condition for the successful rise of states.[6] Internal migrations, such as those from rural areas to cities during industrialization, did not *cause* nationalism, but they did generate needs that nationalism could address. Across Europe, the movement of people that spurred nationalism was migration *within* the state. A key function of the modern state was to facilitate the free flow of people within its boundaries. Indeed the essence of full-fledged state citizenship, as distinct from earlier town or district citizenship, was its uniform applicability throughout the state's domain.[7]

One definition of the nation holds that it is a "territorial community of shared history and mass culture, a unified economy and common rights and duties for all members."[8] Though the European economy is more unified than some national ones, the continuing enlargements of the Union mean that it has not yet established stable territorial limits. Nor, for the foreseeable future, is it reasonable to attribute a shared history and mass culture to the wide variety of regional histories and cultures contained within the EU, despite the EU's efforts in the field of education, discussed in §6.4. Yet this book has explained how the prohibition on nationality-based discrimination, coupled with the ever-increasing growth of European rights, ensure that Europeans *do* share common rights and duties. The dynamic institution of EU citizenship has not yet reached a stable equilibrium.

Some lament that a genuine European political community can never come into existence because robust local identities preclude the formation of an overarching European identity. But the strength or depth of national affiliations might be overestimated—after all, national political institutions remain malleable rather than fixed. It would be a mistake to assume that political identification with the member states will simply disappear, but a mass European identity has progressively emerged and is growing stronger.[9] EU citizenship may eventually replace national citizenship in terms of importance. But if this occurs, it will come about because of a sustained political will rather than some natural or inevitable process. The continued existence of citizenship rights, like that of other rights, depends on constant political and institutional support.

The rights of EU citizenship are not the same as human rights. It is undeniable that noncitizens have gained important social rights in democratic states around the world; it is even possible that a "paradigmatic shift" changed the very nature of citizenship, relocating it from nation-state sovereignty to the international human rights regime.[10] But this book demonstrated the ever-present desire or need to develop specifically *European* rights that would apply only to EU citizens—even though that desire was and remains contentious, with many advocating the extension of European rights to all European residents. Rights have traditionally been coupled with identity—national identity in the case of sovereign states; guild, religious, or other identities in earlier times. But some rights (most notably human rights) do not depend on any particular identity; thus, it is worth asking whether European rights are more like human rights or more like traditional citizenship rights. The outcome of the struggle between inclusion and exclusion matters because the European developments analyzed above are only part of a larger trend of the proliferation of rights beyond borders and the consequent transformation of state sovereignty into regional, and perhaps ultimately global, governance arrangements: Europe might well become a model of post-Westphalian, postsovereign political organization that is emulated by regions elsewhere.[11] At the same time, perhaps the conditions present in Europe were unique. For Spinelli, the Second World War and its aftermath "greatly reduced the habitual respect of citizens for their states and their myths and opened the way to the united European transformation."[12] This popular reaction against state myths may have been a necessary condition for the creation of EU citizenship, and it is unclear whether it can easily be replicated elsewhere.

A major thrust of European integration has been to lower barriers, to break down impediments to movement, and to make borders disappear or at least lose the significance they once had. Support for this project transcends national origins. It is to some extent an ideology, and those inspired by it differentiate themselves from the view of the Union as a simple free trade market. Since the end of Europe's most destructive war, men and women who share the aim of creating European citizens have occupied key institutions, not only supranational ones such as the European Commission, Parliament, or Court, but also influential positions in national governments, industry and labor groups, and civil society. Together they have worked to integrate Europeans not only economically but also socially and politically by conferring upon them European rights. There has been opposition, but the goal of continental integration through rights is increasingly being realized as European citizens are created.

Notes

Introduction

1. Aristotle (1984 [circa 330 BCE]: Bk. 3, Ch. 1).
2. Case C-184/99, *Rudy Grzelczyk v Centre public d'aide sociale d'Ottignies-Louvain-la-Neuve* (2001), ECR I-6193, discussed in §4.1.
3. McNeely (1995: 10); Sassen (2002: 135). For Brubaker (1992: 72), the "emergence of the institution of citizenship cannot be understood apart from the formation of the modern state and state system. But the reverse is equally true." Linz and Stepan (1996: 28) note, "Without a state, there can be no citizenship."
4. The reunification of Germany following the fall of the Berlin Wall is a special case that should be understood as a return to a previously existing political community rather than the creation of a new one. Indeed, West Germany never recognized a separate east German citizenship and had declared in 1957 that east Germans should be considered West German citizens under Community law.
5. Gabriel and Macdonald (2006). For Falk (1994: 136) EU citizenship thus represents "the most significant political innovation" since the emergence of the state at Westphalia.
6. Balibar (1988); Kymlicka and Norman (1994).
7. Tilly (1995: 8).
8. Benhabib (2002, 2004, 2006).
9. Pocock (1995). Aron (1974) answered the question, "Is multinational citizenship possible?" with an emphatic "No!"
10. Maas (2001). Kelemen (forthcoming-a) argues that the EU has become a federation, while Elkins (1995) considers alternative nonterritorial forms of political organization. For McNeely (1995: 3), the modern state's roots were visible by 1300, but

122 Notes to the Introduction

Westphalia marks the historical shift to a new international order, with nation-states as the dominant form of political organization.

11. Giddens (1985); McNeely (1995: 11).

12. Salter (2003: 14–15). Bolkestein (2004: 22) notes that the EU "requires an outer limit, a fixed border. This is a major problem. Europe does not like to talk of 'inside' or 'outside.' That is considered egoistic, anti-social and lacking in solidarity: in short, not in keeping with the European ideal."

13. De Haan (1993: 23–25); Manin (1997: 84, 157); Maas (2001). Echoing Grotius, Hobbes (1996 [1651]: I, Ch. 13, 13) affirmed that states create laws, which create rights: "Where there is no common Power, there is no Law: where no Law, no Injustice."

14. O'Manique (2003: Ch. 8). For Bentham (1843), "Right is the child of law: from real laws come real rights; but from imaginary laws come imaginary rights, a bastard brood of monsters."

15. European Commissioner (later Commission vice president from 1981 to 1985) Viscount Étienne Davignon in European Parliament (1979: 25).

16. Barbalet (1988); Isin (2002).

17. Marshall (1950: 28) traced the historical development of individual rights in England since the eighteenth century, showing how *civil* rights (equality before the law, the right to own property and sign binding contracts, freedom of religion and of speech) led to *political* rights (the passive and active franchise), which in turn led to *social* rights (the right to a minimal level of social and economic welfare).

18. The ambiguity is not resolved in the Universal Declaration of Human Rights: "Everyone has the right to education. Education shall be free, at least in the elementary and fundamental stages" (Art. 26). It is unclear where the distinction between "elementary" or "fundamental" and higher education should lie.

19. Ignatieff (2000); Hirschl (2004).

20. Shapiro (1986: 302).

21. Schuman was the French foreign minister who on 9 May 1950 announced the plan for the European Coal and Steel Community, the basis for future integration. See Ch. 4, n1.

22. Zolberg (1989: 406) claimed that "all the countries to which people would like to go restrict entry." But European states no longer restrict entry or residence for EU citizens, and (as discussed in §5.3) they also increasingly cooperate on immigration from outside the Union.

23. Commissioner Lionello Levi Sandri (1961: 5, 6).

24. Levi Sandri (1961: 5, 6). This idea is often repeated: European Commission (1982, 1998a); Bolkestein (2000).

25. Conant (2002). Milward (1992: 437) argues that when Italian governments prioritized emigration, "an interdependent international order advanced such policies better than an integrationist one." But this is a politically incomplete picture. Calculating that both emigration and political integration could be better secured through supranational institutions than ad hoc bargains, Italian negotiators pushed

hard to achieve an "integrationist" solution. It is they who are primarily responsible for the inclusion of free movement rights in the treaties. Mediterranean states—and Italians in particular—remain among the most strident proponents of an autonomous European citizenship. Delegazione PDS del Gruppo del PSE al Parlamento Europeo (1995).

26. Streeck (1995: 413).
27. Brubaker (1992); Torpey (2000).
28. Milward (1992); Moravcsik (1998); Grin (2003).
29. Meehan (1993); Bru (1994); Marias (1994); Springer (1994); Jessurun d'Oliveira (1995); O'Leary (1996); Orlandi (1996); Menegazzi munari (1996); Shaw (1997); Wiener and Della Sala (1997); Wihtol de Wenden (1997); Wiener (1998, 2006); Dollat (1998); Weiler (1999); Arnold (1999); Magnette (1999); Schmitter (2000); Koslowski (2000); Baier (2000); Parsi (2001); Lehning (2001); Eder and Giesen (2001); Borja, Dourthe, and Peugeot (2001); Besussi and Leonini (2001); La Torre (2004); Guild (2004); Hanf (2006); Bellamy, Castiglione, and Shaw (2006). Costa (2004b) writes that EU citizenship's "novelty . . . should not be underestimated," while Schönlau (2005: 40) claims that introducing EU citizenship "marked an important statement with regard to what kind of polity the Union is."
30. Moravcsik (1998: 472).
31. Haas (1958: 16). Haas (2004: *xxi) now argues that both his original neofunctionalist position and a later version by Stone Sweet, Sandholtz, and Fligstein (2001) mistakenly assumed "the 'automaticity' of the integration process," where integration and institutionalization are seen as irreversible. I agree with Haas that they are neither automatic nor irreversible, as the development of EU citizenship demonstrates.
32. Richardson (2001: 99); Pierson and Leibfried (1995).
33. Héritier (1999). For Streeck (1995: 417), "Nation-states and the relations among them are the most important impediments to welfare-state federalism. Insofar as the Union's member states derive domestic legitimacy from social policies, they are unlikely to cede control over these to supranational agencies."
34. The quotation is from Guy Mollet, vice president of the Socialist International and French prime minister; the list of values is from French Christian Democrat leader Pierre-Henri Teitgen, cited in Mahant (2004: 37, 11).
35. Mahant (2004: 38, 10). On the wars' destructiveness and aftermath, see Mazower (2000) and Judt (2005). For the Italian commitment to the European idea, see Arfé (1986) and Preda (2004).
36. Moravcsik (2005: 10).
37. N. P. Ludlow (2006).
38. Belgian foreign minister Paul-Henri Spaak (1971). Compare Wales (1963: 39).
39. By "low politics" I do not mean dirty political tactics, grassroots organizing, or Keohane and Nye's (1977: 24) view that "the 'high politics' of military security dominates the 'low politics' of economic and social affairs." Instead, I mean the specific

connotation it has acquired in studies of European integration: high politics are issues of prime importance to leaders, whereas low politics are less important and relegated to lesser levels of authority. This recalls its use by Stanley Hoffmann (1966) and Ernst Haas (1968: xxiii): "Integrative decisions based on high politics and basic commitment are undoubtedly more durable than decisions based on converging pragmatic expectations."

Chapter 1

1. Levi Sandri (1961: 10).
2. Pagden (2002). The MFE was cofounded by Altiero Spinelli, later European Commissioner for Industry (1970–1976), deputy in the Italian Parliament (1976–1983), and Communist member of the European Parliament (1979–1986). Imprisoned between 1927 and 1943 for his opposition to Mussolini, in 1941 on the island of Ventotene, Spinelli cowrote the eponymous Ventotene Manifesto, which argued that a "free and united Europe" was necessary because national sovereignty caused war. Both the MFE (www.mfe.it) and its youth organization, the Young European Federalists (www.jef-europe.net/), remain active prointegrationists.
3. Cited in Malvestiti (1959: 58).
4. Churchill (1949: 200)
5. Bitsch (1997); G. T. Miller (1995: 371–72).
6. Milward (2006: 400–407).
7. Spaak (1950: 95).
8. Sassen (1996: 87–92); Mason (1955: 5); Pella (1956); Serra (1995: 132); Willis (1971: 150).
9. Taviani (1954: 176–80).
10. Ranieri (1986: 22).
11. Vignes (1956); Griffiths (1988: 42); Kersten (1988: 296).
12. European Coal and Steel Community (1953: 54).
13. This was the position of Pierre Mendès France, discussed in Marjolin (1989: 289). Institut français de l'opinion publique (1951: 23); Racine (1954); Monnet (1976).
14. Dumoulin (1988); Milward (1988).
15. Martens (1973: 158–63). I discuss this agreement further at page 25 in this chapter.
16. Ranieri (1986: 22–23); Diebold (1959); European Coal and Steel Community (1958).
17. European Coal and Steel Community (1958: 131).
18. Americans would "deport French workers with the aid of the Treaty's clauses guaranteeing free movement of labor. . . . A huge army of French unemployed would be created to provide slave labor for American bases in France, where atom bombs and bacteriological weapons would be stored" (Mason 1955: 30). French Communists long remained opposed to European unification. In September 1957, 55 percent

of French Communists thought that a union of France with the other five Community states was of little or no use (5 percent thought it was indispensable; 25 percent thought it was somewhat or very useful; 15 percent did not respond), compared to only 11 percent of Socialists (31 percent indispensable; 46 percent somewhat or very useful; 12 percent no response), and single digits of partisans of the other parties (Institut français de l'opinion publique 1957: 12–13).

19. European Coal and Steel Community (1958: 131–32). The focus later shifted to the question of whether or not workers originally admitted for the coal or steel industry could subsequently change occupations. European Coal and Steel Community (1954c: 171).

20. High Authority of the European Coal and Steel Community (1954: 157–58).
21. European Coal and Steel Community (1954a).
22. Bok (1955: 56).
23. Bok (1955: 56).
24. Mason (1955: 101–2).
25. Mason (1955: 100).
26. Confederazione Italiana Sindicati Lavoratori (1959: 70–71); Willis (1971).
27. Kreyssig (1958: 24, 25).
28. Council of Europe (1953: 67).
29. Speech at the second session of the Common Assembly, Strasbourg, France, 15 June 1953. Cited in Monnet (1955).
30. Speech of 30 April 1952, cited in Monnet (1955: 132).
31. Poidevin (1998); European Coal and Steel Community (1954b).
32. Belgian Liberal representative Motz in Council of Europe (1953: 71).
33. European Coal and Steel Community (1956).
34. Everson (1995).
35. European Coal and Steel Community (1957).
36. Romero (1991).
37. European Parliament (1960: 9).
38. O'Grada (1969: 80); European Council (1968a, 1968b).
39. Romero (1993: 34).
40. Spinelli (1966: 108).
41. European Parliament (1960).
42. European Council (1961).
43. Lyon-Caen and Lyon-Caen (1991: 180).
44. Robert Marjolin in Bull. EC 1-1961, 31.
45. Levi Sandri (1961: 5, 6).
46. European Commission (1966).
47. Gallup International (1963: 115, 23).
48. European Council (1964b, 1964c).
49. European Council (1964a: Arts. 3.1, 3.2, 4.3).
50. A labor union official, cited in Rosenthal (1975: 74).
51. Bonnet (1969).

52. European Council (1968b: Art. 1).
53. European Council (1968a: Art. 2). See the annual reports in European Commission (1958–).
54. Grabitz (1970: 7).
55. Kitzinger (1963: 46).
56. European Parliament (1960: 12). Directive 15/61 was "the first appearance of a European citizenship," Debates EP no. 48, 135, 22 November 1961. See Evans (1982, 1984: 683).
57. Hallstein (1972 [1969]: 173–74). Hallstein was Commission president from 1958 until 1969.
58. Levi Sandri (1968: 6).
59. Spinelli (1966: 108). For more on Spinelli, see note 2 above.
60. Booth (1992: 19).
61. Feldstein (1967: 31).
62. ILO Convention 97, www.ilo.org/ilolex/cgi-lex/convde.pl?C097.
63. Soviet policy distinguished between large cities, whose residents were issued with internal passports and were thus eligible to change their place of residence upon receiving a new *propiska*, and small towns and villages, whose residents were not issued with internal passports until the last years of the Soviet Union and were therefore not even eligible to move to urban areas without obtaining special permission. Light (2006).
64. Dowty (1987).
65. European Coal and Steel Community (1955: 95).
66. European Coal and Steel Community (1955: 94).
67. Plender (1988: 288); Handoll (1997: 55); Fischer and Straubhaar (1996).
68. Meehan (2000) concludes that Ireland should persuade the UK to merge the Common Travel Area into the Schengen system.
69. United Nations Economic Commission for Europe (1979).
70. United Nations Economic Commission for Europe (1979).
71. Miège and Brichant (1994).
72. European Parliament (1960: 3).
73. European Parliament (1960: 3).
74. European Parliament (1960: 3).
75. Hofstede (1964).
76. European Parliament (1960: 3).
77. European Parliament (1960: 3).
78. Morelli (1992: 200) describes the recruitment efforts.
79. European Parliament (1960: 3); Martens (1973).
80. Morelli (1992: 200).
81. Morelli (1992: 195, 2004).
82. Alter (1998: 131).
83. Alter (1998: 130). Compare Burley and Mattli (1993); Garrett (1995).
84. Alter (1998: 132).

85. Case 26/62, *Van Gend en Loos v Nederlandse Administratie der Belastingen* (1963), ECR 1.
86. Case 26/62, *Van Gend en Loos v Nederlandse Administratie der Belastingen* (1963), ECR 1.
87. Egan (2001: 83); Maduro (1998).
88. Plender (1976).
89. Kostakopoulou (2001: 42).
90. Alter (2001).
91. O'Leary (1999: 377). Dehousse (1998: 45) claims that the ECJ paid increasing attention to individual rights, while national courts generally failed to question its decisions, perhaps because they too were empowered by case law. Kelemen (forthcoming-b) adds that the EU's institutional structure encourages the proliferation of rights and that private parties have strong incentives to launch EU rights litigation.
92. Case 6/64, *Flaminio Costa v Enel* (1964), ECR 585.
93. Caporaso (2002: 94–95). Once the ECJ hands down its judgment, the domestic court applies it to the facts of the case.
94. Lenaerts (1996: 139). For Stone Sweet (2004: 111), the enactment of direct effect and supremacy demonstrate that the "Court is a trustee of the Treaty, not an agent of national governments."
95. Hallstein (1972 [1969]: 33). He continued, "Of course, this is not a new experience for citizens of countries with federal constitutions."

Chapter 2

1. European Council (1972a: 46).
2. European Commission (1975: 28).
3. European Council (1972a: 30).
4. European Council (1972a: 30).
5. European Council (1972a: 39, 46).
6. European Council (1972a: 58–59).
7. Hantrais (1995: 32–33).
8. European Council (1973: pt. 2).
9. European Council (1974: pt. 1104).
10. European Commission (1975: 28).
11. Bull. EC 7/8-1975, pt. 1303.
12. European Commission (1975: 30).
13. European Commission (1975: 32). The report noted, "If the idea of amending national laws on naturalization is to be taken further, this should be as an additional measure while the main emphasis continues to be on promoting greater equality with the nationals of the host State. The situation could however be different if acquiring a new nationality did not involve losing the former one or if it was possible to change nationality easily."
14. European Commission (1975: 28).

128   Notes to Chapter Two

15. Tindemans (1976). Grabitz (1977) discusses the report's promotion of European citizenship.
16. Tindemans (1976: 1).
17. Tindemans (1976: 26). For more on the democratic deficit, see §4.4 in this book.
18. Tindemans (1976: 26).
19. Dinan (2005).
20. Supplement 5/75, Bull. EC, 21; Supplement 9/75, Bull. EC, 26. The Economic and Social Committee, composed of representatives of employers' organizations, trade unions, farmers, consumer groups, professional associations, and other civil society interest groups, was established by the Treaty of Rome to comment on Community policies.
21. Case 48/75, *Royer* (1976), ECR 497, para. 12.
22. Case 2/74, *Reyners v Belgian State* (1974), ECR 631; Case 33/74, *Van Binsbergen v Bestuur van de Bedrijfsvereniging voor de Metaalnijverheid* (1974), ECR 1299; Case 41/74, *Van Duyn v Home Office* (1974), ECR 1337.
23. Case 36/74, *Walrave v Union Cycliste Internationale* (1974), ECR 1405, para. 28: "The rule on non-discrimination applies in judging all legal relationships in so far as these relationships, by reason either of the place where they are entered into or of the place where they take effect, can be located within the territory of the Community."
24. Case 48/75, *Royer* (1976), ECR 497.
25. George (1990: 87).
26. European Parliament (1977).
27. Klaus von Dohnanyi, German foreign minister during its presidency, in European Parliament (1979: 29); European Commission (1994).
28. Belgian MEP Dehousse, cited in Marchal-Van Belle (1968).
29. President Emilio Colombo in European Parliament (1979: 21).
30. European Commission (1979: 14).
31. European Commission (1980: 3).
32. Quoted in Taschner (1993: 430).
33. Taschner (1993: 431–32).
34. O'Leary (1999: 381).
35. European Council (1981).
36. European Parliament (1983).
37. Palmer (1981).
38. European Parliament (1984: Art. 3).
39. European Council (1985a: 5); Schönlau (2005: 56).
40. According to Hoffmann (1989: 32), "Delors is as important to the enterprise today as Jean Monnet was in the 1950s."
41. Case 293/83, *Gravier v Ville de Liège* (1985), ECR 593, 13 February 1985. *Gravier* extended the principle introduced in Case 252/82, *Forcheri* (1983), ECR 2323, which involved the spouse of a Community official who claimed that the im-

position of an additional enrollment fee on nonnationals was unlawful. O'Leary (1996: 160).
42. Case 293/83, *Gravier v Ville de Liège* (1985), ECR 593, 13 February 1985.
43. European Council (1985b).
44. European Commission (1985: 25). In the process of preparing the White Paper, the Commission had contracted out a report on the effects of completely eliminating border controls. But instead of carrying out this study, the contractors wrote a report on relaxing some borders in some fields so that, when the White Paper was released, it was done without an impact assessment. Interview at the Commission, 20 March 2001.
45. European Commission (1985: 26).
46. Anderson, Boer, and Miller (1994: 107).
47. Maas (2005a).
48. "Five EC Members Agree to Eliminate Border Checks," *United Press International*, 14 June 1985.
49. Over two-thirds of journeys leaving Ireland were to the UK, so the Irish government calculated as too high the cost of leaving the Common Travel Area to join Schengen. See §1.3 in this book.
50. European Council (1985a).
51. Gillespie and Laffan (2006) discuss the EU's "deliberate" use of such symbols to create a European identity, arguing that Europeans have indeed started to feel more European.
52. European Council (1985a). See §3.2 in this book.
53. Bull. EC 7/8-1985, pt. 1.1.10.
54. United Kingdom (1985: 226).
55. DTEU, Art. 47.
56. R. Corbett (1998: 231).
57. R. Corbett (1998: 248).
58. R. Corbett (1998: 230); Schmuck (1987).
59. European Commission (1988). Marín had been Spain's minister responsible for negotiating accession. Following Spain's entry, he became Commission vice president, responsible for social affairs, education, and employment and serving under Jacques Delors, then Jacques Santer, then becoming interim president himself until the selection of Romano Prodi as president. Marín returned to Spain in 1999 to become president of the Spanish parliament.
60. D. Morgan (2005: 15).
61. European Council (1987).
62. European Council (1989).
63. Sherrington (2000: 150–52).
64. Garth (1985: 108).
65. Ferreira do Amaral (1993: 243) concluded that "the main consequence of free movement of labour for Portugal will be renewed emigration to Europe." P. Ludlow (2004: 12n18) notes that the member states decided to admit Greece *against* the Commission's advice.

130 ◊ Notes to Chapter Three

66. Former Portuguese president Mario Soares noted, "I am a federalist. I have always been in favour of a federation of states, I am for a political Europe, a Europe of citizens. A Europe that votes by majority" (Bolkestein 2004: 275).

67. European Council (1986a, 1986b, 1988b).

68. Agence Europe 4991, 8 April 1989. United Kingdom (1990).

69. Taschner (1993: 432–33); European Commission (1989).

70. This satisfied the British government that the directives would "prevent abuse" and that "the overall effect on the United Kingdom and its citizens will be beneficial. The Government [does] not consider that the number of people who might take advantage of the directive, if made, will significantly increase the numbers of persons entering the United Kingdom." UK House of Commons, *Debates*, 8 February 1990, column 1103.

71. Case C-295/90, *European Parliament v Council* (1992), ECR I-4193.

72. O'Leary (1999: 381).

73. O'Leary (1999: 382). In Case C-70/88, *European Parliament v Council* (1990), ECR I-2041, the Court had held that Parliament enjoys *locus standi* since the right to intervene is an essential element in the institutional balance established by the treaties.

74. European Council (1988c: 5).

75. European Parliament (1991b).

76. "Britain Prepares to Sign Social Chapter," *BBC News*, 5 May 1997.

Chapter 3

1. Europe Documents 1611, 10 April 1990, in Wiener (1998). Similarly, Guigou (2004: 161) claims that "the 'Europe of peoples' constructed itself even before political Europe."

2. The concept of "constitutional moment" comes from Ackerman (1991).

3. Spanish memorandum to the other member states, 4 May 1990, discussed at p. 48 in this book.

4. European Council (1990a: 15–16).

5. European Parliament (1988: 62).

6. European Parliament (1990).

7. Resolution of 21 March 1990 and Europe Documents 1611, 10 April 1990, 2, cited in Wiener (1998: 253).

8. Belgian memorandum of 19 March 1990, cited in Laursen and Vanhoonacker (1992: 269–75). R. Corbett (1998: 405n22) notes that the Belgian permanent representative, De Schoutheete, met David Martin while preparing the memorandum. Closa (1992: 1154) claims that the Belgian delegation saw citizenship as a "rather vague notion" and "an objective to be achieved" rather than something to entrench in the treaty. See pp. 74–75 in this book for a discussion of the democratic deficit.

9. Magnette (1999: 128–29).

10. Memorandum of 10 April 1990.

11. Memorandum of 15 May 1990. Habermas (1991) developed the concept of "constitutional patriotism" as a way of reconciling the demands of patriotism and cultural diversity, prompting responses from Walzer (1994), Taylor (1999), and other political theorists about how best to reconcile them.

12. R. Corbett (1998: 286). Agence Europe 5238, 20 April 1990. For Tiersky (2003: xiii), the Kohl-Mitterrand partnership was "central to the future of European integration."

13. SEC (90) 1084. SEC (90) 1015/2.

14. SEC (90) 1015/2.

15. "Martin II Report," 11 July, cited in R. Corbett (1998: 287).

16. Council Document SN 3940/90 of 24 September 1990.

17. Europe Documents 1653, 2 October 1990; Solbes Mira (1991); Handoll (1995: 275–76).

18. Danish memorandum of 4 October, in European Commission (1990: 19).

19. Magnette (1999: 133).

20. The vote was 150 to 13. R. Corbett (1998: 296). Unlike the conventions later convened to write the Charter of Fundamental Rights (see §4.3) and the European Constitution (see §5.2), the assizes left the work of drafting a text to the intergovernmental conference.

21. European Council (1990b).

22. Laursen and Vanhoonacker (1992: 325); European Commission (1991b).

23. The European Commission (1991a: 5) proposal continued, "This obligation entails respect for each person's dignity and the rejection of any form of social marginalization."

24. Mazzucelli (1997: 145). Comparing "the Maastricht negotiations and the Single European Act, the big difference was that in the SEA there were a number of positive aspects that Britain wanted, such as the internal market. However, there was very little that it wanted in the Maastricht negotiations, while its main stance was negative." A former Council secretariat official quoted in Blair (1999).

25. European Parliament (1991c).

26. European Parliament (1991a).

27. Belgian ambassador Philippe de Schoutheete de Tervarent, cited in R. Corbett (1998: 314).

28. "La citoyenneté divise les Douze," *Libération*, 15 May 1991, 32; Guigou (1994: 49); Mazzucelli (1997: 197). The debate in France is discussed in more detail further in the chapter.

29. Cited in Tiersky (2003: 115).

30. Cameron (1992: 65).

31. European Council (1993). The 1994 European Parliament elections were the first in which this voting right was tested. Participation of nonnational European voters in their state of residence varied between 44.11 percent in Ireland, where this right had been available since 1979, to 1.55 percent in Greece. The average turnout of nonnational Union citizens was less than 12 percent, compared with an overall

turnout of 56.5 percent. Only one nonnational candidate, a Dutch citizen living in Germany, was elected in her state of residence, of fifty-three Europeans who stood for election outside their state of citizenship (European Commission 1998b).

32. Stanley Hoffmann in Schoutheete (2000: xvi).
33. European Council (1994).
34. Strudel (2003); Connolly, Day, and Shaw (2006).
35. Weyland (1994).
36. European Council (1995a).
37. European Council (1995a: Art. 5.2); Obwexer (1996).
38. European Council (1996b).
39. R. Corbett, Jacobs, and Shackleton (2005: 309–10).
40. Pierucci (1994); Bignami (2005).
41. Söderman (2005).
42. Anderson, Boer, and Miller (1994: 104); Weiler (1999: prologue). Jessurun d'Oliveira (1995: 82) described EU citizenship as "nearly exclusively a symbolic plaything without substantive content."
43. Standard Eurobarometer 39 (April and March 1993). Germany was divided: while West Germans opposed extending the right to vote (40 percent to 45 percent), East Germans supported doing so (50 percent to 34 percent).
44. Government of Denmark, "Denmark in Europe," reprinted in Laursen and Vanhoonacker (1994: 508).
45. European Council (1992).
46. In fact, 43.3 percent voted to reject the treaty even with the Edinburgh concessions. Turnout increased to 86.5 percent from 83.1 percent in the 1992 referendum. Laursen (1994: 73–78).
47. Case C-159/90, *Society for the Protection of Unborn Children Ireland Ltd. v Grogan* (1991), ECR 4685.
48. When X and her parents went to England for an abortion, they asked the Irish police if a DNA test should be done on the fetus for evidence in the rape trial. The next day, the attorney general obtained an expedited ruling from the Irish High Court that, though X had threatened suicide, only an immediate and inevitable risk to the woman's life justifies abortion. The High Court asserted that member states could abrogate free movement rights on public policy grounds, and thus Ireland could restrict X's freedom of movement on grounds of the abortion prohibition. Case, *Attorney General v. X* (1992), IESC 1; Case, *Attorney General v. X* (1992), 1 IR 1; Cole (1993).
49. Van Wijnbergen (1994: 183–85).
50. Declaration of the High Contracting Parties to the Treaty on European Union.
51. Quoted in van Wijnbergen (1994: 188). In the Irish abortion referendum in November 1992, over 62 percent of voters voted to permit women to travel abroad to obtain an abortion, and 60 percent voted to make information about abortion available in Ireland. Simultaneously, over 65 percent of voters rejected the government's third proposal, which would have restricted abortions to those necessary to

save the woman's life. Cole (1993: 140). In a 2002 referendum, a slim majority of voters rejected the government's renewed attempt to remove a suicide threat as grounds for abortion.

52. Vanhoonacker (1994: 47–48).
53. Keraudren and Dubois (1994: 148).
54. "French Gaullists Will Try to Block Maastricht Pact," *Financial Times*, 19 February 1992, 2.
55. "Les sénateurs souhaitent des garanties supplémentaires sur la citoyenneté européenne," *Le Monde*, 22 May 1992, 8.
56. Clark (1992).
57. Balducci (1994).
58. Hartog (1994: 225–26) presciently writes, "The confined national debate in The Netherlands may be seen to raise critical questions regarding public acceptance of the Treaty. At a time when the European Union is fostering the idea of a European citizenship, do the Dutch citizens still foster a European Union?"
59. The Dutch word for citizen is *burger*, thus the reference to the EU citizen as *unieburger*. Bolkestein (1992).
60. Koliopoulos (1994: 120).
61. Koliopoulos (1994: 116–17).
62. Pauly (1994: 209).
63. European Council (1993). Luxembourg continues to limit the right to vote to EU citizens who resided in Luxembourg for five of the last six years, and the right to stand as a candidate to those who lived in Luxembourg for ten of the last twelve years. European Commission (2003c).
64. Marinho (1994: 236).
65. The Council of State ruled that a constitutional amendment was not strictly necessary, but some of those who had written the Constitution disagreed, arguing that "borders still meant a great deal" in 1978, when the Constitution was written (Gil Ibáñez 1994: 131).
66. The only party to vote against was Herri Batasuna, the separatist Basque party, because Maastricht did not recognize Basque specificity (Gil Ibáñez 1994: 135).
67. Cited in Best (1994: 267).
68. Cited in Koslowski (2000: 128).
69. Betten (1991: 327).
70. Beuter (1994: 88).
71. Cited in Beuter (1994: 102).
72. Bundesverfassungsgericht, 2 BvR 2134/92–2 BvR 2159/92, 12 October 1993. Cited in Weatherill (2003: 686).

Chapter 4

1. Schuman (1963).
2. Declaration to the President of the European Council, 6 December 1995.

3. This is how François Mitterrand defined his "*grand projet*," cited in Tiersky (2003: 115).
4. European Parliament (1998).
5. Jacobs (1993). On the historical evolution of EU social policy, see Johnson (2005) and Schierup, Hansen, and Castles (2006).
6. Regulations 36/63, 73/63, 2/64, 3/64, and 108/64; Schmutzer (1967: 57).
7. Leibfried and Pierson (1995); Hallstein (1972 [1969]: 170).
8. Holloway (1981: 52).
9. Holloway (1981: 53–57).
10. Hantrais (1995); Cardoni (1993).
11. Caporaso (2000: 137); Streeck (1995).
12. Majone (1993: 156); Kravaritou (2000).
13. Ackers and Dwyer (2002: 3).
14. Case C-85/96, *Martínez Sala v Freistaat Bayern* (1998), ECR I-2691.
15. Case C-184/99, *Rudy Grzelczyk v Centre public d'aide sociale d'Ottignies-Louvain-la-Neuve* (2001), ECR I-6193.
16. The Court repeated this reasoning in Case C-224/98, *D'Hoop v Office National d'Emploi* (2002), ECR I-6191.
17. Holloway (1981: 291). For an argument that both the ECJ and the European Court of Human Rights in Strasbourg have extended social rights "well beyond the original intentions of member countries," see Conant (2006).
18. European Commission (2003a; 2004d)
19. Tindemans (1976: 28).
20. "EU Plans to Issue 'Identity Number' for Every Citizen," *The Independent*, 5 February 2001, 1; "Mobilität ist Schlüssel zu Vollbeschäftigung in Europa: EU sollte Zugangsbeschränkungen abbauen und Steuersysteme aufeinander abstimmen," *Financial Times Deutschland*, 23 January 2001, 29; Golynker (2006).
21. European Commission (2006d: 6).
22. European Council (1971, 1972b). Pennings (2005) argues that the rise of European citizenship makes obsolete these various categories, particularly the focus on the active working population. Yet he concludes that changing the coordination principle will be difficult without harmonizing contribution rates among the member states.
23. Veil and European Commission (1998).
24. European Council (1995c, 1995d: Annex 15); Petite (1997).
25. McDonagh (1998: 37); Duff (1997: 155).
26. Corrado (2002: 233).
27. United Kingdom (1996); Best (2002).
28. European Council (1996c: 2).
29. European Council (1996a); Tonra (1997).
30. Neuhold (2002: 34, 28).
31. Corrado (2002: 241).
32. Finland (1995); Antola (2002: 125–26).

33. Marinho (2002: 298).
34. Hug and König (2002).
35. Denmark (1998). A poster for the "No" campaign warned about the coming enlargement: "Welcome to 40 million Poles in the EU" ("Sceptical Danes Eye EU Exit Door: Immigration Fears Are Dominating Denmark's Poll on Amsterdam," *The Guardian*, 23 May 1998, 20).
36. Laffan (1997). Luxembourg—which in Maastricht obtained the transition period for voting rights—opposed introducing qualified majority voting on a range of issues, including citizenship. But it also pushed with Belgium and the Netherlands for a greater EU role in free movement of persons (Kerremans 2002: 50).
37. Jacobson and Ruffer (2006).
38. European Council (1999a: Annex IV).
39. European Council (1999a: Annex IV).
40. Schönlau (2005: 86).
41. European Parliament (1999: preamble T).
42. Schönlau (2005: 110–11).
43. Iñigo Méndez de Vigo, chair of the European Parliament delegation to the Convention, cited in Schönlau (2005: 112); Deloche-Gaudez (2001).
44. European Council (2000: 10).
45. Von Danwitz (2001).
46. Treaty preamble. OJ C 80, 10 March 2001, 6.
47. The treaty was not immediately ratified in Ireland: in a June 2001 referendum, with turnout of barely one in three, 53.6 percent of voters rejected it. In a second referendum held in October 2002, with turnout of 49.5 percent, the "Yes" campaign garnered 62.3 percent.
48. P. Ludlow (2004: 47); European Commission (2001g).
49. European Commission (2001e).
50. European Commission (2003b).
51. European Council (2004b: 78).
52. European Council (2004b: 82).
53. European Council (2004b: 84): "It should be left to the host Member State to decide whether it will grant social assistance during the first three months of residence, or for a longer period in the case of job-seekers, to Union citizens other than those who are workers or self-employed persons or who retain that status or their family members, or maintenance assistance for studies, including vocational training, prior to acquisition of the right of permanent residence, to these same persons."
54. Case C-413/99, *Baumbast* (2002), ECR I-7091.
55. European Commission (2002b: 11).
56. In this book, see chapter 2 for the Tindemans report and chapter 3 for the Maastricht negotiations. Similarly, the White Paper on Governance (European Commission 2001h) argues that national and European representative institutions "must try to connect Europe with its citizens."

57. Spinelli (1966: 11). Similarly, Schmidt (2005: 773) argues that the EU is no longer an elite project supported by a permissive consensus but is not yet a peoples' project grounded in a democratic consensus; Rittberger (2005) convincingly shows that concern with the democratic deficit was present already in the European Coal and Steel Community; and Scully (2005) argues that socialization of members of the European Parliament does not explain the European Parliament's consistently prointegration position.

58. European Commission (1993a, 1997b, 2001f, 2004b); Siedentop (2001); Costa (2004a: 216–17) argues that there "is no European 'people' to which we can attribute an identity comparable to the presupposed *demos* of the individual member states," but there is "a 'people' in a different sense: a 'people' as a group of individuals who find their point of convergence in an order of shared rights and duties."

Chapter 5

1. Quoted in European Economic and Social Committee (2003).
2. Quoted in "Europe Drafting Its Constitution," *New York Times*, 15 June 2003, 1.
3. European Council (2001a), section entitled "The Democratic Challenge Facing Europe."
4. For example, see Moravcsik (2002, 2005).
5. European Council (2001a), sections entitled "The Democratic Challenge Facing Europe" and "The Expectations of Europe's Citizens."
6. European Council (2001a), section entitled "Towards a Constitution for European Citizens."
7. See the discussion of the *propiska* in chapter 1 of this book.
8. European Commission (2001a).
9. European Commission (2001a).
10. Case C-244/04, *Commission v Federal Republic of Germany* (2006).
11. European Commission (2001b).
12. European Commission (2001c: 29). On the benefits of legalization programs for unauthorized migrants, see Maas (2006b). It is possible that one reason for the insistence that candidate states protect minority rights before accession was to discourage emigration. See European Council (2001b); Vachudová (2005: 52–56); and the extended discussion in Maas (2006a).
13. European Commission (2001c); De la Porte (2001: 11).
14. Bolkestein (2000).
15. European Parliament (2001: pt. 35).
16. European Commission (2006e: 13–14).
17. European Commission (2006b: 7–8).
18. Waterbury (2006).
19. Cleveland (2002: 171–81). In the end, citizenship was extended though the U.S. Constitution was not amended.

20. The exclusion of ethnic Russian minorities from citizenship in the Baltic states, for example, struck many as problematic.

21. Jileva (2002).

22. European Commission (2006c: 4). Kochenov (2006) argues that the "second class citizenship" of citizens of the new member states will cause prejudice and division and lead the European Court of Justice (ECJ) to reduce European citizenship rights (223).

23. The Economic and Social Committee (three representatives), the Committee of the Regions (six representatives), the social partners (three representatives), and the European Ombudsman attended as observers. The Laeken Declaration provided for the candidate states to participate in the proceedings but not to block consensus among the member states.

24. European Convention (2002g).

25. European Convention (2002b). "Above all," he added, "we must abandon the dangerous idea that democracy goes without saying and always will."

26. European Convention (2002b).

27. European Convention (2002i).

28. European Convention (2002d: 13).

29. "Europe's leaders have been too snobbish to manufacture patriotism, but we need to inject Europe with a sense of patriotism" (speech by Ambassador Bruton at New York University, 22 March 2006).

30. European Convention (2002a: 5). Longo (2006) argues that a common citizenship is a symbolic and material prerequisite for any constitution (9, 164–68).

31. European Convention (2002e).

32. European Convention (2002c).

33. European Convention (2002f).

34. European Convention (2002h: Art. 5).

35. Jens-Peter Bonde, "Nation States Get Same Status as Bavaria!" *EU Observer*, 5 November 2002. Bonde had been an MEP since 1979. From 1999, he chaired the Parliament's Euroskeptic group EDD (Europe of Democracies and Diversities). After the 2004 election, the EDD merged into the IND/DEM (Independence and Democracy) group, with Bonde remaining chair.

36. Interview with Jan Kavan, Czech member of the Convention, 5 March 2004.

37. European Commission (2004a: 19); the relevant section is entitled "Giving Full Content to European Citizenship."

38. Piris (2006).

39. Quoted in "Europe Drafting Its Constitution," *New York Times*, 15 June 2003, 1.

40. As of December 2006, the Constitution had not yet been approved by the Czech Republic, Denmark, France, Ireland, the Netherlands, Poland, Portugal, Sweden, and the UK. Bulgaria and Romania approved it as part of their accession agreements.

41. Verhofstadt (2006). Similarly, Kölliker (2006) reminds us that "differentiated integration," leading to what is sometimes termed "multispeed Europe" or "variable

138 • Notes to Chapter Five

geometry Europe"—in which some member states integrate ahead of others—has a long history and might lead to a more stable European democracy.

42. European Commission (2005b: 3). Rejecting the idea that the French and Dutch "no" votes constitute a "crisis," one academic observer concludes that they in fact represent the creation of a genuine European public sphere: "We witnessed the birth of the European citizen," writes Van Gunsteren (2006: 411).

43. European Commission (2006c).

44. European Commission (2006f: 4–5).

45. European Commission (2006a: 3).

46. European Parliament (2006).

47. European Commission (2006a: 10).

48. International Convention on Certain Questions relating to the Conflict of Nationality Laws (signed at The Hague, 12 April 1930), Art. 1, reprinted in *American Journal of International Law* 24 (3) (Supplement: Official Documents, July 1930): 192–200.

49. Weil (1991).

50. European Commission (2003d: 30).

51. Though, as noted in §4.3 of this book, some of the Charter's rights were restricted to EU citizens.

52. European Convention (2003).

53. European Economic and Social Committee (2002: point 2.11).

54. European Economic and Social Committee (2003: point 3.4).

55. European Economic and Social Committee (2003: point 4.6).

56. Weiss and Wooldridge (2002: 168).

57. European Council (1999b: pt. 21). For examples of concerns, see UK House of Commons European Standing Committee B, minutes of 1 July 2002, www.publications.parliament.uk/pa/cm200102/cmstand/eurob/st020701/20701s01.htm.

58. European Council (2003b). Absences shorter than six months or for specific reasons (military service, secondment for work purposes, serious illness, maternity, research, or studies) do not interrupt the period of residence.

59. European Council (2003a). See also chapter 2 in this book.

60. European Commission (2000, 2001d, 2004a: 19).

61. Geddes (2000: 58).

62. Preuss et al. (2003); Hansen and Weil (2001).

63. Koopmans et al. (2005: 235).

64. www.aedh.net/petition-million.htm; Dell'Olio (2005). Allowing third-country nationals to acquire European citizenship without acquiring national citizenship is also advocated by many academic authors, such as Becker (2004).

65. Maduro (1998); Conant (2002: 5). See also §1.4 in this book.

66. Citing civil rights and abortion cases, Rosenberg (1991: 342) finds "no evidence that court decisions mobilize supporters of significant social reform, [but] the data suggest that they may mobilize opponents."

67. European Commission (1996b: 14).

68. Verdun (forthcoming). Former Commission president Jacques Santer writes that "currency is also an expression of the identity of a nation, a community, which the citizen can comprehend" (Bolkestein 2004: 240).

69. Interview with Commission official, 6 April 2001. DG Employment and Social Affairs runs the EURES website, intended to be the "European Job Mobility Portal," http://europa.eu/eures/.

70. Finnish prime minister Matti Vanhanen at the plenary session of the European Parliament, 5 July 2006. Russell (2005: 9).

Chapter 6

1. Cited in Gstöhl (2002: ix).
2. Weber (1946: 175).
3. Plato (1992 [circa 380 BCE]: 423b).
4. D. Miller (1995: 185). Kymlicka (1995: 13) uses this formulation to describe Canada, and it is a key theme of Habermas (2006).
5. Borja, Dourthe, and Peugeot (2001); Bonduelle (1997). On political agency and contingency in nationalism, see Hossay (2002).
6. For an analysis of the role of public opinion in restricting immigration to Europe, see Lahav (2003).
7. Front National (2006: 71).
8. Fokas (2000: 75). The church also opposed the common European format for passports and frequently engaged in "Europe-bashing" (Fokas 2006).
9. In 1990 there were 650,000 Portuguese and 614,000 Algerians resident in France (White 1999: 213).
10. Handoll (1995: 269).
11. Suleiman (1995: 67). For a discussion of defenses of particular European nation-states' virtues, see Van Gunsteren (1998); Vincent (2002); and D. Miller (1998). According to D. Miller (2000: 93), "Where domestic protection of citizens' rights is feasible, as it is in all liberal democracies, citizenship is better served by constitutional reform within those states than by the creation of transnational bodies, whose likely effect is to dilute the quality of citizenship by applying uniform criteria in fields where uniformity is neither necessary nor appropriate." G. Morgan (2005: 66–69) questions these assumptions, arguing that there are many different conceivable forms of the "horizontal solidarity" that D. Miller assumes only nation-states promote, while Weale (2005) discusses the end of the "permissive consensus" that allowed European integration to progress. Delanty (2005) argues that an EU based on rights and citizenship does not need "a fully articulated cultural or political identity comparable [to] national societies" but simply a public sphere or discursive space in which people can participate (141).
12. Etzioni (2001); Guéhenno (1993).
13. Habermas (2001: 108).
14. Weber (1946: 175); Shore (2000).

15. Cited in Gstöhl (2002: ix). For the second observation, see R. M. Smith (2003).
16. Debates, 17 January 2006, in European Parliament (2006).
17. Carens (2000); Taylor and Gutmann (1994); Benhabib (2002); D. Miller (2000); Kymlicka (1995).
18. Habermas (1998: 227).
19. Ignatieff (2000).
20. Laible (2002).
21. Hobsbawm (1992: 191).
22. Acton (1948 [1862]).
23. Trudeau (1968); Laforest (1992); McRoberts (1997).
24. Mettler (2002: 231).
25. In contrast to the emphasis in Mettler (2002: 233, 237) on the institutions of federalism as the cause of these "semifeudal" welfare provisions, R. M. Smith (1997) focuses on illiberal and undemocratic racial, class, ethnic, and gender hierarchies to explain exclusionary citizenship in the United States. Both would agree that federalism is often an instrument intended to maintain hierarchies. But how support for federalism relates to attempts to preserve exclusionary hierarchies is unclear, because it is possible to support states' rights for their own sake rather than as a means of entrenching local hierarchies. I thank Rogers Smith for this point.
26. Jefferson (1904: xvi, 163); Kettner (1978). Durand (1979) makes similar points for the EU.
27. R. M. Smith (1997: 5).
28. Warren (1970: 216).
29. Mettler (2002: 231).
30. Bussemaker (1999). See §4.1 in this book.
31. "Quotum voor studiebeurzen in het buitenland," *RNW Nederlands Nieuws*, 21 June 2002, personal e-mail.
32. Heffernan (1998).
33. "Vlaamse gemeenten eisen belasting van Nederlanders," *RNW Nederlands Nieuws*, 8 September 2002, personal e-mail.
34. Thompson (1964: 11).
35. Tully (1995).
36. There were 179,248 non-Spanish EU15 (Austria, Belgium, Denmark, Finland, France, Germany, Greece, Ireland, Italy, Luxembourg, Netherlands, Portugal, Spain, Sweden, UK) citizens officially resident in Spain in 1987, and 677,097 (plus 23,090 citizens of the ten 2004 enlargement countries) in 2005.
37. Naturalization and dual citizenship helps explain why, in 2000, there were 18,500 persons born in France or its overseas territories resident in the Netherlands, but only 12,500 non-Dutch French citizens; 45,000 persons born in Belgium, but only 25,000 non-Dutch Belgian citizens; 124,237 persons born in Germany, but only 54,272 non-Dutch German citizens. Similarly, in the UK in 1999, there were 105,000 people born in Italy, but only 94,000 non-British Italian citizens; 40,000

people born in the Netherlands, but only 32,000 non-British Dutch citizens; 56,000 people born in Spain, but only 47,000 non-British Spanish citizens, and so forth.

38. Cavaco (1993). Braun and Arsene (2006) argue that labor migrants from Italy to Germany are lower-class individuals.

39. Statistical Office of the European Communities (2002: 28).

40. Union citizenship was most familiar in Portugal, Finland, Denmark, Luxembourg, and Ireland, where about 80 percent were familiar with the term. The Luxembourgers knew the exact meaning best with 55 percent, while Union citizenship was the least known in Belgium, Sweden, Greece, and the UK, where more than 40 percent of people interviewed had never heard about it. In these member states, the proportion of those who knew the exact meaning was only about 20 percent. Flash Eurobarometer 133: "10 Years of European Citizenship" (October 2002).

41. Flash Eurobarometer 142: "Convention on the Future of Europe" (June 2003).

42. Flash Eurobarometer 133: "10 Years of European Citizenship" (October 2002); "European citizenship opinion poll." Nevertheless, some prointegrationists have advocated granting EU citizens the right to vote in all elections, including national ones (Wistrich 1991: 89).

43. European Commission (2004a: 5).

44. Standard Eurobarometer 64 (autumn 2005).

45. Standard Eurobarometer 64 (autumn 2005).

46. Standard Eurobarometer 40 (autumn 1993).

47. Favell (forthcoming).

48. Vink (2005: 4) argues that "it is too early to announce the devaluation, or even the end, of national citizenship."

49. A. Corbett (2005); Papatsiba (2006). On the importance of European civic education, see Molinini and Parisotto (1989).

50. Petit (2005).

51. Balibar (2004: 199).

52. European Commission (1993b).

53. European Parliament (1982).

54. European Council (1988a: 143–44).

55. European Council (1988a: 11).

56. European Council (1988a: 143–44).

57. European Council (1988d).

58. Case 242/87, *Commission v Council (Erasmus)* (1989), ECR 1425, 30 May 1989.

59. European Commission (1995b: 10, 44–45).

60. European Commission (2002a).

61. King and Ruiz-Gelices (2003); Papatsiba (2005: 183). According to the PIONEUR project, EU citizens who reside in a member state other than their own have "far more positive attitudes toward the EU than stayers" (Rother and Nebe 2006: 17).

62. European Commission (2005a).

63. European Commission (1995b: 9–10).
64. European Commission (1996a: 1).
65. European Council (2004a).
66. European Commission (2004c: 4).
67. European Commission (1995a).
68. European Commission (1995b: 47).
69. European Council (1995b).
70. European Economic and Social Committee (2005: point 1.3). The title of a European Commission (1997a) report, "Accomplishing Europe through Education and Training," expresses the same goal, as do EU efforts in the field of audiovisual policy (Harrison and Woods 2000).
71. European Commission (1995b: 3).
72. "Realizing the European Higher Education Area," Communiqué of the Conference of Ministers responsible for Higher Education in Berlin, 19 September 2003.
73. Berglund et al. (2006: 54). Díez Medrano (2003) makes a similar argument.

Conclusion

1. "Europe is but one nation, composed of many" (Montesquieu 2002 [1734]).
2. Tocqueville (1994 [1835]: Ch. 14).
3. Grotius (1962 [1625]: Bk. 1, Ch. 1, § XIV).
4. Yashar (2005); Tilly (2005). Cohen (2003) argues that states never distinguished neatly between citizens and noncitizens but have always created "semi-citizenships."
5. Garrett (1998: 822).
6. Deutsch (1957).
7. Wiebe (2002: 20).
8. A. Smith (1995: 46). Some, like La Torre (1998: 457), argue that there *is* a common European historical and cultural identity.
9. Bruter (2005).
10. Soysal (1994); Jacobson (1996).
11. Linklater (1998: 204); Slaughter (2004); Magnette (2005).
12. Spinelli (1966: 7).

Selected Bibliography

Ackerman, Bruce A. 1991. *We the People*. Cambridge, Mass.: Harvard University Press.

Ackers, Louise, and Peter Dwyer. 2002. *Senior Citizenship? Retirement, Migration and Welfare in the European Union*. Bristol, UK: Policy Press.

Acton, John Emerich Edward Dalberg (Lord). 1948 [1862]. *Nationality: Essays on Freedom and Power*, 166–95. Boston: Beacon Press.

Alter, Karen J. 1998. Who Are the "Masters of the Treaty"? European Governments and the European Court of Justice. *International Organization* 52 (1): 121–47.

———. 2001. *Establishing the Supremacy of European Law: The Making of an International Rule of Law in Europe*. Oxford: Oxford University Press.

Anderson, Malcolm, Monica den Boer, and Gary Miller. 1994. European Citizenship and Cooperation in Justice and Home Affairs. In *Maastricht and Beyond: Building the European Union*, ed. Andrew Duff, John Pinder, and Roy Pryce, 104–22. London: Routledge.

Antola, Esko. 2002. Finland: From Cautious to Hard-Core Member. In *The Amsterdam Treaty: National Preference Formation, Interstate Bargaining and Outcome*, ed. Finn Laursen, 121–38. Odense, Denmark: Odense University Press.

Arfé, Gaetano. 1986. *L'Idea d'Europa nel movimento di liberazione, 1940–1945*. Rome: Bonacci.

Aristotle. 1984 [circa 330 BCE]. *The Politics*. Translated by Carnes Lord. Chicago: University of Chicago Press.

Arnold, Hans. 1999. *Europa neu denken: Warum und wie weiter Einigung?* Bonn, Germany: Bouvier.

Aron, Raymond. 1974. Is Multinational Citizenship Possible? *Social Research* 41 (4): 638–55.

Baier, Stephan. 2000. *Welches Europa? Überstaat oder Rechtsgemeinschaft*. Vienna, Austria: Amalthea.

Balducci, Massimo. 1994. Italy and the Ratification of the Maastricht Treaty. In *The Ratification of the Maastricht Treaty: Issues, Debates and Future Implications*, ed. Finn Laursen and Sophie Vanhoonacker, 195–201. Dordrecht, The Netherlands: Martinus Nijhoff.

Balibar, Étienne. 1988. Propositions sur la citoyenneté. In *La Citoyenneté et les changements de structures sociale et nationale de la population française*, ed. Catherine Wihtol de Wenden, 221–34. Paris: Edilig/Fondation Diderot.

———. 2004. *We, the People of Europe? Reflections on Transnational Citizenship*. Translated by James Swenson. Princeton, N.J.: Princeton University Press.

Barbalet, J. M. 1988. *Citizenship: Rights, Struggle and Class Equality*. Milton Keynes, UK: Open University Press.

Becker, Michael A. 2004. Managing Diversity in the European Union: Inclusive European Citizenship and Third-Country Nationals. *Yale Human Rights & Development Law Journal* 7:132–52.

Bellamy, Richard, Dario Castiglione, and Jo Shaw, ed. 2006. *Making European Citizens: Civic Inclusion in a Transnational Context*. New York: Palgrave Macmillan.

Benhabib, Seyla. 2002. *The Claims of Culture: Equality and Diversity in the Global Era*. Princeton, N.J.: Princeton University Press.

———. 2004. *The Rights of Others: Aliens, Residents and Citizens*. Cambridge: Cambridge University Press.

———. 2006. *Another Cosmopolitanism: Hospitality, Sovereignty, and Democratic Iterations*. New York: Oxford University Press.

Bentham, Jeremy. 1843. Anarchical Fallacies. In *The Works of Jeremy Bentham, Volume II*, 489–534. Edinburgh: William Tait.

Berglund, Sten, Joakim Ekman, Henri Vogt, and Frank H. Aarebrot. 2006. *The Making of the European Union: Foundations, Institutions and Future Trends*. Cheltenham, UK: Edward Elgar.

Best, Edward. 1994. The United Kingdom and the Ratification of the Maastricht Treaty. In *The Ratification of the Maastricht Treaty: Issues, Debates and Future Implications*, ed. Finn Laursen and Sophie Vanhoonacker, 245–78. Dordrecht, The Netherlands: Martinus Nijhoff.

———. 2002. The United Kingdom: From Isolation towards Influence? In *The Amsterdam Treaty: National Preference Formation, Interstate Bargaining and Outcome*, ed. Finn Laursen, 359–78. Odense, Denmark: Odense University Press.

Besussi, Antonella, and Luisa Leonini. 2001. *L'Europa tra società e politica: Integrazione europea e nuove cittadinanze*. Milan, Italy: Guerini studio.

Betten, Lammy. 1991. The Free Movement of Persons. In *German Unification in European Perspective*, ed. Wolfgang Heisenberg, 317–41. London: Brassey's.

Beuter, Rita. 1994. Germany and the Ratification of the Maastricht Treaty. In *The Ratification of the Maastricht Treaty: Issues, Debates and Future Implications*, ed. Finn

Laursen and Sophie Vanhoonacker, 87–112. Dordrecht, The Netherlands: Martinus Nijhoff.

Bignami, Francesca. 2005. Creating European Rights: National Values and Supranational Interests. *Columbia Journal of European Law* 11:241–353.

Bitsch, Marie-Thérèse, ed. 1997. *Jalons pour une histoire du Conseil de l'Europe.* Berne, Switzerland: Peter Lang.

Blair, Alasdair. 1999. *Dealing With Europe: Britain and the Negotiation of the Maastricht Treaty.* Aldershot, UK: Ashgate.

Bok, Derek Curtis. 1955. *The First Three Years of the Schuman Plan.* Princeton, N.J.: Princeton University Press.

Bolkestein, Frits. 1992. Een unieburger vindt men alleen bij McDonald's. *Internationale Spectator* 46 (9): 511–16.

———. 2000. De uitbreiding en het effect ervan op de vrijheden van de interne markt. Beraad voor de bouw, The Hague, The Netherlands.

———. 2004. *The Limits of Europe.* Tielt, Belgium: Lannoo.

Bonduelle, Bruno. 1997. *Aux armes, Européens!* Paris: France-Empire.

Bonnet, René. 1969. L'Europe du travail est-elle réalisée? *Droit Social* 3.

Booth, Heather. 1992. *The Migration Process in Britain and West Germany: Two Demographic Studies of Migrant Populations.* Aldershot, UK: Avebury.

Borja, Jordi, Geneviève Dourthe, and Valérie Peugeot. 2001. *La Ciudadanía Europea.* Barcelona, Spain: Ediciones Península.

Braun, Michael, and Camelia Arsene. 2006. The Demographics of Movers and Stayers in the European Union. PIONEUR conference, Florence, 10 March. www.obets.ua.es/pioneur/resultados.php.

Bru, Carlos Maria. 1994. *La Ciudadanía Europea.* Madrid: Editorial Sistema.

Brubaker, Rogers. 1992. *Citizenship and Nationhood in France and Germany.* Cambridge, Mass.: Harvard University Press.

Bruter, Michael. 2005. *Citizens of Europe? The Emergence of a Mass European Identity.* New York: Palgrave Macmillan.

Burley, Anne-Marie, and Walter Mattli. 1993. Europe before the Court: A Political Theory of Legal Integration. *International Organization* 47 (1): 41–76.

Bussemaker, Jet, ed. 1999. *Citizenship and Welfare State Reform in Europe.* London: Routledge.

Cameron, David R. 1992. The 1992 Initiative: Causes and Consequences. In *Euro-Politics: Institutions and Policymaking in the New European Community,* ed. Alberta M. Sbragia, 23–74. Washington, D.C.: Brookings Institution.

Caporaso, James A. 2000. *The European Union: Dilemmas of Regional Integration.* Boulder, Colo.: Westview Press.

———. 2002. The European Union and the Democratic Deficit: The Emergence of an International Rechtsstaat? In *Federalism Doomed? European Federalism between Integration and Separation,* ed. Andreas Heinemann-Grüder, 83–99. New York: Berghahn Books.

Cardoni, Giovanni. 1993. Libera circolazione dei lavoratori e sicurezza sociale nella Comunità Europea. In *Il Sistema Previdenziale Europeo*, ed. Roberto Pessi, 211–39. Padua, Italy: CEDAM.

Carens, Joseph H. 2000. *Culture, Citizenship, and Community: A Contextual Exploration of Justice as Evenhandedness*. Oxford: Oxford University Press.

Cavaco, Carminda. 1993. A Place in the Sun: Return Migration and Rural Change in Portugal. In *Mass Migrations in Europe: The Legacy and the Future*, ed. Russell King, 174–94. London: Belhaven Press.

Churchill, Winston. 1949. *The Sinews of Peace: Post-War Speeches*. Boston: Houghton Mifflin.

Clark, Alan. 1992. François Mitterand and the Idea of Europe. In *The Idea of Europe: Problems of National and Transnational Identity*, ed. Brian Nelson, David Roberts, and Walter Veit, 152–70. Oxford: Berg.

Cleveland, Sarah H. 2002. Powers Inherent in Sovereignty: Indians, Aliens, Territories, and the Nineteenth Century Origins of Plenary Power over Foreign Affairs. *Texas Law Review* 81 (1): 1–284.

Closa, Carlos. 1992. The Concept of Citizenship in the Treaty on European Union. *Common Market Law Review* 29:1137–69.

Cohen, Elizabeth. 2003. The Myth of Full Citizenship: A Comparative Study of Semi-Citizenship in Democratic Polities. PhD diss., Yale University, New Haven, Conn.

Cole, David. 1993. Going to England: Irish Abortion Law and the European Community. *Hastings International and Comparative Law Review* 17:113–42.

Conant, Lisa. 2002. *Justice Contained: Law and Politics in the European Union*. Ithaca, N.Y.: Cornell University Press.

———. 2006. Individuals, Courts, and the Development of European Social Rights. *Comparative Political Studies* 39 (1): 76–100.

Confederazione Italiana Sindicati Lavoratori. 1959. *La politica sociale della Comunità Economica Europea: Atti del terzo convegno di studi di economia e politica del lavoro*. Rome: Confederazione Italiana Sindicati Lavoratori.

Connolly, Anthea, Stephen Day, and Jo Shaw. 2006. The Contested Case of EU Electoral Rights. In *Making European Citizens: Civic Inclusion in a Transnational Context*, ed. Richard Bellamy, Dario Castiglione, and Jo Shaw, 31–55. New York: Palgrave Macmillan.

Corbett, Anne. 2005. *Universities and the Europe of Knowledge: Ideas, Institutions, and Policy Entrepreneurship in European Union Higher Education Policy, 1955–2005*. New York: Palgrave Macmillan.

Corbett, Richard. 1998. *The European Parliament's Role in Closer EU Integration*. Houndmills, UK: Macmillan.

Corbett, Richard, Francis Jacobs, and Michael Shackleton. 2005. *The European Parliament*. 6th ed. London: John Harper Publishing.

Corrado, Laura. 2002. Italy: From the "Hard Core" to Flexible Integration. In *The Amsterdam Treaty: National Preference Formation, Interstate Bargaining and Outcome*, ed. Finn Laursen, 225–54. Odense, Denmark: Odense University Press.

Costa, Pietro. 2004a. From National to European Citizenship: A Historical Comparison. In *Lineages of European Citizenship: Rights, Belonging and Participation in Eleven Nation-States*, ed. Richard Bellamy, Dario Castiglione, and Emilio Santoro, 207–26. New York: Palgrave Macmillan.

———. 2004b. From National to European Citizenship: A Historical Comparison. In *Lineages of European Citizenship: Rights, Belonging, and Participation in Eleven Nation-States*, ed. Richard Bellamy, Dario Castiglione, and Emilio Santoro, x, 235. New York: Palgrave.

Council of Europe. 1953. *First Joint Meeting of the Members of the Consultative Assembly of the Council of Europe and of the Members of the Common Assembly of the European Community of Coal and Steel, Official Report of the Debate, 22 June 1953*. Strasbourg, France: Consultative Assembly.

de Haan, Ido. 1993. *Zelfbestuur en staatsbeheer: het politieke debat over burgerschap en rechtsstaat in de twintigste eeuw*. Amsterdam: Amsterdam University Press.

Dehousse, Renaud. 1998. *The European Court of Justice: The Politics of Judicial Integration*. New York: St. Martin's Press.

Delanty, Gerard. 2005. The Quest for European Identity. In *Making the European Polity: Reflexive Integration in the EU*, ed. Erik Oddvar Eriksen, 127–42. London: Routledge.

De la Porte, Caroline. 2001. De inzet van de sociale dimensie van de uitbreiding en de toekomstverwachtingen. *Belgisch Tijdschrift voor Sociale Zekerheid* 43:275–95.

Delegazione PDS del Gruppo del PSE al Parlamento Europeo. 1995. *Idee programmatiche per l'Europa*. Rome: Sapere 2000.

Dell'Olio, Fiorella. 2005. *The Europeanization of Citizenship: Between the Ideology of Nationality, Immigration, and European Identity*. Aldershot, UK: Ashgate.

Deloche-Gaudez, Florence. 2001. *The Convention on a Charter of Fundamental Rights: A Method for the Future?* Paris: Fondation Notre Europe.

Denmark. 1998. *Amsterdam-traktaten og Danmark: de danske forbehold*. Copenhagen, Denmark: Ministry of Foreign Affairs.

Deutsch, Karl Wolfgang. 1957. *Political Community and the North Atlantic Area: International Organization in the Light of Historical Experience*. Princeton, N.J.: Princeton University Press.

Diebold, William, Jr. 1959. *The Schuman Plan: A Study in Economic Cooperation 1950–1959*. New York: Council on Foreign Relations.

Díez Medrano, Juan. 2003. *Framing Europe: Attitudes to European Integration in Germany, Spain, and the United Kingdom*. Princeton, N.J.: Princeton University Press.

Dinan, Desmond. 2005. *Ever Closer Union: An Introduction to European Integration*. 3rd ed. Boulder, Colo.: Lynne Rienner.

Dollat, Patrick. 1998. *Libre circulation des personnes et citoyenneté européenne: enjeux et perspectives*. Brussels, Belgium: Bruylant.

Dowty, Alan. 1987. *Closed Borders: The Contemporary Assault on Freedom of Movement*. New Haven, Conn.: Yale University Press.

Duff, Andrew, ed. 1997. *The Treaty of Amsterdam: Text and Commentary*. London: Federal Trust/Sweet and Maxwell.

Dumoulin, Michel. 1988. La Belgique et les débuts du Plan Schuman. mai 1950—février 1952. In *Die Anfänge des Schuman-Plans, 1950/51*, ed. Klaus Schwabe, 271–84. Baden-Baden, Germany: Nomos.

Durand, Andrew. 1979. European Citizenship. *European Law Review* 4 (1): 3–14.

Eder, Klaus, and Bernhard Giesen. 2001. *European Citizenship: Between National Legacies and Postnational Projects*. New York: Oxford University Press.

Egan, Michelle P. 2001. *Constructing a European Market: Standards, Regulations, and Governance*. Oxford: Oxford University Press.

Elkins, David J. 1995. *Beyond Sovereignty: Territory and Political Economy in the Twenty-first Century*. Toronto: University of Toronto Press.

Etzioni, Amitai. 2001. *Political Unification Revisited: On Building Supranational Communities*. Lanham, Md.: Lexington Books.

European Coal and Steel Community. 1953. *Recueil Statistique de la Communauté Européenne du Charbon et de l'Acier*. Luxembourg: Haute Autorité.

———. 1954a. *Bulletin from the European Community for Coal and Steel*. Luxembourg: Publications Service of the European Coal and Steel Community.

———. 1954b. Rapport sur l'application du traité instituant la Communauté européenne du charbon et de l'acier pendant la période du 1er Janvier au 30 avril 1954. Luxembourg: Assemblée Commune.

———. 1954c. *Second General Report on the Activities of the Community*. Luxembourg: Publications Service of the European Coal and Steel Community.

———. 1955. Inventaire des organismes existants dans les domaines visés par la résolution de Messine. Comité intergouvernemental créé par la Conférence de Messine.

———. 1956. Rapport des Chefs de Délégation aux Ministres des Affaires Étrangères. Comité intergouvernemental créé par la Conférence de Messine.

———. 1957. Rapport de M. Bertrand sur la migration et la libre circulation des travailleurs dans la CECA. Rapport no.5. Luxembourg: Assemblée Commune.

———. 1958. *Le Traité C.E.C.A. devant les Parlements Nationaux*. Luxembourg: Assemblée Commune.

European Commission. 1958–. *Exposé sur l'évolution de la situation sociale dans la Communauté*. Brussels, Belgium: Services des publications des Communautés européennes.

———. 1966. Portée des règlements communautaires sur la sécurité sociale des travailleurs migrants. Commission administrative pour la sécurité sociale des travailleurs migrants.

———. 1975. Towards European Citizenship. Supplement 7/75—Bull. EC.

———. 1979. Proposal for a Council Directive on a Right of Residence for Nationals of Member States in the Territory of Another Member State. COM(79) 215.

———. 1980. Amended Proposal for a Council Directive on a Right of Residence for Nationals of Member States in the Territory of Another Member State. COM(80) 358.

———. 1982. *Freedom of Movement for Persons in the European Community*. Luxembourg: Office for Official Publications of the European Communities.
———. 1985. Completing the Internal Market. White Paper. COM(85) 310.
———. 1988. *Social Europe: The Social Dimension of the Internal Market. Interim Report of the Interdeparmental Working Party. Special Edition*. Luxembourg.
———. 1989. Proposal for a Council Directive on the Right of Residence. COM(89) 275.
———. 1990. Commission Opinion of 21 October 1990 on the Proposal for Amendment of the Treaty Establishing the European Economic Community with a View to Political Union. COM(90) 600.
———. 1991a. Initial Contribution by the Commission to the Intergovernmental Conference on Political Union. Composite Working Paper of 15 May. SEC(91) 500.
———. 1991b. Union Citizenship. Supplement 2/91—Bull. EC.
———. 1993a. First Report on Citizenship of the Union. COM(93) 702.
———. 1993b. Report from the Commission to the Council, the European Parliament and the Economic and Social Committee—EC Education and Training Programmes 1986–1992—Results and Achievements: An Overview. COM(93) 151.
———. 1994. Proposal for a Council Directive Laying Down Detailed Arrangements for the Exercise of the Right to Vote and to Stand as a Candidate to Municipal Elections by Citizens of the Union Residing in a Member State of Which They Are Not Nationals. COM(94) 38.
———. 1995a. Report from the Commission to the Council LINGUA Programme—1994 Activity Report. COM(95) 458.
———. 1995b. White Paper on Education and Training. Teaching and Learning: Towards the Learning Society. COM(95) 590.
———. 1996a. Education—Training—Research—The Obstacles to Transnational Mobility—Green Paper. COM(96) 462.
———. 1996b. *Fourth Report from the Commission to the Council, the European Parliament and the Economic and Social Committee on the Application of the Community Charter of the Fundamental Social Rights of Workers*. Luxembourg: Office for Official Publications of the European Communities.
———. 1997a. Accomplishing Europe through Education and Training.
———. 1997b. Second Report on Citizenship of the Union. COM(97) 230.
———. 1998a. *Report of the High Level Panel on the Free Movement of Persons (Veil report)*. Luxembourg: Office for Official Publication of the European Communities.
———. 1998b. Report on the Application of Directive 93/109/EC. Voting Rights of EU Citizens Living in a Member State of Which They Are Not Nationals in European Parliament Elections. COM(97) 731.
———. 2000. A Community Immigration Policy. COM(2000) 757.
———. 2001a. Commission Proposes Transition Periods for Purchase of Real Estate in Candidate Countries. IP/01/645.

———. 2001b. Enlargement: Commission Proposes Flexible Transitional Arrangements for the Free Movement of Workers. IP/01/561.
———. 2001c. The Free Movement of Workers in the Context of Enlargement.
———. 2001d. An Open Method of Coordination for the Community Immigration Policy. COM(2001) 387.
———. 2001e. Proposal for a European Parliament and Council Directive on the Right of Citizens of the Union and Their Family Members to Move and Reside Freely within the Territory of the Member States. COM(2001) 257.
———. 2001f. Third Report on Citizenship of the Union. COM(2001) 506.
———. 2001g. The Treaty of Nice: A Comprehensive Guide.
———. 2001h. European Governance. A White Paper. COM(2001) 428.
———. 2002a. "One Million Erasmus Students": A European Success Story.
———. 2002b. A Project for the European Union. COM(2002) 247.
———. 2003a. Communication from the Commission concerning the Introduction of a European Health Insurance Card. COM(2003) 73.
———. 2003b. Effects of the Entry into Force of the Nice Treaty on Current Legislative Procedures. COM(2003) 61.
———. 2003c. Granting a Derogation Pursuant to Article 19(2) of the EC Treaty, Presented under Article 14(3) of Directive 93/109/EC on the Right to Vote and to Stand as a Candidate in Elections to the European Parliament. COM(2003) 31.
———. 2003d. Immigration, Integration and Employment. COM(2003) 336.
———. 2004a. Building Our Common Future: Policy Challenges and Budgetary Means of the Enlarged Union 2007–2013. COM(2004) 101.
———. 2004b. Fourth Report on Citizenship of the Union. COM(2004) 695.
———. 2004c. Making Citizenship Work: Fostering European Culture and Diversity through Programmes for Youth, Culture, Audiovisual and Civic Participation. COM(2004) 154.
———. 2004d. More Europe in Your Pocket—the European Health Insurance Card.
———. 2005a. Another Successful Year for Erasmus: Student and Teacher Mobility Rose by Almost 10% in 2003/2004. IP/05/190.
———. 2005b. The Commission's Contribution to the Period of Reflection and Beyond: Plan-D for Democracy, Dialogue and Debate. COM(2005) 494.
———. 2006a. A Citizens' Agenda: Delivering Results for Europe. COM(2006) 211.
———. 2006b. Enlargement, Two Years After—An Economic Success. COM(2006) 200.
———. 2006c. The Period of Reflection and Plan D. COM(2006) 212.
———. 2006d. Proposal for a Regulation Laying Down the Procedure for Implementing Regulation. EC. No 883/2004 on the Coordination of Social Security Systems. COM(2006) 16.
———. 2006e. Report on the Functioning of the Transitional Arrangements Set Out in the 2003 Accession Treaty (period 1 May 2004–30 April 2006). COM(2006) 48.
———. 2006f. White Paper on a European Communication Policy. COM(2006) 35.

European Convention. 2002a. Communication from the Commission, forwarded by Mr. Barnier and Mr. Vitorino, Members of the Convention: "Communication from the Commission to the Convention, 22 May 2002: A Project for the European Union." CONV 229/02.

———. 2002b. Contribution by H. A. F. M. O. van Mierlo, Dutch Government Representative, 21 March.

———. 2002c. Contribution by Josep Borrel, Member of the Convention, Carlos Carnero and Diego López Garrido, Alternate Members of the Convention: "A European Constitution for Peace, Solidarity and Human rights." CONV 455/02.

———. 2002d. Contribution from Mr. John Bruton, Member of the Convention. CONV 27/02.

———. 2002e. Contribution Submitted by Mr. Eduardo Zaplana Hernandez-Soro, Mr. Jos Chabert, Mr. Manfred Dammeyer, Mr. Patrick Dewael, Ms. Claude du Granrut and Mr. Claudio Martini, Observers of the Committee of the Regions and Members of the Convention. CONV 195/02.

———. 2002f. Final Text Adopted by the European Youth Convention. CONV 205/02.

———. 2002g. Introductory Speech by President V. Giscard D'Estaing. 26 February.

———. 2002h. Preliminary Draft Constitutional Treaty. CONV 369/02.

———. 2002i. Speech by John Bruton, 22 March.

———. 2003. Contribution from Ms. Pervenche Berès: "Which Citizenship for the Union?" CONV 576/03.

European Council. 1961. Regulation 15/61 of 16 August 1961 on the First Measures for the Realization of Free Movement of Workers within the Community.

———. 1964a. Directive 64/221 of 25 February 1964 on the Co-ordination of Special Measures concerning the Movement and Residence of Foreign Nationals Which Are Justified on Grounds of Public Policy, Public Security or Public Health.

———. 1964b. Directive 64/240 of 25 March 1964 on the Abolition of Restrictions on the Movement and Residence of Member States' Workers and Their Families within the Community.

———. 1964c. Regulation 38/64 of 25 March 1964 on the Free Movement of Workers within the Community.

———. 1968a. Directive 68/360 of 15 October 1968 on the Abolition of Restrictions on Movement and Residence within the Community for Workers of Member States and Their Families.

———. 1968b. Regulation 1612/68 of 15 October 1968 on Freedom of Movement for Workers within the Community.

———. 1971. Regulation 1408/71 of 14 June 1971 on the Application of Social Security Schemes to Employed Persons and Their Families Moving within the Community.

———. 1972a. First Summit Conference of the Enlarged Community, 19–21 October. Bull. EC 11–72.

———. 1972b. Regulation 574/72 of 21 March 1972 Fixing the Procedure for Implementing Regulation 1408/71 on the Coordination of Social Security Schemes for Persons Moving within the Community.
———. 1973. Document on the European Identity Published by the Nine Foreign Ministers, Copenhagen European Council, 14 December.
———. 1974. Summit Conference of Heads of State or Government, 9 and 10 December. Bull. EC 12–74.
———. 1981. Resolution of the Representatives of the Governments of the Member States of the European Communities, meeting within the council of 23 June 1981. OJ C 241, 19 September, p. 1.
———. 1985a. A People's Europe. Adonnino Report. Supplement 7/85—Bull. EC.
———. 1985b. Report of the Ad Hoc Committee for Institutional Affairs to the European Council. Dooge Report.
———. 1986a. Presidency Conclusions, London European Council, 5 and 6 December.
———. 1986b. Presidency Conclusions, The Hague European Council, 26 and 27 June.
———. 1987. Decision 87/327 of 15 June 1987 Adopting the European Community Action Scheme for the Mobility of University Students. Erasmus.
———. 1988a. *European Educational Policy Statements*. 3rd ed. Luxembourg: Office for Official Publications of the European Communities.
———. 1988b. Presidency Conclusions, Hanover European Council, 27 and 28 June.
———. 1988c. Presidency Conclusions, Rhodes European Council, 2 and 3 December.
———. 1988d. Resolution of the Council and the Ministers of Education Meeting within the Council on the European Dimension in Education. 24 May.
———. 1989. Decision of 28 July 1989 Establishing an Action Programme to Promote Foreign Language Competence in the European Community. Lingua.
———. 1990a. Presidency Conclusions, Dublin European Council, 25 and 26 April.
———. 1990b. Presidency Conclusions, Rome European Council, 14 and 15 December.
———. 1992. Decision of the Heads of State and Government, Meeting within the European Council, concerning Certain Problems Raised by Denmark on the Treaty on European Union.
———. 1993. Directive 93/109 of 6 December 1993 Laying Down Detailed Arrangements for the Exercise of the Right to Vote and Stand as a Candidate in Elections to the European Parliament for Citizens of the Union Residing in a Member State of Which They Are Not Nationals.
———. 1994. Directive 94/80/EC of 19 December 1994 Laying Down Detailed arrangements for the Exercise of the Right to Vote and to Stand as a Candidate in Municipal Elections by Citizens of the Union Residing in a Member State of Which They Are Not Nationals.
———. 1995a. Decision 95/553/EC of the Representatives of the Governments of the Member States Meeting within the Council of 19 December 1995 regarding Protection for Citizens of the European Union by Diplomatic and Consular Representations.

———. 1995b. Parliament and Council Decision 819/95/EC of 14 March 1995 Establishing the Community Action Programme "Socrates."
———. 1995c. Presidency Conclusions, Cannes European Council, 26 and 27 June.
———. 1995d. Presidency Conclusions, Madrid European Council, 15 and 16 December.
———. 1996a. Contribution sur la citoyenneté de l'Union présentée par les délégations autrichienne et italienne au Groupe des représentants à la Conférence intergouvernementale. 3 October. CONF 3941/96.
———. 1996b. Decision 96/409/CSFP of the Representatives of the Governments of the Member States, Meeting within the Council of 25 June 1996 on the Establishment of an Emergency Travel Document.
———. 1996c. Presidency Introductory Note on Citizenship. 26 July. CONF 3878/96.
———. 1999a. Presidency Conclusions, Cologne European Council, 3 and 4 June.
———. 1999b. Presidency Conclusions, Tampere European Council, 15 and 16 October.
———. 2000. Submission of the Permanent Forum of Civil Society, Draft European Citizen's Charter. Charter 4104/00, Contrib. 4, 7 January.
———. 2001a. The Future of the European Union: Laeken Declaration.
———. 2001b. Regulation 539/2001 of 15 March 2001 Listing the Third Countries Whose Nationals Must Be in Possession of Visas When Crossing the External Borders and Those Whose Nationals Are Exempt from That Requirement.
———. 2003a. Council Directive 2003/86/EC of 22 September 2003 on the Right to Family Reunification. OJ L 251, 3 October.
———. 2003b. Directive 2003/109/EC of 25 November 2003 Concerning the Status of Third-Country Nationals Who Are Long-Term Residents. OJ L 16, 23 January 2004.
———. 2004a. Decision 2004/100 of 26 January 2004 Establishing a Community Action Programme to Promote Active European Citizenship (Civic Participation).
———. 2004b. Directive 2004/38/EC of the European Parliament and of the Council of 29 April 2004 on the Right of Citizens of the Union and Their Family Members to Move and Reside Freely within the Territory of the Member States Amending Regulation. EEC. No. 1612/68 and Repealing Directives 64/221/EEC, 68/360/EEC, 72/194/EEC, 73/148/EEC, 75/34/EEC, 75/35/EEC, 90/364/EEC, 90/365/EEC, and 93/96/EEC. OJ L 158, 30 April, p. 77.
European Economic and Social Committee. 2002. Resolution Addressed to the European Convention. CES 1069/2002.
———. 2003. Opinion of the European Economic and Social Committee on Access to European Union Citizenship. CES 593/2003.
———. 2005. Opinion of the European Economic and Social Committee on the Proposal for a Decision of the European Parliament and of the Council Creating the Youth in Action Programme for the Period 2007–2013 (COM [2004] 471 final—2004/0152 [COD]). CES 253/2005.

European Parliament. 1960. Rapport sur le règlement relatif aux premières mesures pour la réalisation de la libre circulation des travailleurs dans la Communauté (Rubinacci report). Document 67.

———. 1977. Resolution on the Granting of Special Rights to the Citizens of the European Community (16 November). OJ C 299, 12 December.

———. 1979. Proceedings of the Round Table on "Special Rights and a Charter of the Rights of the Citizens of the European Community" and Related Documents.

———. 1982. Resolution on a Community Programme in the Field of Education. OJ C 87, 5 April, p. 90.

———. 1983. Resolution on the Right of Citizens of a Member State Residing in a Member State Other than Their Own to Stand for and Vote in Local Elections (Macciocchi Report). OJ C 184, 11 July, p. 28.

———. 1984. Resolution on the Draft Treaty Establishing the European Union. OJ C 77, 19 March, p. 53.

———. 1988. Resolution on the Results Obtained from Implementation of the Single Act (Graziani Report). OJ C 309, 27 October.

———. 1990. Resolution on the Intergovernmental Conference in the Context of the Parliament's Strategy for European Union (14 March). OJ C 96, 17 April, p. 114.

———. 1991a. Report of the Committee on Institutional Affairs of the European Parliament on Union Citizenship (Bindi Report). Document A3-0300/91, PE 153.099/fin, 6 November.

———. 1991b. Resolution on the Social Dimension of the Single Market (15 March). OJ C 96, 17 March, p. 61.

———. 1991c. Resolution on Union Citizenship (14 June). OJ C 183, 15 July, p. 473.

———. 1998. Resolution on the Second Commission Report on Citizenship of the Union (2 July). OJ C 226, 20 July, p. 61.

———. 1999. Resolution on the Establishment of the Charter of Fundamental Rights (16 September). OJ 2000 C 54/04, 25 February, p. 93.

———. 2001. Resolution on the Enlargement of the European Union (5 September) OJ 2001 C 72, 21 March, p. 160.

———. 2006. Discours du Président Barroso au Parlement européen en vue du Conseil européen des 15 et 16 juin 2006. 14 June. SPEECH/06/373.

Evans, Andrew C. 1982. European Citizenship. *Modern Law Review* 45: 497–515.

———. 1984. European Citizenship: A Novel Concept in EEC Law. *American Journal of Comparative Law* 32 (4): 679–715.

Everson, Michelle. 1995. The Legacy of the Market Citizen. In *New Legal Dynamics of European Union*, ed. Jo Shaw and Gillian More, 73–89. Oxford: Oxford University Press.

Falk, Richard. 1994. The Making of Global Citizenship. In *The Condition of Citizenship*, ed. Bart van Steenbergen, 127–40. London: Sage.

Favell, Adrian. forthcoming. *Eurostars and Eurocities: Free Moving Urban Professionals in an Integrating Europe*. Oxford: Blackwell.

Feldstein, Helen S. 1967. A Study of Transaction and Political Integration: Transnational Labour Flow within the European Economic Community. *Journal of Common Market Studies* 6 (1): 24–55.

Ferreira do Amaral, João. 1993. Portugal and the Free Movement of Labour. In *Portugal and EC Membership Evaluated*, ed. José da Silva Lopes, 240–46. London: Pinter Publishers.

Finland. 1995. Memorandum Concerning Finnish Points of View with Regard to the 1996 Intergovernmental Conference of the European Union. Helsinki, 18 September.

Fischer, Peter A., and Thomas Straubhaar. 1996. *Migration and Economic Integration in the Nordic Common Labour Market*. Copenhagen, Denmark: Nordic Council of Ministers.

Fokas, Efterpe. 2000. Greek Orthodoxy and European Identity. In *Contemporary Greece and Europe*, ed. Achilleas Mitsos and Elias Mossialos, 275–300. Aldershot, UK: Ashgate.

———. 2006. Greece: Religion, Nation, and Membership in the European Union. In *Citizenship and Ethnic Conflict: Challenging the Nation-State*, ed. Haldun Gülalp, 39–60. New York: Routledge.

Front National. 2006. *Pour un avenir français: Le programme de gouvernement du Front national*. www.frontnational.com/pdf/programme.pdf.

Gabriel, Christina, and Laura Macdonald. 2006. Regional Integration in North America and Europe: Lessons about Civil Rights and Equal Citizenship. International Studies Association, San Diego.

Gallup International. 1963. Public Opinion and the European Community. *Journal of Common Market Studies* 2 (2): 101–26.

Garrett, Geoffrey. 1995. The Politics of Legal Integration in the European Union. *International Organization* 49 (1): 171–81.

———. 1998. Global Markets and National Politics: Collision Course or Virtuous Circle? *International Organization* 52 (4): 787–824.

Garth, Bryant. 1985. Migrant Workers and Rights of Mobility in the European Communities and the United States. In *Integration through Law: Europe and the American Federal Experience, volume 3: Forces and Potential for a European Identity*, ed. Mauro Cappelletti, Monica Seccombe, and Joseph Weiler, 85–163. Berlin: Walter de Gruyter.

Geddes, Andrew. 2000. *Immigration and European Integration: Towards Fortress Europe?* Manchester, UK: Manchester University Press.

George, Stephen. 1990. *An Awkward Partner: Britain in the European Community*. Oxford: Oxford University Press.

Giddens, Anthony. 1985. *The Nation-State and Violence, Volume Two of a Contemporary Critique of Historical Materialism*. Cambridge: Polity Press.

Gil Ibáñez, Alberto. 1994. Spain and the Ratification of the Maastricht Treaty. In *The Ratification of the Maastricht Treaty: Issues, Debates and Future Implications*, ed.

Finn Laursen and Sophie Vanhoonacker, 129–45. Dordrecht, The Netherlands: Martinus Nijhoff.

Gillespie, Paul, and Brigid Laffan. 2006. European Identity: Theory and Empirics. In *Palgrave Advances in European Union Studies*, ed. Michelle Cini and Angela K. Bourne, 131–50. New York: Palgrave Macmillan.

Golynker, Oxana. 2006. *Ubiquitous Citizens of Europe: The Paradigm of Partial Migration*. Antwerp, Belgium: Intersentia.

Grabitz, Eberhard. 1970. *Europäisches Bürgerrecht zwischen Marktbürgerschaft und Staatsbürgerschaft*. Cologne, Germany: Europa Union Verlag.

———. 1977. Die Grundrechte der Europäischen Union, Das Europa der Bürger. In *Auf dem Weg zur Europäischen Union? Diskussionsbeiträge zum Tindemans-Bericht*, ed. Heinrich Schneider and Wolfgang Wessels, 167–88. Bonn, Germany: Europa-Union-Verlag.

Griffiths, Richard T. 1988. The Schuman Plan Negotiations: The Economic Clauses. In *Die Anfänge des Schuman-Plans, 1950/51*, ed. Klaus Schwabe, 35–71. Baden-Baden, Germany: Nomos.

Grin, Gilles. 2003. *The Battle of the Single European Market: Achievements and Economic Thought 1985–2000*. London: Kegan Paul.

Grotius, Hugo. 1962 [1625]. *The Law of War and Peace: De jure belli ac pacis libri tres*. Translated by Francis W. Kelsey. Indianapolis: Bobbs-Merrill.

Gstöhl, Sieglinde. 2002. *Reluctant Europeans: Norway, Sweden, and Switzerland in the Process of Integration*. Boulder, Colo.: Lynne Rienner.

Guéhenno, Jean-Marie. 1993. *La fin de la démocratie*. Paris: Flammarion.

Guigou, Elisabeth. 1994. *Pour les Européens*. Paris: Flammarion.

———. 2004. *Je vous parle d'Europe*. Paris: Seuil.

Guild, Elspeth. 2004. *The Legal Elements of European identity: EU Citizenship and Migration Law*. The Hague, The Netherlands: Kluwer Law International.

Haas, Ernst B. 1958. *The Uniting of Europe: Political, Social, and Economic forces, 1950–1957*. Stanford, Calif.: Stanford University Press.

———. 1968. *The Uniting of Europe: Political, Social, and Economic forces, 1950–1957*. 2nd ed. Stanford, Calif.: Stanford University Press.

———. 2004. *The Uniting of Europe: Political, Social, and Economic Forces, 1950–1957*. Notre Dame, Ind.: University of Notre Dame Press.

Habermas, Jürgen. 1991. *Staatsbürgerschaft und nationale Identität: Überlegungen zur europäischen Zukunft*. St. Gallen, Switzerland: Erker.

———. 1998. Struggles for Recognition in the Democratic Constitutional State. In *The Inclusion of the Other: Studies in Political Theory*, ed. Ciarran Cronin and Pablo De Greiff, 203–36. Cambridge, Mass.: MIT Press.

———. 2001. *The Postnational Constellation: Political Essays*. Translated by Max Pensky. Cambridge, Mass.: MIT Press.

———. 2006. *Time of Transitions*. Translated by Ciaran Cronin and Max Pensky. Cambridge: Polity Press.

Hallstein, Walter. 1972 [1969]. *Europe in the Making*. London: Allen and Unwin.

Handoll, John. 1995. *Free Movement of Persons in the EU*. New York: John Wiley & Sons.

———. 1997. The Free Movement of Persons. In *Amsterdam: What the Treaty Means*, ed. Ben Tonra, 133–45. Dublin: Institute of European Affairs.

Hanf, Dominik. 2006. Le développement de la citoyenneté de l'Union européenne. Bruges, Belgium: European Legal Studies, Research Papers in Law 1/2006.

Hansen, Randall, and Patrick Weil, eds. 2001. *Towards a European Nationality: Citizenship, Immigration, and Nationality Law in the EU*. New York: Palgrave.

Hantrais, Linda. 1995. *Social policy in the European Union*. New York: St. Martin's Press.

Harrison, Jackie, and Lorna Woods. 2000. European Citizenship: Can Audio-Visual Policy Make a Difference? *Journal of Common Market Studies* 38 (3): 471–95.

Hartog, Arthur den. 1994. The Netherlands and the Ratification of the Maastricht Treaty. In *The Ratification of the Maastricht Treaty: Issues, Debates and Future Implications*, ed. Finn Laursen and Sophie Vanhoonacker, 213–29. Dordrecht, The Netherlands: Martinus Nijhoff.

Heffernan, Michael J. 1998. *The Meaning of Europe: Geography and Geopolitics*. London: Arnold.

Héritier, Adrienne. 1999. *Policy-Making and Diversity in Europe: Escaping Deadlock*. Cambridge: Cambridge University Press.

High Authority of the European Coal and Steel Community. 1954. *Second General Report on the Activities of the Community*. Luxembourg: Publications Service of the European Coal and Steel Community.

Hirschl, Ran. 2004. *Towards Juristocracy: The Origins and Consequences of the New Constitutionalism*. Cambridge, Mass.: Harvard University Press.

Hobbes, Thomas. 1996 [1651]. *Leviathan*. Cambridge: Cambridge University Press.

Hobsbawm, Eric J. 1992. *Nations and Nationalism since 1780: Programme, Myth, Reality*. 2nd ed. Cambridge: Cambridge University Press.

Hoffmann, Stanley. 1966. Obstinate or Obsolete? The Fate of the Nation-State and the Case of Western Europe. *Daedalus* 95 (2): 862–915.

———. 1989. The European Community and 1992. *Foreign Affairs* 68 (4): 27–47.

Hofstede, B. P. 1964. *Thwarted Exodus: Post-war Overseas Migration from the Netherlands*. The Hague, The Netherlands: Martinus Nijhoff.

Holloway, John. 1981. *Social Policy Harmonisation in the European Community*. Farnborough, UK: Gower.

Hossay, Patrick. 2002. *Contentions of Nationhood: Nationalist Movements, Political Conflict, and Social Change in Flanders, Scotland, and French Canada*. Lanham, Md.: Lexington Books.

Hug, Simon, and Thomas König. 2002. In View of Ratification: Governmental Preferences and Domestic Constraints at the Amsterdam Intergovernmental Conference. In *International Organization* 56 (2): 447–76.

Ignatieff, Michael. 2000. *The Rights Revolution*. Toronto: House of Anansi Press.

Institut français de l'opinion publique. 1951. *Sondages: Revue française de l'opinion publique* 13 (1).

———. 1957. *Sondages: Revue française de l'opinion publique* 19 (3).
Isin, Engin F. 2002. *Being Political: Genealogies of Citizenship*. Minneapolis: University of Minnesota Press.
Jacobs, Lesley A. 1993. *Rights and Deprivation*. Oxford: Oxford University Press.
Jacobson, David. 1996. *Rights across Borders: Immigration and the Decline of Citizenship*. Baltimore: Johns Hopkins University Press.
Jacobson, David, and Galya Benarieh Ruffer. 2006. Social Relations on a Global Scale: The Implications for Human Rights and for Democracy. In *Dialogues on Migration Policy*, ed. Marco Giugni and Florence Passy, 25–44. Lanham, Md.: Lexington Books.
Jefferson, Thomas. 1904. *The Writings of Thomas Jefferson*. Washington, D.C.: Thomas Jefferson Memorial Association of the United States.
Jessurun d'Oliveira, Hans Ulrich. 1995. Union Citizenship: Pie in the Sky? In *A Citizen's Europe: In Search of a New Order*, ed. Allan Rosas and Esko Antola, 58–84. London: Sage.
Jileva, Elena. 2002. Larger than the European Union: The Emerging EU Migration Regime and Enlargement. In *Migration and the Externalities of European Integration*, ed. Sandra Lavenex and Emek M. Uçarer, 75–89. Lanham, Md.: Lexington Books.
Johnson, Ailish M. 2005. *European Welfare States and Supranational Governance of Social Policy*. New York: Palgrave Macmillan.
Judt, Tony. 2005. *Postwar: A History of Europe since 1945*. New York: Penguin Press.
Kelemen, R. Daniel. forthcoming-a. Built to Last? The durability of EU federalism. In *The State of the European Union*, vol. 8, ed. Kathleen McNamara and Sophie Meunier. Oxford: Oxford University Press.
———. forthcoming-b. *Suing for Europe? The Rise of Adversarial Legalism in the European Union*. Cambridge, Mass.: Harvard University Press.
Keohane, Robert O., and Joseph S. Nye. 1977. *Power and Interdependence: World Politics in Transition*. Boston: Little, Brown.
Keraudren, Philippe, and Nicolas Dubois. 1994. France and the Ratification of the Maastricht Treaty. In *The Ratification of the Maastricht Treaty: Issues, Debates and Future Implications*, ed. Finn Laursen and Sophie Vanhoonacker, 147–80. Dordrecht, The Netherlands: Martinus Nijhoff.
Kerremans, Bart. 2002. Belgium: From Orthodoxy to Pragmatism. In *The Amsterdam Treaty: National Preference Formation, Interstate Bargaining and Outcome*, ed. Finn Laursen, 43–70. Odense, Denmark: Odense University Press.
Kersten, Albert. 1988. A Welcome Surprise? The Netherlands and the Schuman Plan Negotiations. In *Die Anfänge des Schuman-Plans, 1950/51*, ed. Klaus Schwabe, 284–304. Baden-Baden, Germany: Nomos.
Kettner, James H. 1978. *The Development of American Citizenship, 1608–1870*. Chapel Hill: University of North Carolina Press.
King, R., and E. Ruiz-Gelices. 2003. International Student Migration and the European "Year Abroad": Effects on European Identity and Subsequent Migration Behaviour. *International Journal of Population Geography* 9:229–52.

Kitzinger, Uwe W. 1963. *The Politics and Economics of European Integration: Britain, Europe, and the United States*. Revised ed. New York: Praeger.

Kochenov, Dimitry. 2006. European Integration and the Gift of Second Class Citizenship. *Murdoch University Electronic Journal of Law* 13 (1): 209–24.

Koliopoulos, Kostas. 1994. Greece and the Ratification of the Maastricht Treaty. In *The Ratification of the Maastricht Treaty: Issues, Debates and Future Implications*, ed. Finn Laursen and Sophie Vanhoonacker, 113–28. Dordrecht, The Netherlands: Martinus Nijhoff.

Kölliker, Alkuin. 2006. *Flexibility and European Integration: The Logic of Differentiated Integration*. Lanham, Md.: Rowman & Littlefield.

Koopmans, Ruud, Paul Statham, Marco Giugni, and Florence Passy. 2005. *Contested Citizenship: Immigration and Cultural Diversity in Europe*. Minneapolis: University of Minnesota Press.

Koslowski, Rey. 2000. *Migrants and Citizens: Demographic Change in the European State System*. Ithaca, N.Y.: Cornell University Press.

Kostakopoulou, Theodora. 2001. *Citizenship, Identity and Immigration in the European Union: Between Past and Future*. Manchester, UK: Manchester University Press.

Kravaritou, Yota. 2000. Social Rights and Women's Citizenship in Europe. In *The Europeanisation of Law: The Legal Effects of European Integration*, ed. Francis Snyder, 321–33. Oxford: Hart.

Kreyssig, Gerhard. 1958. *Révision du Traité instituant la Communauté Européenne du Charbon et de l'Acier*. Strasbourg, France: Communauté Européenne du Charbon et de l'Acier.

Kymlicka, Will. 1995. *Multicultural Citizenship: A Liberal Theory of Minority Rights*. Oxford: Clarendon Press.

Kymlicka, Will, and Wayne Norman. 1994. Return of the Citizen: A Survey of Recent Work on Citizenship Theory. *Ethics* 104:352–81.

Laffan, Brigid. 1997. The Governance of the Union. In *Amsterdam: What the Treaty Means*, ed. Ben Tonra, 29–48. Dublin: Institute of European Affairs.

Laforest, Guy. 1992. *Trudeau et la fin d'un rêve canadien*. Sillery, Quebec, Canada: Septentrion.

Lahav, Gallya. 2003. *Immigration and Politics in the New Europe: Reinventing Borders*. Cambridge: Cambridge University Press.

Laible, Janet Marie. 2002. Choosing Compromised Sovereignty: Nationalist Movements Negotiate European Integration. PhD diss., Yale University, New Haven, Conn.

La Torre, Massimo. 1998. Citizenship, Consitution, and the European Union. In *European Citizenship: An Institutional Challenge*, ed. Massimo La Torre, 435–57. The Hague, The Netherlands: Kluwer Law International.

———. 2004. *Cittadinanza e ordine politico: Diritti, crisi della sovranità e sfera pubblica: una prospettiva europea*. Turin, Italy: G. Giappichelli.

Laursen, Finn. 1994. Denmark and the Ratification of the Maastricht Treaty. In *The Ratification of the Maastricht Treaty: Issues, Debates and Future Implications*, ed. Finn

Laursen and Sophie Vanhoonacker, 61–86. Dordrecht, The Netherlands: Martinus Nijhoff.

Laursen, Finn, and Sophie Vanhoonacker, eds. 1992. *The Intergovernmental Conference on Political Union*. Maastricht, The Netherlands: European Institute of Public Administration.

Laursen, Finn, and Sophie Vanhoonacker. 1994. *The Ratification of the Maastricht Treaty: Issues, Debates and Future Implications*. Dordrecht, The Netherlands: Martinus Nijhoff.

Lehning, P. B. 2001. European Citizenship: Towards a European Identity? *Law and Philosophy* 20 (3): 239–82.

Leibfried, Stephan, and Paul Pierson, eds. 1995. *European Social Policy: Between Fragmentation and Integration*. Washington, D.C.: Brookings Institution.

Lenaerts, Koen. 1996. Federalism and Rights in the European Community. In *Federalism and Rights*, ed. Ellis Katz and G. Alan Tarr, 139–72. Lanham, Md.: Rowman & Littlefield.

Levi Sandri, Lionello. 1961. The Free Movement of Workers in the Countries of the European Economic Community. Bull. EC 6/61, p. 5–10.

———. 1968. Free Movement of Workers in the European Community. Bull. EC 11/68.

Light, Matthew A. 2006. Regional Migration Policies in Post-Soviet Russia: From Pervasive Control to Insecure Freedom. PhD diss., Yale University, New Haven, Conn.

Linklater, Andrew. 1998. *The Transformation of Political Community: Ethical Foundations of the Post-Westphalian Era*. Columbia: University of South Carolina Press.

Linz, Juan J., and Alfred C. Stepan. 1996. *Problems of Democratic Transition and Consolidation: Southern Europe, South America, and Post-Communist Europe*. Baltimore: Johns Hopkins University Press.

Longo, Michael. 2006. *Constitutionalising Europe: Processes and Practices*. Aldershot, UK: Ashgate.

Ludlow, N. Piers. 2006. *The European Community and the Crises of the 1960s: Negotiating the Gaullist Challenge*. London: Routledge.

Ludlow, Peter. 2004. *The Making of the New Europe: The European Councils in Brussels and Copenhagen 2002*. Brussels, Belgium: EuroComment.

Lyon-Caen, Gérard, and Antoine Lyon-Caen. 1991. *Droit social international et européen*. 7th ed. Paris: Dalloz.

Maas, Willem. 2001. Grotius on Citizenship and Political Community. *Grotiana* 21:163–78.

———. 2005a. Freedom of Movement inside "Fortress Europe." In *Global Surveillance and Policing: Borders, Security, Identity*, ed. Elia Zureik and Mark B. Salter, 233–45. Portland, Oreg.: Willan.

———. 2005b. The Genesis of European Rights. *Journal of Common Market Studies* 43 (5): 1009–25.

———. 2006a. Free Movement after EU Enlargement. In *Towards the Completion of*

Europe: Analysis and Perspectives of the new European Union Enlargement, ed. Joaquín Roy and Roberto Domínguez. Coral Gables: University of Miami, Florida, European Union Center.

———. 2006b. The Politics of Immigration, Employment, and Amnesty in Spain. International Studies Association conference, San Diego, 24 March.

———. forthcoming. The Evolution of EU Citizenship. In *The State of the European Union, vol.8*, ed. Kathleen McNamara and Sophie Meunier. Oxford: Oxford University Press.

Maduro, Miguel Poiares. 1998. *We the Court: The European Court of Justice and the European Economic Constitution.* Oxford: Hart Publishing.

Magnette, Paul. 1999. *La citoyenneté européenne: Droits, politiques, institutions.* Brussels, Belgium: Éditions de l'Université de Bruxelles.

———. 2005. *Citizenship: The History of an Idea.* Translated by Katya Long. Colchester, UK: ECPR.

Mahant, Edelgard E. 2004. *Birthmarks of Europe: The Origins of the European Community Reconsidered.* Aldershot, UK: Ashgate.

Majone, Giandomenico. 1993. The EC between Social Policy and Social Regulation. *Journal of Common Market Studies* 31 (2): 153–70.

Malvestiti, Piero. 1959. *There Is Hope in Europe: Addresses Delivered on the Occasion of the Inauguration of the High Authority of the European Coal and Steel Community, 16–23 September, 1959.* Luxembourg: Publications Department of the European Communities.

Manin, Bernard. 1997. *The Principles of Representative Government.* Cambridge: Cambridge University Press.

Marchal-Van Belle, Graziella. 1968. *Les socialistes belges et l'intégration européenne.* Brussels, Belgium: Éditions de l'Institut de sociologie, Université libre de Bruxelles.

Marias, Epaminondas A., ed. 1994. *European Citizenship.* Maastricht, The Netherlands: European Institute of Public Administration.

Marinho, Clotilde. 1994. Portugal and the Ratification of the Maastricht Treaty. In *The Ratification of the Maastricht Treaty: Issues, Debates and Future Implications*, ed. Finn Laursen and Sophie Vanhoonacker, 231–44. Dordrecht, The Netherlands: Martinus Nijhoff.

———. 2002. Portugal: Preserving Equality and Solidarity among Member States. In *The Amsterdam Treaty: National Preference Formation, Interstate Bargaining and Outcome*, ed. Finn Laursen, 291–310. Odense, Denmark: Odense University Press.

Marjolin, Robert. 1989. *Architect of European Unity: Memoirs, 1911–1986.* London: Weidenfeld and Nicolson.

Marshall, T. H. 1950. *Citizenship and Social Class and other Essays.* Cambridge: Cambridge University Press.

Martens, Albert. 1973. *25 Jaar Wegwerparbeiders: Het Belgisch Immigratiebeleid na 1945.* Leuven, Belgium: Sociologisch Onderzoeksinstituut.

Mason, Henry L. 1955. *The European Coal and Steel Community: Experiment in Supranationalism.* The Hague, The Netherlands: Martinus Nijhoff.

Mazower, Mark. 2000. *Dark Continent: Europe's Twentieth Century*. New York: Vintage.
Mazzucelli, Colette. 1997. *France and Germany at Maastricht: Politics and Negotiations to Create the European Union*. New York: Garland.
McDonagh, Bobby. 1998. *Original Sin in a Brave New World: An Account of the Negotiation of the Treaty of Amsterdam*. Dublin: Institute of European Affairs.
McNeely, Connie L. 1995. *Constructing the Nation-State: International Organization and Prescriptive Action*. Westport, Conn.: Greenwood Press.
McRoberts, Kenneth. 1997. *Misconceiving Canada: The Struggle for National Unity*. Toronto: Oxford University Press.
Meehan, Elizabeth M. 1993. *Citizenship and the European Community*. London: Sage.
———. 2000. *Free Movement between Ireland and the UK: From the "common travel area" to the Common Travel Area*, Trinity Studies in Public Policy. Dublin: University of Dublin.
Menegazzi munari, Francesca. 1996. *Cittadinanza europea: Una promessa da mantenere*. Turin, Italy: G. Giappichelli.
Mettler, Suzanne. 2002. Social Citizens of Separate Sovereignties: Governance in the New Deal Welfare State. In *The New Deal and the Triumph of Liberalism*, ed. Sidney M. Milkis and Jerome M. Mileur, 231–71. Amherst: University of Massachusetts Press.
Miège, Jean Louis, and Colette Dubois Brichant, ed. 1994. *L'Europe retrouvée: Les migrations de la décolonisation*. Paris: L'Harmattan.
Miller, David. 1995. *On Nationality*. Oxford: Oxford University Press.
———. 1998. The left, the nation-state, and European citizenship. *Dissent* 45 (3): 47–51.
———. 2000. *Citizenship and National Identity*. Cambridge: Polity Press.
Miller, Gary T. 1995. Citizenship and European Union: A Federalist Approach. In *Federal-type Solutions and European Integration*, ed. C. Lloyd Brown-John, 461–99. Lanham, Md.: University Press of America.
Milward, Alan S. 1988. The Belgian Coal and Steel Industries and the Schuman Plan. In *Die Anfänge des Schuman-Plans, 1950/51*, ed. Klaus Schwabe, 437–54. Baden-Baden, Germany: Nomos.
———. 1992. *The European Rescue of the Nation-State*. London: Routledge.
———. 2006. *The Reconstruction of Western Europe, 1945–51*. London: Routledge.
Molinini, Gioacchino, and Orazio Parisotto. 1989. *Cittadini d'Europa*. Turin, Italy: Nuova Eri.
Monnet, Jean. 1955. *Les États-Unis d'Europe ont Commencé: La Communauté Européenne du Charbon et de l'Acier, Discours et Allocutions 1952–1954*. Paris: Robert Laffont.
———. 1976. *Mémoires*. Paris: Fayard.
Montesquieu, Charles de Secondat. 2002 [1734]. *Réflexions sur la Monarchie universelle en Europe*, ed. Michel Porret. Geneva, Switzerland: Librairie Droz.

Moravcsik, Andrew. 1998. *The Choice for Europe: Social Purpose and State Power from Messina to Maastricht*. Ithaca, N.Y.: Cornell University Press.

———. 2002. In Defence of the Democratic Deficit: Reassessing Legitimacy in the European Union. *Journal of Common Market Studies* 40 (4): 603–24.

———. 2005. Europe without Illusions. In *Europe without Illusions: The Paul-Henri Spaak Lectures, 1994–1999*, ed. Andrew Moravcsik, 3–44. Lanham, Md.: University Press of America.

Morelli, Anne. 1992. L'Immigration italienne en Belgique aux XIXe et XXe siècles. In *Histoire des étrangers et de l'immigration en Belgique de la préhistoire á nos jours*, ed. Anne Morelli, 195–206. Brussels, Belgium: Éditions Vie ouvrière.

———. 2004. *Gli italiani del Belgio: Storia e storie di due secoli di migrazioni*. Foligno, Perugia, Italy: Editoriale Umbra.

Morgan, David. 2005. Is EU Media Coverage Biased? *European Affairs* 6 (1): 14–16.

Morgan, Glyn. 2005. *The Idea of a European Superstate: Public Justification and European Integration*. Princeton, N.J.: Princeton University Press.

Neuhold, Christine. 2002. Austria: Trailing Behind and Raising the Flag. In *The Amsterdam Treaty: National Preference Formation, Interstate Bargaining and Outcome*, ed. Finn Laursen, 23–41. Odense, Denmark: Odense University Press.

Obwexer, Walter. 1996. Das Recht der Unionsbürger auf diplomatischen und konsularischen Schutz. *Ecolex: Fachzeitschrift für Wirtschaftsrecht* 7:323–28.

O'Grada, Cormac. 1969. The Vocational Training Policy of the EEC and the Free Movement of Skilled Labour. *Journal of Common Market Studies* 8 (2): 79–109.

O'Leary, Síofra. 1996. *The Evolving Concept of Community Citizenship: From the Free Movement of Persons to Union Citizenship*. The Hague, The Netherlands: Kluwer Law International.

———. 1999. The Free Movement of Persons and Services. In *The Evolution of EU Law*, ed. Paul Craig and Gráinne De Búrca, 377–416. Oxford: Oxford University Press.

O'Manique, John. 2003. *The Origins of Justice: The Evolution of Morality, Human Rights, and Law*. Philadelphia: University of Pennsylvania Press.

Orlandi, Maurizio. 1996. *Cittadinanza europea e libera circolazione delle persone*. Naples, Italy: Edizioni scientifiche italiane.

Pagden, Anthony. 2002. *The Idea of Europe: From Antiquity to the European Union*. Cambridge: Cambridge University Press.

Palmer, John. 1981. Nationality Bill Irks Expatriates. *Guardian Weekly*, 29 March, Manchester, UK, 6.

Papatsiba, Vassiliki. 2005. Political and Individual Rationales of Student Mobility: A Case-Study of ERASMUS and a French Regional Scheme for Studies Abroad. *European Journal of Education* 40 (2): 173–88.

———. 2006. Making Higher Education More European through Student Mobility? Revisiting EU Initiatives in the Context of the Bologna Process. *Comparative Education* 42 (1): 93–111.

Parsi, Vittorio Emanuele, ed. 2001. *Cittadinanza e identità costituzionale europea*. Bologna, Italy: Il Mulino.
Pauly, Alexis. 1994. Luxembourg and the Ratification of the Maastricht Treaty. In *The Ratification of the Maastricht Treaty: Issues, Debates and Future Implications*, ed. Finn Laursen and Sophie Vanhoonacker, 203–11. Dordrecht, The Netherlands: Martinus Nijhoff.
Pella, Giuseppe. 1956. *La Comunità Europea del Carbone e dell'Acciaio: Risultati e Prospettivo*. Rome: Edizioni 5 Lune.
Petit, Isabelle. 2005. Agir par mimétisme: la Commission européenne et sa politique d'éducation. *Canadian Journal of Political Science* 38 (3): 627–52.
Petite, Michel. 1997. Le traité d'Amsterdam: ambition et réalisme. *Revue du Marché Unique Européen* 3:17–52.
Pierson, Paul, and Stephan Leibfried. 1995. The Dynamics of Social Policy Integration. In *European Social Policy: Between Fragmentation and Integration*, ed. Stephan Leibfried and Paul Pierson, 432–65. Washington, D.C.: Brookings Institution.
Pierucci, Andrea. 1994. Les recours au médiateur européen. In *European Citizenship*, ed. Epaminondas A. Marias, 103–18. Maastricht, The Netherlands: European Institute of Public Administration.
Piris, Jean-Claude. 2006. *The Constitution for Europe: A Legal Analysis*. Cambridge: Cambridge University Press.
Plato. 1992 [circa 380 BCE]. *The Republic*. Translated by G. M. A. Grube and revised by C. D. C. Reeve. Indianapolis: Hackett.
Plender, Richard. 1976. An Incipient Form of European Citizenship. In *European Law and the Individual*, ed. F. G. Jacobs, 39–53. Amsterdam: Elsevier/North-Holland.
———. 1988. *International Migration Law*. 2nd revised ed. Dordrecht, The Netherlands: Martinus Nijhoff.
Pocock, J. G. A. 1995. The Ideal of Citizenship since Classical Times. In *Theorizing Citizenship*, ed. Ronald Beiner, 29–52. Albany: State University of New York Press.
Poidevin, Raymond. 1998. Le rôle de la C.E.C.A. dans la prise de conscience d'une identité européenne. In *Institutions européennes et identités européennes*, ed. Marie-Thérèse Bitsch, Wilfried Loth, and Raymond Poidevin, 155–64. Brussels, Belgium: Bruylant.
Preda, Daniela. 2004. *Alcide De Gasperi federalista europeo, Storia del federalismo e dell'integrazione europea sull'integrazione europea*. Bologna, Italy: Il mulino.
Preuss, Ulrich K., Michelle Everson, Mathias Koenig-Archibugi, and Edwige Lefebvre. 2003. Traditions of Citizenship in the European Union. *Citizenship Studies* 7 (1): 3–14.
Racine, Raymond. 1954. *Vers une Europe nouvelle par le plan Schuman*. Neuchâtel, Switzerland: La Baconnière.
Ranieri, Ruggero. 1986. *Italy and the Schuman Plan Negotiations, EUI working paper no. 86/215*. Florence, Italy: European University Institute.
Richardson, Jeremy. 2001. Policy-Making in the EU: Familiar Ambitions in Unfamiliar Settings. In *From the Nation State to Europe? Essays in Honour of Jack Hay-*

ward, ed. Anand Menon and Vincent Wright, 97–117. Oxford: Oxford University Press.

Rittberger, Berthold. 2005. *Building Europe's Parliament: Democratic Representation Beyond the Nation State*. Oxford: Oxford University Press.

Romero, Federico. 1991. *Emigrazione e integrazione europea 1945–1973*. Rome: Edizioni Lavoro.

———. 1993. Migration as an Issue in European Interdependence and Integration: The Case of Italy. In *The Frontier of National Sovereignty: History and Theory, 1945–1992*, ed. Alan S. Milward, Frances M. B. Lynch, Ruggero Ranieri, Federico Romero, and Vibeke Sørensen, 33–58. London: Routledge.

Rosenberg, Gerald N. 1991. *The Hollow Hope: Can Courts Bring About Social Change?* Chicago: University of Chicago Press.

Rosenthal, Glenda G. 1975. *The Men behind the Decisions: Cases in European Policymaking*. Lexington, Mass.: Lexington Books.

Rother, Nina, and Tina M. Nebe. 2006. The Question of European Identity. PIONEUR conference, Florence, 10 March. www.obets.ua.es/pioneur/resultados.php.

Russell, Peter H. 2005. The Future of Europe in an Era of Federalism. In *The Changing Faces of Federalism: Institutional Reconfiguration in Europe from East to West*, ed. Sergio Ortino, Mitja Žagar, and Vojtech Mastny, 4–20. Manchester, UK: Manchester University Press.

Salter, Mark B. 2003. *Rights of Passage: The Passport in International Relations*. Boulder, Colo.: Lynne Rienner.

Sassen, Saskia. 1996. *Migranten, Siedler, Flüchtlinge: Von der Massenauswanderung zur Festung Europa*. Frankfurt am Main, Germany: Fischer Taschenbuch Verlag.

———. 2002. Economic Globalization and the Redrawing of Citizenship. In *Moral Imperialism: A Critical Anthology*, ed. Berta Esperanza Hernández-Truyol, 135–50. New York: New York University Press.

Schierup, Carl-Ulrik, Peo Hansen, and Stephen Castles. 2006. *Migration, Citizenship, and the European Welfare State: A European Dilemma*. Oxford: Oxford University Press.

Schmidt, Vivien. 2005. Democracy in Europe: The Impact of European Integration. *Perspectives on Politics* 3 (4): 761–79.

Schmitter, Philippe C. 2000. *How to Democratize the European Union—and Why Bother?* Lanham, Md.: Rowman & Littlefield.

Schmuck, Otto. 1987. The European Parliament's Draft Treaty Establishing the European Union. In *The Dynamics of European Union*, ed. Roy Pryce, 188–216. London: Croom Helm.

Schmutzer, A. K. M. 1967. Los problemas sociales y la integración europea. In *La Integración de Europa desde la perspectiva española*, 39–62. Madrid, Spain: Centro de Estudios Sociales de la Santa Cruz del Valle de los Caidos.

Schönlau, Justus. 2005. *Drafting the EU Charter: Rights, Legitimacy, and Process*. New York: Palgrave Macmillan.

Schoutheete, Philippe de. 2000. *The Case for Europe: Unity, Diversity, and Democracy in the European Union*. Boulder, Colo.: Lynne Rienner.

Schuman, Robert. 1963. *Pour l'Europe*. Paris: Éditions Nagel.

Scully, Roger. 2005. *Becoming Europeans? Attitudes, Behaviour, and Socialization in the European Parliament*. Oxford: Oxford University Press.

Serra, Francesca. 1995. Alcune osservazioni sulla presenza della rappresentanza degli interessi nella delegazione italiana al Piano Schuman. In *L'altra via per l'Europa: Forze sociali e organizzazione degli interessi nell'integrazione europea (1947–1957)*, ed. Andrea Ciampani, 137–48. Milan, Italy: FrancoAngeli.

Shapiro, Ian. 1986. *The Evolution of Rights in Liberal Theory: An Essay in Critical Anthropology*. Cambridge: Cambridge University Press.

Shaw, Jo. 1997. The Many Pasts and Futures of Citizenship in the European Union. *European Law Review* 22 (6): 554–72.

Sherrington, Philippa. 2000. *The Council of Ministers: Political Authority in the European Union*. London: Pinter.

Shore, Cris. 2000. *Building Europe: The Cultural Politics of European Integration*. London: Routledge.

Siedentop, Larry. 2001. *Democracy in Europe*. New York: Columbia University Press.

Slaughter, Anne-Marie. 2004. *A New World Order*. Princeton, N.J.: Princeton University Press.

Smith, Anthony. 1995. The Nations of Europe after the Cold War. In *Governing the New Europe*, ed. Jack Hayward and Edward C. Page, 44–66. Durham, N.C.: Duke University Press.

Smith, Rogers M. 1997. *Civic Ideals: Conflicting Visions of Citizenship in U.S. History*. New Haven, Conn.: Yale University Press.

———. 2003. *Stories of Peoplehood: The Politics and Morals of Political Membership*. Cambridge: Cambridge University Press.

Söderman, Jacob. 2005. The Early Years of the European Ombudsman. In *The European Ombudsman: Origins, Establishment, Evolution*, 83–105. Luxembourg: Office for Official Publications of the European Communities.

Solbes Mira, P. 1991. La citoyenneté européenne. *Revue du Marché Commun* 345:168–70.

Soysal, Yasemin Nuhoglu. 1994. *Limits of Citizenship: Migrants and Postnational Membership in Europe*. Chicago: University of Chicago Press.

Spaak, Paul-Henri. 1950. The Integration of Europe: Dreams and Realities. *Foreign Affairs* 29 (October): 94–100.

———. 1971. *The Continuing Battle: Memoirs of a European, 1936–1966*. London: Weidenfeld.

Spinelli, Altiero. 1966. *The Eurocrats: Conflict and Crisis in the European Community*. Baltimore: Johns Hopkins Press.

Springer, Beverly. 1994. *The European Union and its Citizens: The Social Agenda*. Westport, Conn.: Greenwood Press.

Statistical Office of the European Communities. 2002. *The Social Situation in the European Union*. Luxembourg: Office for Official Publications of the European Communities.

Stone Sweet, Alec. 2004. *The Judicial Construction of Europe*. Oxford: Oxford University Press.

Stone Sweet, Alec, Wayne Sandholtz, and Neil Fligstein. 2001. *The Institutionalization of Europe*. Oxford: Oxford University Press.

Streeck, Wolfgang. 1995. From Market-Making to State-Building: Reflections on the Political Economy of European Social Policy. In *European Social Policy: Between Fragmentation and Integration*, ed. Stephan Leibfried and Paul Pierson, 389–431. Washington, D.C.: Brookings Institution.

Strudel, Sylvie. 2003. Polyrythmie européenne: Le droit de suffrage municipal au sein de l'Union, une règle électorale entre détournements et retardements. *Revue Française de Science Politique* 53 (1): 3–34.

Suleiman, Ezra. 1995. Is Democratic Supranationalism a Danger? In *Nationalism and Nationalities in the New Europe*, ed. Charles A. Kupchan, 66–84. Ithaca, N.Y.: Cornell University Press.

Taschner, Hans Claudius. 1993. Free Movement of Students, Retired Persons and Other European Citizens—A Difficult Legislative Process. In *Free Movement of Persons in Europe: Legal Problems and Experiences*, ed. Henry G. Schermers et al., 427–36. Dordrecht, The Netherlands: Martinus Nijhoff.

Taviani, Paolo Emilio. 1954. *Solidarietà atlantica e comunità europea*. Milan, Italy: Edizioni Atlante.

Taylor, Charles. 1999. Democratic Exclusion (and Its Remedies)? In *Citizenship, Diversity, and Pluralism: Canadian and Comparative Perspectives*, ed. Alan Cairns, John Courtney, Peter MacKinnon, Hans Michelmann, and David Smith, 265–87. Montreal: McGill-Queen's University Press.

Taylor, Charles, and Amy Gutmann. 1994. *Multiculturalism: Examining the Politics of Recognition*. Princeton N.J.: Princeton University Press.

Thompson, E. P. 1964. *The Making of the English Working Class*. New York: Pantheon Books.

Tiersky, Ronald. 2003. *François Mitterrand: A Very French President*. Lanham, Md.: Rowman & Littlefield.

Tilly, Charles. 1995. Citizenship, Identity and Social History. *International Review of Social History* 40 (3): 1–17.

———. 2005. *Identities, Boundaries, and Social Ties*. Boulder, Colo.: Paradigm Publishers.

Tindemans, Leo. 1976. European Union, Report to the European Council. Supplement 1/76—Bull. EC.

Tocqueville, Alexis de. 1994 [1835]. *Democracy in America*. New York: Knopf.

Tonra, Ben. 1997. EU Policy Development: Environment, Public Health, Consumer Protection and Citizenship. In *Amsterdam: What the Treaty Means*, ed. Ben Tonra, 85–93. Dublin: Institute of European Affairs.

Torpey, John C. 2000. *The Invention of the Passport: Surveillance, Citizenship, and the State*. Cambridge: Cambridge University Press.
Trudeau, Pierre Elliott. 1968. *Federalism and the French Canadians*. Toronto: Macmillan.
Tully, James. 1995. *Strange Multiplicity: Constitutionalism in an Age of Diversity*. Cambridge: Cambridge University Press.
United Kingdom. 1985. *European Union*. London: House of Lords Select Committee on the European Communities.
―――. 1990. *Free Movement of People and Right of Residence in the European Community*. London: House of Lords Select Committee on the European Communities.
―――. 1996. *A Partnership of Nations: The British Approach to the European Union Intergovernmental Conference 1996*. London: HMSO.
United Nations Economic Commission for Europe. 1979. *Economic Survey of Europe: Labour Supply and Migration in Europe, Demographic Dimensions 1950–1975*. Geneva, Switzerland: Author.
Vachudová, Milada Anna. 2005. *Europe Undivided: Democracy, Leverage, and Integration after Communism*. Oxford: Oxford University Press.
van Gunsteren, Herman. 1998. *A Theory of Citizenship: Organizing Plurality in Contemporary Democracies*. Boulder, Colo.: Westview Press.
―――. 2006. The Birth of the European Citizen out of the Dutch No Vote. *European Constitutional Law Review* 1 (3): 406–11.
Vanhoonacker, Sophie. 1994. Belgium and the Ratification of the Maastricht Treaty. In *The Ratification of the Maastricht Treaty: Issues, Debates and Future Implications*, ed. Finn Laursen and Sophie Vanhoonacker, 47–60. Dordrecht, The Netherlands: Martinus Nijhoff.
van Wijnbergen, Christa. 1994. Ireland and the Ratification of the Maastricht Treaty. In *The Ratification of the Maastricht Treaty: Issues, Debates and Future Implications*, ed. Finn Laursen and Sophie Vanhoonacker, 181–93. Dordrecht, The Netherlands: Martinus Nijhoff.
Veil, Simone, and European Commission. 1998. *Report of the High Level Panel on the Free Movement of Persons*. Luxembourg: Office for Official Publication of the European Communities.
Verdun, Amy. forthcoming. Economic and Monetary Union. In *The State of the European Union, vol.8*, ed. Kathleen McNamara and Sophie Meunier. Oxford: Oxford University Press.
Verhofstadt, Guy. 2006. *The United States of Europe: Manifesto for a New Europe*. London: Federal Trust.
Vignes, Daniel. 1956. *La Communauté européenne du charbon et de l'acier: Un exemple d'administration économique internationale*. Liège, Belgium: Georges Thone.
Vincent, Andrew. 2002. *Nationalism and Particularity*. Cambridge: Cambridge University Press.
Vink, Maarten. 2005. *Limits of European Citizenship: European Integration and Domestic Immigration Policies*. New York: Palgrave Macmillan.

von Danwitz, Thomas. 2001. Zwischen Symbolismus und Realismus: Die Grundrechtsscharta der Europaïschen Union. *Internationale Politik* 56 (2): 37–42.
Wales, Peter. 1963. *Europe Is My Country: The Story of West European Co-operation since 1945*. London: Methuen.
Walzer, Michael. 1994. Notes on the New Tribalism. In *Political Restructuring in Europe: Ethical Perspectives*, ed. Chris Brown, 187–200. London: Routledge.
Warren, Earl. 1970. Fourteenth Amendment: Retrospect and Prospect. In *The Fourteenth Amendment*, ed. Bernard Schwartz. New York: New York University Press.
Waterbury, Myra A. 2006. Internal Exclusion, External Inclusion: Diaspora Politics and Party-Building Strategies in Post-Communist Hungary. *East European Politics and Societies* 20 (3): 483–515.
Weale, Albert. 2005. *Democratic Citizenship and the European Union*. Manchester, UK: Manchester University Press.
Weatherill, Stephen. 2003. *Cases and Materials on EU Law*. 6th ed. Oxford: Oxford University Press.
Weber, Max. 1946. Structures of Power. In *From Max Weber: Essays in Sociology*, ed. H. H. Gerth and C. Wright Mills, 159–79. New York: Oxford University Press.
Weil, Patrick. 1991. *La France et ses étrangers: l'aventure d'une politique de l'immigration, 1938–1991*. Paris: Calmann-Lévy.
Weiler, J. H. H. 1999. *The Constitution of Europe*. Cambridge: Cambridge University Press.
Weiss, Friedl, and Frank Wooldridge. 2002. *Free Movement of Persons within the European Community*. The Hague, The Netherlands: Kluwer Law International.
Weyland, Joseph. 1994. La protection diplomatique et consulaire des citoyens de l'Union européene. In *European Citizenship*, ed. Epaminondas A. Marias, 63–68. Maastricht, The Netherlands: European Institute of Public Administration.
White, Paul. 1999. Ethnicity, Racialization and Citizenship as Divisive Elements in Europe. In *Divided Europe: Society and Territory*, ed. Ray Hudson and Allan M. Williams, 210–30. London: Sage.
Wiebe, Robert H. 2002. *Who We Are: A History of Popular Nationalism*. Princeton, N.J.: Princeton University Press.
Wiener, Antje. 2006. Europäische Bürgerschaftspraxis. In *Moderne (Staats)Bürgerschaft. Vom klassischen Modell zu Debatten der Citizenship Studies*, ed. Jürgen Mackert. Hamburg: VS Verlag.
———. 1998. *"European" Citizenship Practice: Building Institutions of a Non-State*. Boulder, Colo.: Westview Press.
Wiener, Antje, and Vincent Della Sala. 1997. Constitution-Making and Citizenship Practice: Bridging the Democracy Gap in the EU? *Journal of Common Market Studies* 35:595–614.
Wihtol de Wenden, Catherine. 1997. *La citoyenneté européenne*. Paris: Presses de la Fondation nationale des sciences politiques.
Willis, F. Roy. 1971. *Italy Chooses Europe*. New York: Oxford University Press.

Wistrich, Ernest. 1991. *After 1992: The United States of Europe*. Revised ed. London: Routledge.
Yashar, Deborah J. 2005. *Contesting Citizenship in Latin America: The Rise of Indigenous Movements and the Postliberal Challenge*. Cambridge: Cambridge University Press.
Zolberg, Aristide. 1989. The Next Waves: Migration Theory for a Changing World. *International Migration Review* 23 (3): 403–30.

Index

abortion, 54, 132nn47–51
Acton, Lord, 101
Adams, John Quincy, 82
Adenauer, Konrad, 13
Adonnino, Pietro, 35. *See also* People's Europe
Africa, 24
African Americans, 102
African Union, 2
Ahern, Bertie, 65
Algeria, 24
Algerians in France, 24, 97
Amato, Giuliano, 82
Amsterdam Treaty, 10, 61, 62, 67–70, 72, 75, 85
Andreotti, Giulio, 29, 30
anthem, European, 38
Aristotle, 1, 2
assizes, parliamentary, 48, 70
asylum, 68–70, 84, 87, 93
atomic energy, 18, 124n18
Australia, 1
Austria: accession, 75; and Amsterdam Treaty, 68; and European constitution, 86; Freedom Party, 97, 99; migration from, 25, 106; migration to, 80, 81, 97
Austro-Hungarian empire, 81, 82

Balkans, 83
Basque nationalism, 101, 133n66
Bavaria, 85
Belgium, 36, 51, 64; and Amsterdam Treaty, 69, 135n36; and DTEU, 35; and European Coal and Steel Community, 11, 13–26; and European constitution, 86; Flemish nationalism, 55, 99, 101; and Lingua, 40; and Maastricht Treaty, 46, 49, 54, 55, 59, 130n8; migration from, 105; migration to, 14, 16, 25, 26, 81, 103, 104, 106; support for EU citizenship in, 9, 20. *See also* Benelux; Schengen agreement
Benelux, 8, 13, 17, 18, 23, 24, 26
Bentham, Jeremy, 122n14
Berès, Pervenche, 89
Berlin Wall, 24, 45, 46, 59, 81, 121n4
Berlusconi, Silvio, 67
Blair, Tony, 43, 67

171

Bolkestein, Frits, 56, 80, 122n12
Bologna process, 112
Bonde, Jens-Peter, 85, 137n35
borders, vii, 3–6, 64, 82, 117–120; cross-border workers, 20, 25, 33, 66, 81, 103; external borders of EU, 68, 87, 93, 103, 122n12; intra-EU, 19, 22, 37, 38, 46, 61, 82, 96, 118. *See also* Schengen agreement
Brandt, Willy, 30
Britain. *See* United Kingdom
Bruton, John, 84
Bulgaria, 78, 83, 137n40
Bureau International du Travail, 22

Canada, 1, 32, 63, 101, 105, 139n4
Catalan nationalism, 101
Catania report, 98–100
Cavaco Silva, Aníbal, 57
Channel Islands, 24. *See also* Common Travel Area
Charter of Fundamental Rights. *See* European Charter of Fundamental Rights
Chirac, Jacques, 55, 61, 67
Churchill, Winston, 12
citizenship, vii, 1–3, and passim; commonwealth, 32; federalism and, 32; naturalization, 32, 84, 88, 90, 105, 127n13, 140n37
coal and steel workers, 14–18, 25, 26
Cold War, 2, 9, 13, 30,
Commission. *See* European Commission
Committee of the Regions, 84, 137n23
Common Assembly, 16–18
common foreign and security policy, 47, 52, 53, 56, 67
Common Travel Area, 24, 26, 37, 126n68, 129n49
Communism, 12, 22, 23, 30; Communist parties, 15, 56, 58, 98, 99, 124n2, 124n18

Community Charter on the Fundamental Social Rights of Workers, 42, 43. *See also* European Social Charter
constitution, draft European, 75, 77–91, 93, 98, 100, 101, 107; constitutional moment, 45. *See also* Maastricht Treaty
consular and diplomatic protection, common European, 48, 50, 51, 59
consumer protection, 69, 128n20
Convention, European, 70–72, 74, 75, 78, 83–89, 93, 98, 107, 131n20
Cook, Robin, 43
corruption, 56
Costa v. Enel case, 28, 127n92
Coudenhove-Kalergi, Richard de, 13
Council of Europe, 116
court. *See* European Court of Human Rights; European Court of Justice; International Criminal Court
credentials. *See* qualifications
Croatia, 83
cross-border workers, 20, 25, 33, 66, 81, 103
culture, 69, 100–111, 119
currency. *See* euro
customs union
Cyprus, 78, 80, 86
Czechoslovakia, 2, 101
Czech Republic, 78, 137n40

Davignon, Étienne, 122n15
defense. *See* common foreign and security policy
De Gasperi, Alcide, 13
De Gaulle, 27
Dehaene, Jean-Luc, 83
Delors, Jacques, 36, 46, 54, 59, 95, 98, 128n40, 129n59
democratic deficit, 10, 32, 46–48, 84, 136n57; definition, 74, 75
Denmark: and Amsterdam Treaty, 68, 69, 135n35; and EU citizenship, 9,

10, 29, 36, 41, 43, 64, 107; and Maastricht Treaty, 10, 48, 49, 51–54, 56, 59; migration to, 81, 97; Nordic Common Labor Market, 24, 26; and Schengen, 37; and SEA, 36, 38
diplomatic and consular protection, common European, 48, 50, 51, 59
direct effect of European law, 12, 26–28, 33, 49, 50, 127n94
direct elections to European Parliament, 34, 75
discrimination. See nondiscrimination
Dooge, James, 35
DTEU (Draft Treaty Establishing European Union), 35–38, 43

economic and monetary union, 46–48, 53, 57, 69
Economic and Social Committee, 32, 39, 42, 89, 128n20, 137n23
ECSC. See European Coal and Steel Community; Paris, Treaty of
Eden, Anthony, 13
education: EU role in, 39, 40, 69, 84, 109–113, 119; national role in, 3, 36, 103, 109–113; right to, 4, 20, 63, 68, 122n18; in United States, 91. See also *Gravier* case; *Grzelczyk* case; students
EEC Treaty. See Rome, Treaty of
Eisenhower, Dwight, 91
employment, 16–25, 58, 62, 66, 69, 72, 79–81, 88, 102, 106, 139n69. See also unemployment
EMU, 46–48, 53, 57, 69
environment, EU role in 69
equality. See nondiscrimination
Erasmus program, 39, 110–12
Estonia, 78, 86
Euratom, 18, 124n18
euro, 52, 53, 86, 92, 108, 139n68. See also European Central Bank
European Action, 12

European anthem, 38
European Association for the Protection of Human Rights, 90
European Central Bank, 55, 92. See also euro
European Charter of Fundamental Rights, 4, 70–72, 74, 75, 78, 83, 84, 88, 92, 93, 98, 131n20. See also Community Charter on the Fundamental Social Rights of Workers; European Social Charter
European Coal and Steel Community, viii, 9, 11–17, 23, 61, 90, 122n21. See also Paris, Treaty of
European Commission, 9, 10, 18, 21, 28, 30–32, 34, 36–39, 41, 42, 46–49, 51, 56, 59, 62, 63, 66, 68, 70, 72–74, 79, 80, 83, 84, 86–88, 90–93, 99, 102, 109, 111, 117, 120; DG Internal Market, 80, 92; DG Employment and Social Affairs, 39, 92, 129n59, 139n69; DG Justice and Home Affairs, 70, 92, 93. See also internal market
European Convention, 70–72, 74, 75, 78, 83–89, 93, 98, 107, 131n20
European Convention on Human Rights (ECHR), 47–49, 68–70, 78
European Council: meetings in 1970s, 31–33; meetings in 1980s, 35, 36, 38–40, 42; meetings in 1990s, 46–50, 53, 56, 67–70, 89; meetings in 2000s, 72, 77; qualified majority voting, 36, 38, 41, 42, 68, 72, 73, 135n36; and social affairs, 62, 63
European Court of Human Rights, 116, 134n17
European Court of Justice, 1, 3, 4, 9, 12, 26–28, 33, 37, 39, 42, 46, 46, 54, 63–65, 68, 70, 74, 91, 92, 103, 116, 117, 127n91, 127n94, 137n22; *Costa v. Enel*, 28, 127n92; direct effect of European law, 12, 26–28, 33, 49, 50,

127n94; *Gravier* case, 36; *Grzelczyk* case, 64, 65; *Martínez Sala* case, 64, 65; supremacy of EU law, 12, 28, 127n94; *Van Gend en Loos* case, 27
European Federalist Movement, 12, 124n2
European flag, 38
European health insurance card, 65
European idea, 6, 8, 9, 11–13, 17, 19, 20, 50, 123n35
European Movement, 71
European Ombudsman, 38, 48, 50, 52, 59, 137n23
European Parliament, 9, 10, 17, 19, 21, 30, 33–36, 38–42, 45–52, 62, 68, 70, 72–75, 81, 83–87, 89–91, 98, 107, 110, 117, 120; direct elections, 34, 75
European Social Charter, 38, 70. *See also* Community Charter on the Fundamental Social Rights of Workers; European Charter of Fundamental Rights
European Youth Convention, 85
Europe Day, 85
Euroskepticism, ix, 9, 33, 34, 81, 85–87, 99, 101, 137n35
Eyskens, Gaston, 30

family: definition, 73; effect of free movement on, 15, 62, 105; free movement rights of, 9, 20, 21, 28, 34, 72–74, 79, 90, 104; policy, EU role in, 63; social benefits for, 20, 34, 62, 66, 135n53
farmers, 8, 79, 128n20
federalism, 63, 64, 105, 117; in Europe, 50, 85, 91, 123n33, 127n95, 130n66; in Germany, 70, 85; in the United States, 27, 91, 102, 103, 140n25
Finland: accession, 79; and Amsterdam Treaty, 68; and European constitution, 86; Nordic Common Labor Market, 24, 26; right to vote, 51; and workers from new member states, 82
First World War, 81, 116
flag, European, 38
Flemish nationalism, 55, 99, 101
foreign and security policy, common European, 47, 52, 56, 67
Fortuyn, Pim, 96
Fourteenth Amendment, 102, 103
France, 6, 9, 13, 22–25, 81, 82, 88, 90, 97, 99, 105, 106, 117; 2005 riots in, 90, 99; Algerians in, 24, 97; and Amsterdam Treaty, 67, 68; and European Coal and Steel Community, 11, 13, 14, 16, 124n18; and European constitution, 86, 87, 137n40, 138n42; and European Court of Justice, 26, 65; and Lingua, 40; and Maastricht Treaty, 10, 46–50, 55, 56, 59; *pieds-noirs* in, 24; public opinion in, 8, 10, 14, 20, 56, 86; and Schengen, 37; and Tindemans report, 32
free movement, vii, 3–6, and passim. *See also* family, health, United States of America
frontiers. *See* borders
frontier workers, 19, 20, 23, 62, 66

Germany: and Amsterdam Treaty, 67; and Berlin Wall, 24, 45, 46, 59, 81, 121n4; citizenship in Nazi Germany, 88; and European Coal and Steel Community, 11, 13–16; and European constitution, 86; and European idea, 8, 9, 20, 33; federalism, 70, 85; and Lingua, 40; and Maastricht Treaty, 46, 47, 49, 53, 58, 59, 132n43; *Martínez Sala* case, 64, 65; migration from, 24, 105, 140n37; migration to, 22, 24, 25, 70, 80, 81, 105, 106, 141n38;

reunification of, 58, 121n4; and Schengen, 37; unification of, 1, 6. See also European idea
Giscard d'Estaing, Valéry, 32, 83
Gonzalez, Felipé, 47
Grandi, Achille, 12
Gravier case, 36, 128n41
Greece: accession, 34, 40, 58, 78, 129n65; and European constitution, 86; and Lingua, 40; and Maastricht Treaty, 46, 47, 53, 56, 59; migration from, 22, 24–26, 30, 34, 40, 62, 105, 106; migration to, 81; and Schengen, 37; and SEA, 36, 38
Greek Orthodox Church, 97
Gronchi, Giovanni, 12
Grotius, Hugo, 3, 115, 122n13
Grzelczyk case, 64, 65
Guigou, Élisabeth, 130n1
Gulf War, 48

Haas, Ernst, 123n31
Hague Congress, 12, 13, 71
Hague Convention, 88
Hallstein, Walter, 13, 21, 28, 62, 126n57
health: benefits for EU citizens, 41, 62, 63, 66, 73; EU role in, 66, 69, 87; European insurance card, 65; occupational, 39 ; public policy and security limit to free movement, 15, 18, 20, 73
High Authority of the ECSC, 13–17
Hobbes, Thomas, 3, 122n13
human rights, 31, 38, 47–49, 59, 68, 70, 90, 98, 119, 120. See also European Convention on Human Rights; Universal Declaration of Human Rights
Hungary, 78, 81, 82, 86

immigration, 5, 34, 40, 58, 68–70, 84, 85, 88, 90, 93, 96, 99, 122n22. See also entries for individual states; third-country nationals
industrialization, 119
Institutional Affairs, report on, 35, 36, 38
integration, theories of, 5–7
intergovernmentalism, 5–7
internal market, 12, 23, 36–39, 42, 43, 104, 131n24; directorate general for, 80, 92
International Criminal Court, 116
International Labor Organization, 22
Ireland: abortion, 54, 132nn47–51; and Amsterdam Treaty, 68; and Common Travel Area, 24, 26, 37, 126n68, 129n49; and Lingua, 40; and Maastricht Treaty, 51, 53, 54, 59; migration from, 24, 106; migration to, 81, 106; and Schengen, 37; and Treaty of Nice, 135n47
Isle of Man, 24. See also Common Travel Area
Italy: and Amsterdam Treaty, 67, 68; and DTEU, 35; and EU citizenship, 8, 9, 20, 31, 123n35; and European Coal and Steel Community, 9, 11–16; and European constitution, 86; and Lingua, 40; and Maastricht Treaty, 46, 49, 53, 56, 5; migration from, 4, 13–16, 18–26, 30, 51, 105, 105, 122n25, 140n37, 141n38; migration to, 81, 131n31; unification of, 19; and Schengen, 37

Jacini, Stefano, 12
Jeferson, Thomas, 82
Jospin, Lionel, 67
Juppé, Alain, 55, 67

Kohl, Helmut, 47, 59, 61, 67, 131n12

Laeken, 77, 85, 98, 137n23
language, 39, 57, 58, 68, 111, 112
Latvia, 78, 86

law. *See* European Court of Justice; nondiscrimination
Le Pen, Jean-Marie, 99
Le Pen, Marine, 99
Levi Sandri, Lionello, 11, 21, 122n23, 122n24, 125n45
Lithuania, 78, 86
Locke, John, 3
London bombings, 90, 99
Louisiana Purchase, 82
Luxembourg: and Amsterdam Treaty, 135n36; and EU citizenship, 9, 10, 106, 141n40; and European Coal and Steel Community, 11, 13, 14, 16, 24, 25; and European constitution, 86; and Maastricht Treaty, 49, 51, 53, 55–57, 59; migration to, 22, 23, 51, 81, 106, 133n63; and Schengen, 37. *See also* Benelux

Maastricht Treaty, 1, 7, 10, 29, 30, 38, 40, 42–62, 67–69, 84, 104, 106, 110, 111, 135n36; citizenship provisions, 37, 45–62, 68; negotiations, 42, 45–62, 67, 70, 75
Macmillan, Harold, 13
Major, John, 43, 57, 67, 68
Malta, 78, 80, 86
Mansholt, Sicco, 31
Marín, Manuel, 39, 42, 129n59
Marjolin, Robert, 125n44
Marshall Plan, 14
Marshall, T. H., 122n17
Martin, David, 46, 130n46
Martínez Sala case, 64, 65
Mercosur, 2, 5
Messina, 17, 23
Mexican migrants, 118
Mitsotakis, Konstantine, 56
Mitterrand, François, 13, 47, 50, 55, 56, 59, 67, 131n12, 134n3
Mollet, Guy, 123n34
Monnet, Jean, 14, 17, 36, 87

Montesquieu, Charles de, 115
Morocco, 26, 103
Moscow, residence permits, 23. *See also* Soviet Union
Movimento Federalista Europeo. *See* European Federalist Movement
Mussolini, Benito, 124n2

NAFTA (North American Free Trade Agreement), 2, 5, 118
nationalism, 3, 8, 9, 81, 82, 101, 109, 118, 119, 139n5. *See also* European idea; patriotism
naturalization, 32, 84, 88, 90, 105, 127n13, 140n37
natural law, 3
neofunctionalism, 7
Netherlands, the: and Amsterdam Treaty, 135n36; and European Coal and Steel Community, 11, 13–17, 20, 23–25; and European constitution, 86, 87, 137n40, 138n42; and Lingua, 40; and Maastricht Treaty, 49, 51, 53, 56, 59, 133n58; education policy, 83; migration from, 23–25, 103; migration to, 81, 90, 104, 140n37; and Schengen, 37. *See also* Benelux
Nice, Treaty of, 61, 62, 72–75, 86
nondiscrimination, 16, 20, 23, 33, 36, 41, 42, 64, 65, 69, 82, 86, 89, 91, 92, 100–104, 119, 128n23
Nordic Common Labor Market, 24, 26

ombudsman. *See* European Ombudsman
Organization of European Economic Cooperation, 14
Ottoman empire, 82

Palacio, Ana, 77, 86
Papandreou, Andreas, 56
Paris, Treaty of, 9, 11, 13, 15, 17–19, 22, 26, 28, 30, 31, 38

Pasqua, Charles, 55
passport, 17, 19, 23, 24, 72, 126n63; abolition of controls, 31; EU format, 35, 36, 85, 139n8. *See also* Common Travel Area; Schengen agreement
patriotism, 12, 47, 84, 96, 97, 100, 131n11, 137n29
People's Europe, 32, 35–38, 109
petition, 50, 52, 59, 68, 90
pieds-noirs, 24
Plan D, 87
Plato, 95
Poland, 14, 24, 78, 81, 103, 135n35, 137n40
Portugal: accession, 9, 29, 30, 34, 37, 40, 58, 78; and Amsterdam Treaty, 69; and *Grzelczyk* case, 65; and Lingua, 40; and Maastricht Treaty, 40, 57, 59; migration from, 22, 30, 34, 51, 57, 62, 97, 105, 106, 129n65; migration to, 81
posted workers, 66, 81
Prodi, Romano, 65, 68, 129n59
projet de vie en commun, 87
Pufendorf, Samuel von, 3

qualifications, recognition of, 30, 37, 39, 63, 118; coal and steel workers, 15–17, 26
qualified majority voting, 36, 38, 41, 42, 68, 72, 73, 135n36

religion, 96, 97, 120
Romania, 78, 81–83, 137n40
Rome, Treaty of, 9, 11, 17–19, 21, 22, 26–28, 33, 38, 50, 62, 79, 87, 109, 110
Rousseau, Jean-Jacques, 3
Russia, 82. *See also* Soviet Union

Santer, Jacques, 57, 129n59, 139n68
Schengen agreement, 37, 47, 69, 86, 93, 96, 97

Schoutheete, Philippe de, 130n8, 131n27
Schuman Plan, 13, 14, 122n21
Schuman, Robert, 5, 13, 61, 122n21
Scottish nationalism, 101
SEA (Single European Act), 30, 35, 38–40, 43, 45, 46, 131n24
Second World War, vii, 4, 12, 22, 88, 120
Slovakia, 2, 78, 81, 82, 86
Slovenia, 78, 81, 86
Soares, Mario, 130n66
social affairs, 62, 63, 123n39; Benelux commission, 23; ECSC commission, 15, 17; European Commission DG, 39, 92, 129n59, 139n69
Social Charter, 42, 43
social rights, 16, 17, 23, 40, 41, 62–66, 72, 86, 92. *See also* health; education
Söderman, Jacob, 52
sovereignty, vii, 1, 3, 7, 13, 88, 99, 119–120, 124n2; British, 32; French, 32, 50, 55
Soviet Union, 2, 9, 22, 30, 82, 101, 137n20; residence permit (*propiska*) in, 23, 78, 126n63
Spaak, Paul-Henri, 13, 18, 62, 123n38, 124n7
Spain, 40, 62, 101, 129n59, 133n65; accession, 9, 29, 30, 34, 37, 58; and European constitution, 82, 86; and Lingua, 39, 40; and Maastricht Treaty, 47–51, 53, 57, 59; migration from, 22, 24–26, 30, 34; migration to, 81, 104–107, 140nn36–37
Spinelli, Altiero, 13, 22, 35, 75, 120, 124n2,
sports, 69
structural funds, 39
students, 4, 34, 36, 37, 39, 41, 42, 64–66, 73, 73, 103–106, 109–113,

See also education; Erasmus program; *Gravier* case; *Grzelczyk* case
supremacy of EU law, 12, 28, 127n94
Sweden, 24, 26, 51, 79, 81

Tampere, 70, 71, 89
Taviani, Paolo, 13
Teitgen, Pierre-Henri, 123n34
territoriality, vii, 1, 6, 85, 117–19, 121n10
Thatcher, Margaret, 34, 39, 43, 56, 58, 67
third-country nationals, 34, 37, 68, 72–74, 78, 80, 88–90, 93, 99, 138n64
Thompson, E. P., 104
Tindemans, Leo, 31–33, 37, 65, 75
Tocqueville, Alexis de, 115
Toussas, Georgios, 99, 100
treaty. *See* Amsterdam Treaty; constitution, draft European; DTEU; Maastricht Treaty; Nice, Treaty of; Paris, Treaty of; Rome, Treaty of; SEA
Trudeau, Pierre, 101
Turkey, 22, 26, 62, 78, 83
two-speed Europe, 32, 37, 137n41

unemployment, 14–19, 24, 25, 34, 58, 66, 74, 78, 92, 124n18. *See also* employment
United Kingdom: and Amsterdam Treaty, 67, 68; Citizenship Act, 35; and Common Travel Area, 24, 26, 37, 126n68, 129n49; and EU citizenship, 9, 29, 36, 41, 49, 65; and Lingua, 40; and Maastricht Treaty, 43, 47, 51, 53, 57–59; and membership in European bodies, 13, 23, 33, 34; migration from, 35, 105; migration to, 81, 90, 106; and Schengen, 37; and SEA, 36, 38; and Social Charter, 43; and Tindemans report, 32, 33
United States of America, 1, 27, 63, 64, 82, 91, 101–103, 140n25; African Americans, 102; citizenship, 32, 82, 102; foreign policy, 9, 15, 124n18; Fourteenth Amendment, 102, 103; free movement, 27, 66, 102, 105, 118
Universal Declaration of Human Rights, 4, 88, 116, 122n18
USSR. *See* Soviet Union

Van Gend en Loos case, 27
Van Gogh, Theo, 99
Vanhanen, Matti, 139n70
Van Mierlo, Hans, 84
variable geometry, 32, 37, 137n41
Ventotene Manifesto, 124n2
Vienna Conventions on diplomatic and consular relations, 51
visas, 19, 23, 55, 68, 93. *See also* borders; Schengen agreement
Vitorino, António, 70, 77, 93
vote: right to vote in local and European elections, 30–33, 35, 37, 47, 50–55, 57, 59, 88, 89, 131n31; right to vote in national elections, 32, 68, 107

Weber, Max, 95, 98
welfare. *See* social rights
Western European Union, 23, 26, 56
Westphalia, Peace of, 2, 3, 116, 120, 121n5, 121n10
Wilson, Harold, 33
workers: frontier workers, 19, 20, 23, 62, 66; posted workers, 66, 81
World War I, 81, 116
World War II, vii, 4, 12, 22, 88, 120

Young European Federalists, 124n2
Yugoslavia, 2, 25, 49, 101

About the Author

Willem Maas obtained his PhD in political science from Yale University. He is assistant professor of political science at Glendon College, York University, and faculty affiliate of the Canadian Centre for German and European Studies. His teaching and research focus on comparative politics, European integration, citizenship and migration, sovereignty, nationalism, democratic theory, and federalism.